LOIS LENSKI

Lois as a young girl, reading. R. C. H. Lenski, photographer.
Photograph courtesy of Jan Ferne Haueisen.

LOIS LENSKI
Storycatcher

BOBBIE MALONE

UNIVERSITY OF OKLAHOMA PRESS : NORMAN

Publication of this book is made possible through the generosity of Edith Kinney Gaylord.

The following poems, songs, and hymns by Lois Lenski, are reproduced in this volume on the pages noted by permission of the Lois Lenski Covey Foundation, copyright by Lois Lenski: "Place and People" (p. 22); "People" (p. 79); "I Sing the Life I Live" (p. 242); "House or Home" (p. 256); "A Book Can Take Me" (p. 256–57); "My Garden" (p. 257); and "Dear Child" (p. 265).

The following poems, songs, and hymns by Lois Lenski are reproduced in this volume on the pages noted by permission of Burrell Montz Covey and the Lois Lenski Covey Foundation, copyright by Lois Lenski: "Farewell Song" (p. 187); "We Are Thy Children" (p. 230); "Child of God" (p. 233); and "Big Mr. Small" (p. 236).

LIBRARY OF CONGRESS CATALOGING-IN-PUBLICATION DATA
Name: Malone, Bobbie, 1944– author.
Title: Lois Lenski : storycatcher / Bobbie Malone.
Description: Norman : University of Oklahoma Press, 2016. | Includes
    bibliographical references and index.
Identifiers: LCCN 2015043810 | ISBN 978-0-8061-5386-5 (cloth)
    ISBN 978-0-8061-6560-8 (paper)
Subjects: LCSH: Lenski, Lois, 1893-1974. | Authors, American—20th century—
    Biography. | Children's stories—Authorship.
Classification: LCC PS3523.E575 Z75 2016 | DDC 811/.52—dc23 LC record
    available at http://lccn.loc.gov/2015043810

For my incomparable Bill

And in memory of my mother,

Sylvia Goldinger Scharlack,

A little bundle of strength, beauty, principle, and love

CONTENTS

ILLUSTRATIONS

LOIS LENSKI

INTRODUCTION
TOUCHING YOUNG LIVES

Lois Lenski's career as a children's author-illustrator spanned five decades—from the 1920s through the 1960s—and mirrored the cultural energy and concerns of the mid-twentieth-century United States. Winning the prestigious Newbery Award in 1946 for *Strawberry Girl* cemented her reputation as a writer of realistic children's fiction, the genre she largely dominated through her remarkable and original research methodology, her inviting illustrations, and the sheer number of titles she produced. But in her first decade as a professional artist, she had already harnessed her determination, talents, and skills to become an illustrator for several well-reviewed children's books, including, most notably, the original edition of Watty Piper's *The Little Engine That Could* (1930). Although she had not originally aspired to become an author, by the late 1920s, she wrote and illustrated her first quasi-autobiographical storybooks. During the following decade, she created *The Little Family* (1932), the first picture book designed to fit the small hands of toddlers, and introduced to young readers the irrepressible Mr. Small in his initial guise as the proud owner of *The Little Auto* (1934). Simultaneously, she began to develop historical fiction for an older youth audience, garnering a Newbery Honor for *Phebe Fairchild: Her Book* (1937), Lenski's first book in this field. By the time she wrote *Indian Captive: The Story of Mary Jemison* (1941), another Newbery

Original drawing:
Endpaper for PAPA SMALL

LOIS LENSKI
1951

Mr. Small in his various guises, original drawing for the endpapers of *Papa Small*, 1950. Reprinted by permission of the Lois Lenski Covey Foundation and Burrell Covey, copyright by Lois Lenski. Courtesy of the Lois Lenski Papers, de Grummond Collection, McCain Library, University of Southern Mississippi.

Honor book, Lenski had managed to create an interdependent melding of illustration and text that distinguished her from her contemporaries. Throughout her career, she continued to utilize successfully her signature style, which appealed to readers of all ages and developmental stages.[1]

Once Lenski completely embraced her profession, she became one of the most prolific children's author-illustrators of the twentieth century, working tirelessly to help children understand the world in which they lived. Her simply drawn picture books for younger readers provided answers to many of the how and why questions their curious minds wanted to understand. Yet her greatest contribution to American children's literature, arguably, was her ability to inculcate empathy. As she stated in her

Newbery acceptance speech, "What better way, than through the reading of a book, to enter the minds and hearts of others and find them full of good things? . . . Only when we truly see others as ourselves can we hope to have a world in which all men are brothers."[2] She passionately believed that in order to love one's neighbor as oneself, one had to get to know that neighbor, to become acquainted with that neighbor's social and environmental reality, and to accept that life as decent and as worthwhile as one's own. She realized that children respond instinctively to narratives rich in reality. And through these stories woven from her conscientious study of hard-working families, she implanted intimations of social justice. The illustrations that accompany her texts play a significant role in communicating the realities of the lives of children of sharecroppers and coal miners and migrant field-workers. While these youngsters had been largely invisible in the middle-class mainstream of children's literature, they could now see themselves depicted in books—and other young readers who needed to see worlds beyond their own comfort zone could see them as well.

Such an inclusive vision of American democracy fits squarely within what Gary D. Schmidt explores in *Making Americans: Children's Literature from 1930 to 1960*—years coincident with the heart of Lenski's oeuvre. As the twentieth-century interest in childhood evolved in the takeoff decade of the 1920s, publishers, editors, librarians, and reviewers (or what Schmidt and Leonard Marcus have called cultural "minders") believed that the greater purpose of children's literature "would be to define what America meant, what democracy in America meant, and what being an American meant for a child of the twentieth century. The question was, 'How might a coherent set of social values set in the physical terrain of the nation look as it came into works for children?'"[3]

As a ten-year-old growing up in San Antonio, I would have been unaware of such overarching scholarly concerns. Yet from the day I entered the Cambridge Elementary School library in Alamo Heights and saw Lois Lenski's Newbery Award–winning book prominently displayed, I found that she fired my imagination as no other author had done. Coming from a vastly different cultural background, entrepreneur and celebrity extraordinaire Oprah Winfrey similarly declared that she was "hooked" and read every title in Lenski's regional series that the library held, just as I did.[4] The stories and their settings conveyed a realism I had never found in anything I'd read before, with characters that were not middle class and who struggled to deal with their hardscrabble lives. The combination of dialogue, description, and compelling illustration immediately intrigued me, for Lenski was among the first children's authors to recognize and validate the lives of poor families living in various regions throughout the United States.[5] Her books simultaneously delivered a more inclusive sense of American lives to young readers everywhere experiencing their own challenges growing up.

But I was also fascinated with the books that she wrote for younger readers. I immediately realized that I had found the same author-illustrator who had created the books in my younger brother's room: *Papa Small, Cowboy Small, The Little Auto, The Little Train*—the "boy books" that he pored over with such serious devotion as an already-emerging mechanical engineer. At a younger cousin's, I found *Let's Play House,*[6] in which two little girls mimicked women's typical housekeeping and mothering roles. Lenski's simple line drawings and words were as easily identifiable as those that drew me to her regional books, yet so different in line quality and detail. As Lenski's son, Steven Covey,[7] told me, his mother's gift as an illustrator was the ability to create her signature stylized drawings, whatever the assignment—for another author, for her picture books, or for her regionals—and have readers immediately recognize them as "Lenskiesque."[8] She seemed to have immediately grasped the need to create heavily inked outlines filled with simple color washes for her picture books. Yet it was not until the publication of *Indian Captive* that she mastered the perfect complement of text-and-visual depiction that both embellished and added depth to the narratives of her books for middle-level readers. Both styles were equally captivating for their respective audiences.

I loved to draw and to write, and I wanted to grow up to be an author of children's books myself. Was *Strawberry Girl* the book that fueled that ambition? Were Lenski's books of realistic fiction, lodged in my brain, the reason I was drawn to become a historian—and ultimately a public historian writing for children and classrooms—instead of an author of children's literature?[9] I cannot be certain, but Lenski's stories of children from worlds so different from my own comfortable, upper-middle-class upbringing met fertile ground. My mother, Sylvia Goldinger Scharlack, had nurtured my already questing consciousness. She grew up in Los Angeles and graduated from high school in 1936, in the heart of the Great Depression. Although her family did not suffer nearly so much as many others during those dark economic times, she was instinctively sensitive to those around her who endured more hardship. She studied political science and sociology at UCLA and UC-Berkeley. Her most meaningful encounter as an undergraduate, which she talked about frequently and with great passion, involved visiting a migrant camp near Burbank and interviewing some of those who lived and worked there. When she turned in her paper, her professor accused her of being a "bleeding-heart liberal who wanted to change the world," and I think she relished that criticism. Raising her children in then-segregated Texas only fed her determination that we would grow up free of racism and class bias. Lenski was the first writer I encountered who supported my mother's worldview. That she was neither a family member nor Jewish also impressed me. My world stretched to accommodate that recognition, and it has been stretching ever since, still rooted firmly in the sense of social justice instilled by my mother and affirmed by Lenski's books.

It seems that my response was exactly what Lenski intended. Only as I began researching for this biography nearly sixty years later did I fully realize how much rigorous sociological, historical, and anthropological research she invested in her stories. Such meticulous self-taught methodology is rare in mid-twentieth-century children's literature. She steeped herself in archival research, visited different parts of the country, sketched, and listened to old and young family members as well as to entire classrooms of children who told her about their lives. From this raw material, she created characters embodying those stories, some almost verbatim. Even as a child, I sensed the power of that realism.

Lenski's complete trust in and respect for the intellectual and emotional strength of her young readers gave her the ability to write simply and directly for her preschool audience. For upper elementary readers, she had the confidence to free herself from oversimplifying language to meet generally accepted designations of children's reading levels. She grasped that the language of her narratives—especially regional dialects in dialogue—was essential in expressing both the inner and outer lives of her characters, just as the children from whom she drew her stories had shared them. Lenski believed that the middle-level reading audience would find the lives depicted within her books rich enough to make the reach in comprehension not only challenging but well worth the additional effort. To do otherwise would distort and fail to do justice to the lives of the people whose stories she had "caught." Without Lenski's use of regional dialect, readers' imaginations would not be kindled to accommodate lives well beyond their own.

Remarkably, throughout her life, Lenski retained her insatiable curiosity and the similarly intense joy of discovery that a child experiences in exploring his or her world. As an adult, she directed that energy into the painstaking research that undergirded her ability to envision, capture, and transmit her findings into accurate words and drawings that satisfied her youngest readers' demands. She provided real terminology for a cowboy's equipment and work in *Cowboy Small;* the parts of a train in *The Little Train;* the demanding duties of a fireman in *The Little Fire Engine;* and the rhythm of the seasons in *Spring Is Here, On a Summer Day, Now It's Fall,* and *I Like Winter.*[10]

Other young readers had reactions similar to mine. Growing up on her family's farm near Ladysmith, Wisconsin, in the 1950s, Peggy Marxen was impressed that Lenski's characters "were like the people I knew both flawed and heroic," and her illustrations "looked and felt like me." She also remembered that the books "delivered a hopeful message . . . struggle could be overcome by hard works and good works." In an interview, Oprah Winfrey mentioned that after reading *Strawberry Girl,* "I went through a period of Lois Lenski books." Motivated to read the entire series, she encountered "lots of stories about these little peasant children. . . . I went through a period where I wanted to be them. I would read the character, and whichever book I was reading, that's who I wanted to be that week." She later declared, "Books were my path to personal freedom." *Strawberry Girl* has remained a favorite of Oprah's, and the transformative experience of reading Lois Lenski's regionals led her to recommend that parents should make excellent series books available to their children.[11]

While Lenski opened worlds for young readers, she was reluctant to reveal too much about the day-to-day world that she herself inhabited. She left an autobiography, *Journey into Childhood,* in which she deftly described growing up in Anna, Ohio, the middle daughter in the well-disciplined household of a dedicated Lutheran pastor and his wife. Yet the further she travels on her chronological journey sketching the broad outlines of her personal and professional lives—gathered from correspondence saved by the longtime devoted friends with whom she had worked—the more detached and the less revealing her writing becomes. As a reserved individual endlessly protecting her privacy and promoting her "brand," she certainly wanted to control her legacy. No letters between her and her parents, husband, stepchildren, or children appear in her archives. When I asked prominent children's literature poet and author Lee Bennett Hopkins why he described Lenski as "a tough lady," he told me he interviewed her in 1969 for his anthology of children's authors for young readers, *Books Are by People*. He found her "adamant about reviewing anything that anyone wrote about her," and later wrote him: "I expect you to send me a copy of the piece you write about me and my work, so that I can check it for accuracy. I find that so much inaccurate and untruthful information has been printed about me—largely due to carelessness of the writer—that it is wise to have me go over it before it appears in print." Such reflexive self-protection and censorship unfortunately prevents us from gaining as much insight as we might want into her familial relationships and into the endless sacrifices she made to produce so many books and illustrations in a career spanning more than half a century.[12]

In her personal life she was the devoted wife of her former mentor-teacher, painter and muralist Arthur Covey, and a mother and stepmother to their children and grandchildren. She was also the chief breadwinner during the Great Depression and years following, as the demand for her work grew and commissions for his were few and far between. Too close to her own story, she failed to contextualize her work as a pioneer in the field of American children's literature during its seminal years from the 1920s through the 1960s. She also provided little insight into how that then-growing genre reflected the changes in the American cultural scene and the ever-expanding definition of American democratic education. So, the reader is left wanting to understand more about this courageous and generous author who provided so much grist for the generations of children nourished by her prodigious efforts.

Her writings for parents, teachers, and librarians, on the other hand, collected in *Adventure in Understanding* and scattered elsewhere in articles in a variety of periodicals, give us a fuller introduction to Lenski's worldview and rationale, if not into her personal life.[13] Lenski systematically collected her comprehensive background notes, her carefully identified photographs and sketches, her original illustrations, and the letters saved and returned by her professional and personal contacts. Instead of selecting a single archive at a university, Lenski chose to spread her vast materials

"Children of America, how many kinds are we!

America, America! We all belong to thee!"

L.L.

Lois

FIFTEEN REGIONALS

BAYOU SUZETTE

BLUE RIDGE BILLY

BOOM TOWN BOY

COAL CAMP GIRL

CORN-FARM BOY

COTTON IN MY SACK

FLOOD FRIDAY

HOUSEBOAT GIRL

JUDY'S JOURNEY

MAMA HATTIE'S GIRL

PRAIRIE SCHOOL

SAN FRANCISCO BOY

SHOO-FLY GIRL

STRAWBERRY GIRL

TEXAS TOMBOY

PRAIRIE SCHOOL
South Dakota

SAN FRANCISCO BOY
Calif.

Okla.

BOOM TOWN BOY

PACIFIC OCEAN

TEXAS TOMBOY
Texas

Numbers on map indicate locations of settings in

ROUNDABOUT AMERICA Books

by Lois Lenski

① WE LIVE IN THE SOUTH ② PEANUTS FOR BILLY BEN

③ PROJECT BOY ④ WE LIVE IN THE CITY ⑤ BERRIES IN THE SCOOP

⑥ WE LIVE BY THE RIVER ⑦ LITTLE SIOUX GIRL ⑧ WE LIVE IN THE COUNTRY

⑨ WE LIVE IN THE SOUTHWEST

Lois Lenski's USA, publicity map indicating the regionals' protagonists and their locations, ca. 1957. Reprinted by permission of the Lois Lenski Covey Foundation and Burrell Covey, copyright by Lois Lenski. Courtesy of the Lois Lenski Papers, 1893–1974, MSS 015, Martha Blakeney Hodges Special Collections and University Archives, University Libraries, University of North Carolina at Greensboro.

over two dozen public, college, and university libraries, museums, or archival repositories around the country.[14] These tangible assets of a lifetime of work astound the researcher in their comprehensive breadth and offer even more valuable insights into the complex woman behind the stories. Lenski expended considerable effort in organizing all aspects of her creative process—not so much for a future biographer but for the elementary education and library science professionals whose work, she hoped, would be made richer and deeper because of her efforts to introduce future generations to the processes and production of her book publishing.

Like Lenski, who in many ways felt her work a calling, I felt that I needed to tell her story and, in so doing, gained both more and less than I sought. Although her desire to maintain the privacy of her personal life is understandable, one wishes that she had left more of the elements of that story behind, so that a deeper sense of her familial relationships would be available. Yet tracking down her story, traveling to archives, talking with people who remembered her as a grandparent, great-aunt, neighbor, or visiting author, looking at a staggering array of her illustrations, and reading the letters to those who shared her joys in creating worlds for children to explore—all these experiences delivered far more than I imagined. Lois Lenski bequeathed a legacy of respect for the intellectual and emotional strength of children and in their ability to accept stories from life, thereby widening a path to increasing realism in American children's literature.

CHAPTER 1

GROWING UP
IN THE LENSKI HOUSEHOLD

L
ois Lenski was born in Springfield, Ohio, on October 14, 1893, the
fourth child born to Richard Charles Henry and Marietta Young
Lenski. Her father, Richard Charles Henry Lenski, served as minister
of the Zion Lutheran Church. Her mother, Marietta, had taught school
before marrying and settling into the routine of helpmate, parent, and
household manager. Both parents' professional experiences and their
European American cultural roots contributed to the family's strong
internal organization and self-conscious public representation, which
provided Lois and her siblings with a firm, if narrowly constructed, sense
of self and well-being. Born twenty-seven years before women achieved
the right to vote, Lois died in 1974 as the first wave of feminism entered
the mainstream. Her life and career demonstrate the difficulties she
faced as a woman reared in a culture where submission was considered
a feminine virtue. She had to assail that expectation in order to create
her own professional persona before most middle-class women entered the
workforce.

Lois's autobiography, *Journey into Childhood*, published in 1972, gives a
glimpse of her forebears as she recalled them late in her own life. But over
three decades earlier she actually had begun seriously documenting her
family's story in a lengthy handwritten letter to her son, Stephen, in which

she gathered "some of my memories of my childhood, which may interest you after you are grown." The succession of events in the years immediately preceding Lois's letter-writing undoubtedly affected her perspective:

> It has recently been borne in upon me that my childhood occurred in a Vanished World—a world that is now, 1940, gone, never to return. So this will be in a sense, a record, a document from that world. In this present-day of wars and rumors of wars, turmoil, despotism, labor troubles, etc. etc., it is pleasant to escape to the quiet, simple life of the turn of the century.[1]

Her family roots represent the two main variants of European immigration: her mother's family having arrived in this country several generations earlier, while her father was himself an immigrant. She knew relatively little about her ancestors—especially those on her father's side— some of which she recounted in her letter to Stephen, and other details that she included in a few paragraphs in *Journey*. Nevertheless, within these scant sketches, Lois indicates her grandparents' struggles and ambitions for their children and the sense of hard work, frugality, and dedication to task that they bequeathed to subsequent generations.

Lois's father was often known by his initials, R. C. H., although her mother, Marietta, called him Dick, and his own mother always addressed him in the German form, "Rickart" [*sic*]. The name Lenski is Polish, but R. C. H.'s father and Lois's "Grosspapa," Wilhelm Johann or William John, was born in East Prussia, "the youngest son in an aristocratic family." With primogeniture the rule, William's "oldest brother inherited the family title, while the younger was forced to leave home." He moved to Germany where he trained as a tailor and met his future wife, Lois's "Grossmama," Ernestine Louise Pittlekow. Her family was Russian, but she was born in West Prussia. Both she and William were the same age, born in 1837. Richard and his younger brother, Paul, were born in Greifenburg, Prussia, in 1864 and 1866. Like so many of their central European compatriots, the Lenski family emigrated to the United States after the Franco-Prussian War in April 1872,[2] settling in Jackson, Michigan, where they had friends and William could successfully ply his trade. Even though Ernestine was aware of William's own difficult position as the youngest son, she had her own ambitions for R. C. H., in the favored position of firstborn. Birth order determined the two sons' futures. "Grossmama's one idea was to educate my father for the ministry, which they did, with difficulty." R. C. H. was sent to Capital University, the Ohio Synod Lutheran College & Seminary in Columbus, Ohio. His younger brother, Paul, suffered "a difficult boyhood," and Lois never mentioned what became of him. But in her loosely autobiographical *A Little Girl of Nineteen Hundred*, Uncle Paul must have been the model for "Uncle Phil" and his large family—including a memorable set of twin babies—whom Lois gets to know when the Ohio family visits Michigan.[3] Lois remembered her Grossmama "as being warm and affectionate, especially to . . . my father whom she adored, and whom she had 'given to the Lord.'" Lois felt very differently about her Grosspapa. She found him "cold and cynical," recalling her fear that "he would laugh at me, although he never did."[4]

Marietta Young hailed from Franklin County, Ohio, just south of Columbus, where she was born in 1863. Her grandfather, Philip Helsel (or Heltzel back in York County, Pennsylvania), was of Pennsylvania "Dutch" (German) heritage, pioneering with his wife, Mary Willis Helsel, and their eight children as one of the original settlers in the Scioto Valley of Ohio in the early 1800s. Lois's maternal family had similarly strong ties to Lutheranism. The first Lutheran church in the area was organized in the Helsel barn near Valley Crossing. Despite these strong maternal German roots, Marietta had a real "hatred of all things German," never allowing the language to be spoken in the home. Later in life, Lois wondered why, since she and her siblings were surrounded by the language as children, and often "were taken to German church [services] as well as to English."[5]

Marietta was the middle child, with an older brother and a younger sister, raised almost entirely alone by "our Grandma Young," whose husband (of British ancestry) died before their youngest child was born. Grandma Young had to be "a woman of strong mind and character" to remain with her youngsters in a log cabin on land where she became a truck gardener in order to support and educate them. Once Marietta had received a basic education and was still quite young, she taught at a one-room rural school south of Columbus. Although she had many talents that may have led her to more visually aesthetic pursuits, she needed to be practical. To remind her of Marietta's paths not taken, Lois kept a round plaque on which her mother had painted a "spray of wood-bine" that the daughter judged "well observed & carefully painted."[6] Marietta and R. C. H. met at a box supper at the schoolhouse where she taught, then married in Columbus in February 1888. Their first child, Esther, arrived the following December, with the other children following in short order: Gerhard (1891), Oscar (1892), Lois (1893), and her younger sister, Miriam (1895).

Shortly after Lois was born, the family moved from their home at 422 Cedar Avenue to the parsonage at 416 West Columbia Street, where they lived until Lois was six. The first memory she recounts from these early and "hazy" Springfield years deals with contracting membranous croup, a life-threatening condition that she described as "a membrane growing over the windpipe." At the same time, Oscar had scarlet fever, and the house was under quarantine. A member of her father's congregation, Mrs. Theodore Hax, came daily to help Marietta care for the children. Lois credits Mrs. Hax with saving her life. "I acquired a sort of halo, a reflected glory for not having died. I was so good as to be almost angelic . . . but I am afraid I got over it speedily and my earthly nature began to assert itself."[7] Undoubtedly, Lois heard this story repeatedly and accepted it as part of her persona, which tells us more than a tale of a toddler's valiant struggle to stay alive. Her early brush with death introduces two recurring themes. The first indicates Lois's tendency to contract various illnesses and endure other physical limitations that temporarily inhibited her otherwise headlong rush to be productive. The second demonstrates the pressure she felt "to be almost angelic," even as an adult, in coping with the competing roles of artist, illustrator, author, wife, stepmother, mother, and primary breadwinner. In effect, Lois's earliest memories became a self-fulfilling prophecy.

In 1899 the family relocated to Anna, Ohio, some sixty miles northwest, when R. C. H. became pastor of St. Jacob Lutheran Church. When the Lenskis moved to Anna, it was a little farm village of two hundred residents. As Lois told her story, "When the new Lutheran preacher arrived with his wife and five children, it increased to two hundred and seven." When R. C. H. began his ministry, the church was housed in a small white frame building. Just eight years later, he helped design and proudly oversaw the building of a substantial brick edifice.[8]

While the pastor of St. Jacob Church held the respect and admiration of his congregation, R. C. H.'s annual salary of seven hundred dollars only meagerly supported his large family. The congregation of small farmers and the townspeople who serviced them periodically supplemented the pastor's income by organizing a traditional (at least in Anna) and unannounced

"Donation Party." The Lenskis might glance up from their household activities to see "a long procession of solemn, silent people . . . coming up the sidewalk from the church corner . . . with packages and bundles in their arms." These hard-working congregants brought what they could, including eggs, chicken, hams, or jam and fresh vegetables, and "home furnishings like towels or pillowcases." When they entered the parsonage, where doors were never locked, a party would ensue, where "as if by magic, refreshments appeared on the table," and R. C. H. hung lighted Japanese lanterns that enhanced the festive environment.[9]

As she grew older, Lois learned that her father's role as pastor went far beyond delivering dynamic sermons. She recalled looking out from an open school window to see a man running down the street shouting repeatedly, "Mr. F—— has hung himself." After the final bell, when classes were dismissed and students ran to see the house where the tragedy occurred, Lois was amazed to find her father "standing inside the door, his arms around the stricken young daughter, trying to comfort her." That scene remained fresh in Lois's memory, providing "one of the first intimations" that registered the force and responsibility of her father's role as "spiritual advisor in the community." Even though she had considered the tiny community of Anna "a perfect child's town," offering "all a child could enjoy and comprehend," she realized that "so did tragedy touch the lives of the children, many for the first time."[10]

Lois quickly learned that her family's life was public as well as private. Since the doors of the parsonage were open day and night, she and her siblings witnessed their father's availability to all who entered: "a farmer with a gift of smoked ham, a troubled woman in need of advice, a passing tramp begging for a handout, a visiting preacher to spend the night (they came often); a student selling Bibles, a choir director to make a complaint . . . a bereaved family to arrange for a funeral or a bride and groom to be married." All were treated with equal respect, and the Lenski children "very early learned to treat all people alike no matter who they were." The example set by their parents' dedication to serving others strongly shaped their children—just as R. C. H. and Marietta might have hoped. As Lois wrote in 1954 to a teacher she was mentoring:

As for my brothers and sisters: My older sister, Esther, "Ella," married a preacher, has 3 children & 7 or 8 grandchildren. She

& her husband still live in central Ill. I visited her there in July. "Milly" or Miriam, also married a preacher, and moved to Calif. 30 years ago; brought up her 3 children out there, has come back East only about 4 times, now has her first grandson. . . . Oscar (Ned) became a church architect, later designer of church furnishings. My older bro. Gerhard (Jerry) has been pastor of a large Lutheran church on 16th St., Wash. D.C. for over 30 years. . . . They all stayed pretty close to the church but me. I was the odd one, went to N.Y. to study art and married an artist.[11]

Although moving well beyond the sphere of her family's tight devotional circle, Lois found a way to combine communitarian compassion and creativity to serve children, parents, teachers, caregivers, and librarians.[12]

Both parents managed other aspects of their extremely busy lives in ways that easily impressed their progeny. Marietta was quite a horsewoman and enjoyed decorative flower gardening as well as raising vegetables for the family table. Because of the family's tight budget, she was able to use her eye for fashion and enormous skills as a dressmaker and tailor to provide the entire family with all their clothing, including suits for the boys and R. C. H. Lois remembered her mother's "great love of beauty, which . . . had few outlets."[13] Lois clearly empathized with her mother's inability to spend more of her time fulfilling her own creative imperatives.

In addition to being a pastor and a serious religious scholar, R. C. H. pursued a series of hobbies that included gardening and raising various kinds of fowl. An excellent photographer and the only one in town, he "did all his own developing and printing of negatives (glass plates) and pictures, and mounted them with professional skill." By helping him, Lois learned the entire process. R. C. H. photographed every aspect of the community's family life cycle events—wedding couples, new babies, family parties— the photographs becoming "a social record of a rural Ohio community at the turn of the century." As was customary in the years of her childhood, people often wanted photographs of recently deceased family members. R. C. H. obliged them with photographs of their loved ones in their coffins, and Lois imagined that these mementos must have been "a comfort to the survivors." She and her siblings saw "nothing morbid" in them and often played funeral: "We put the dolls in shoeboxes, dug holes in the ground, buried them with a long sermon and a few hymns, and put flowers on the

Lois and her mother, Marietta Lenski, about 1900. R. C. H. Lenski, photographer. Courtesy of Jeanine Covey Gutowski, Vivian Covey, and Michael Covey.

Lois and her father, R. C. H. Lenski, about 1897. Courtesy of Jeanine Covey Gutowski, Vivian Covey, and Michael Covey.

graves" before digging them up again.[14] The Lenski children accepted darkness and death as a part of life. The value of visually documenting a community in all its aspects resonated with Lois's emerging sensibilities. Such experiences undoubtedly shaped her ability to share the unpleasant realities of daily living that she wove into her realistic books for middle-level readers.

Lois described herself as a child who observed more readily than she participated. Even in play with her beloved younger sister, Miriam, who shared "my every movement and thought and activity. . . . Miriam's play was active, mine was passive. Miriam enacted drama with her dolls, while I, busy sewing for mine, watched her. . . . I watched and listened."[15] Miriam had a best friend across the street; Lois did not. Instead, she "watched and listened" (and remembered) very intently, for she was able to use details of what she experienced when she was very young as fodder for her own fiction over two decades later.

Beyond the handsome, newly constructed St. Jacob Church of 1907, Lois thought that the small town of Anna contained "no particular beauty or grace." Yet its lack of aesthetic appeal was insignificant. The small village contained all the basics needed to service its inhabitants and the surrounding farms, and Lois developed a firm and secure sense of her place within it. Anna, she fondly recalled, "soon became my own, a compound of sights and sounds and smells and buildings and people that became a part of me." Lois remembered her delight in running errands for the family. The parsonage sat in the block just north of St. Jacob. When Lois turned right at the intersection dominated by the church, she immediately passed the doctor's office and his residence just beyond as she headed down Main Street into town. The next block was more exciting to a child, with a fire station, town hall, commercial buildings, saloon, and finally Woehrle's Grocery on the corner where she could dash in, ask for "a pound of Arbuckle's XXXX Coffee," shouting back, "Charge it!" as she dashed out. The ice cream parlor across the street tempted her, and that side of Main Street also held two imposing corner mansions, the drugstore and Finkenbine's Department Store: dry goods on one side, groceries on the other. Further down, she could race by the hotel to pick up mail or deliver a letter to the post office, then take off for the depot by the Cincinnati Hamilton and Dayton railroad tracks to see a train coming into town, or stare at the grain elevator beyond. She soon felt that "the town that looked so commonplace and unpromising at first improved with time. . . . The little stores were places of enchantment . . . The fields and meadows and orchards and vacant lots unexplored kingdoms of thrilling adventure."[16]

The power of Lois's accurate observations and memory supplied enough material to furnish her first two, largely autobiographical, storybooks. The charming cover imagery of streets of Victorian homes and endpapers with a bird's-eye map of "Greenhill" set the nostalgic tone of *Skipping Village* (1927), augmented by the whimsical pen illustrations sprinkled liberally throughout the text. A less generously sized companion volume, *A Little Girl of Nineteen Hundred*, published the following year, was similar in style.[17]

In her autobiography, *Journey into Childhood*, Lois devoted as many pages to describing the parsonage as she did to introducing the members of her family, so intertwined were the *setting* of her childhood and the lives of those who lived within it. She recounted in minute detail every exterior and interior feature of the rambling Anna parsonage built a decade and a

Lutheran parsonage, Anna, Ohio, 1905, with the whole Lenski family in the front yard. R. C. H. Lenski, photographer. Courtesy of Jeanine Covey Gutowski, Vivian Covey, and Michael Covey.

half earlier by German carpenters, "a house like none other in the world . . . with its steep gables and peaks and small porches . . . ornamented with gingerbread trim." She deemed it "a perfect place for children . . . full of mystery and magic."[18]

Given the remarkable gifts of observation Lois acquired as a youngster and retained throughout her life, the Anna parsonage filled her with a keen appreciation for the many lively and memorable scenes the setting offered. More than fodder for her early autobiographical books, the importance of *place* solidly grounded her.

Beloved childhood home! Not a square foot of that house or yard, not a single detail of color or pattern or object but would stay with me till my last day, so vivid are the impressions of childhood!

Small house, small yard, small town—it was a very small world to have been the center of all those activities and dramas and escapades, all those joys and delights, sorrows too, of a family of five growing children. It was a small world made luminous and beautiful . . . bounded only by the unfettered imaginations of five growing children. A small world, a good world, a fortunate world in which to grow up.[19]

Lois translated this intersection of setting and family into a broader understanding of the effects of environment on personal development when she began to delve into the childhoods of the past in her historical works of the 1930s and early 1940s. She applied her emphasis on "place" still more powerfully in her regionals, a series she developed from the 1940s through the 1960s, which included her Newbery Award–winning *Strawberry Girl* (1945). When she wrote *Shoo-Fly Girl* (1963) about an Amish family, Lois recognized the parallels to her own childhood in a world populated by people of German heritage.[20] In a far larger sense, her devotion to depicting family life in a wide variety of circumstances in many geographical locations underscores her belief in the centrality of place in shaping character. In "Place and People," a lecture delivered at Illinois State University in 1965, she describes herself as "the Listener," visiting families in various parts of the country:

> The scene varies. . . .
>
> But the home—underneath all the outward differences—the home is the heart of security for the children. It may not even have a roof—it may be a tent, a trailer, a boat, a Quonset hut, a tumble-down shack. American children live in them all. . . .
>
> The Listener senses the setting and feels at home there. He sits back and drinks in the words, savoring each and hoarding them like treasure. Through words, the story, the plot, the drama takes form. . . .
>
> The Listener is transported into the lives of others.[21]

Although somewhat contrived, Lois's speech describes her self-taught anthropological or sociological research—what she calls elsewhere "getting books from life"—from which her regionals sprung. For each of her regional residencies, she proudly stated, "This is the way it was in this Place. This is the Truth. . . . Where I have gone and what I have sensed,

I will give to my readers." She often expressed her deepest feelings in rhyme or, later, collaborating with the talented children's author and composer Clyde Robert Bulla, in lyrics. She ended the talk with these original lines:

> Land that never knew my birthplace,
> Land accepted, chosen, prized;
> Land unlike my native region,
> By adoption realized.
>
> Land unknown but never alien,
> Land so new of me a part;
> Once I gave it understanding,
> There I buried roots and heart.[22]

As she more fully grasped the depth and power of these childhood associations, Lois carried her sense of the primacy of family and home to its most universal application. The roots of that keen sensitivity were nurtured in the Anna parsonage, under the watchful supervision of devoted parents.

"As a child, I felt that I had the right kind of father," one who "always had a good supply of pins under the lapel of his coat, a sharp penknife in his pants pocket, and a half-a-dozen pencils in his vest pocket. All these things come in handy when a little girl has need of them." Lois admired her studious father,[23] who often spent hours at a time in his study or "*sanctum sanctorum*," and from her sense of her father's personal work space, she "early got the idea that it was a good thing to have a room with a closed door to keep others out, a desk inside with plenty of pens and pencils, a place to write down what one was thinking, a place where ideas came . . . a place to get away from others," in other words, "a most desirable place." Although Lois had to wait until she was married and living in rural Connecticut, she understood that she would need her own *sanctum sanctorum* in which to be a productive artist, illustrator, and author.[24]

Lois knew her father as a well-respected scholar and pastor, a "determined man" who "held fast to his own opinions . . . and the courage of his convictions." Authoritative and authoritarian, R. C. H. was a real "stickler" for the church rules as he interpreted them, and in the pulpit, unafraid to call out by name anyone who deviated, a reputation that was still recalled by congregants decades later.

As Lois sat with her mother and siblings in church, she watched her father in the pulpit

> with his finger pointing at sinners in the congregation! He was a fearful and somewhat terrifying person, speaking in reverberating, ringing tones, with power in his delivery and magnetism in his voice. . . . Papa, important, forbidding, sometimes fiercely angry and unapproachable, who later that same day back home at the dinner table, became just plain Papa, beloved and friendly again. We looked up to him with genuine awe and respect, and at the same time, we loved him dearly.[25]

Lois described R. C. H.'s "intense bright blue eyes" that seemed capable of looking right through a guilty individual. But those same eyes often twinkled with a keen sense of humor, and he passed on both to his middle daughter. When Lois won the Newbery Medal for *Strawberry Girl* in 1946, beloved children's author Maud Hart Lovelace—for whom Lois had illustrated the first several of her popular Betsy-Tacy books—wrote an appreciation in *The Horn Book* in which she mentioned Lois's "very bright blue" eyes, "full of the humor with which her books abound." Lovelace's description of Lois's personality also mirrors some of the traits that Lois attributed to her own father:

> I found her forceful, enthusiastic, gay, but still not vivacious in the manner I had anticipated. For all the animation with which she plunged into discussion of pictures, paper and binding for the book in process of creation, there was in her personality an underlying stratum of calm, the calm which comes from positive convictions, from an assured purpose in life, and from steady continuing accomplishment.[26]

Not surprisingly, R. C. H.'s strict moral dictums "expected obedience . . . without question, delay, or argument," and Lois remembered him "cold and undemonstrative in affection." Like his own father—but "unlike his warm and affectionate, outgoing mother"—R. C. H. found it difficult "to show the soft side of his nature." Lois admired his methodical and self-disciplined nature, adhering to a "regular schedule for work and for play for all the days of the week. . . . Whatever he did, he did with intelligence and intensity and thoroughness." Like her father, Lois was never happier than when working. She, too, was generally reserved in her interpersonal relations with family members, finding her greatest pleasure in exercising her abundant intellectual and creative energies. Actually, both parents taught their children to think of work as "a joy and a delight." Lois grew to regard work as "sacred." Many years later, after a long bout of illness for which she had been hospitalized, she confessed how much that enforced "vacation" had kept her from her "beloved work." Just as when she was sewing for her dolls, Lois was only truly happy when she was working.[27]

Her warmest moments with her mother occurred in the family kitchen when she and Esther were helping with chores, recalling that they "came closer to her at these times than at any other." Lois consciously emulated her mother. "Whatever Mama did, I did . . . and I learned how to do things *right*, too. . . . How she *ever* did *all* she did as *well* as she did, I don't know." Marietta was an extremely frugal housekeeper, a trait she absorbed from her widowed mother and passed directly to Lois, who emulated her scrimping by writing or sketching story lines and illustrations on the reverse sides of manuscript pages returned from publishers and recycling many other materials. Marietta reserved little time for herself, her busy schedule in Anna revolving around her family and her responsibilities as president of the Ladies' Society at the church.

Yet Marietta was a quiet rebel in her own way. In the frame building housing St. Jacob Church, women sat on one side, and men on the other, "in old-world style." Ignoring local custom, she would enter after the service had begun, holding Miriam and Lois by the hand, and defiantly sit with her children on the men's side. As the pastor's wife, and the best-dressed woman and loveliest singer in the congregation, she must have enjoyed the privilege of doing so without fear of retribution. Lois admired her mother's sense of self-worth.

Only as an adult did she learn that her mother had given birth to another baby after Miriam, but the infant either died soon after birth or was stillborn. She recalled her father telling her, "Mama's health was never good from that time on." And Lois agreed, adding that her mother's health declined rapidly in later years because she had "worked far beyond her strength" without a doctor's proper care."[28]

The close-knit family—with occasional impromptu visits from Grandma Young, who always arrived unexpectedly to help her daughter, carrying all her possessions in a suitcase as she moved from one of her children's homes to the next—created a secure setting for the five Lenski children, all of whom seemed to enjoy one another's company. As the oldest, Esther exerted "considerable influence" over her younger siblings. "When she was not coaxing us into carrying out one of her lively schemes, she was always reading." Despite the five years between them, she and Lois built and retained "a congenial companionship and devotion for each other," which remained intact as long as they both lived. Otherwise, Gerhard and Oscar were "the boys," and Lois and Miriam "the girls." Miriam and Lois were loving and inseparable, even though "Miriam was a great favorite of my father's." Lois dedicated *A Little Girl of Nineteen Hundred* to her younger sister, and the reader senses the tenderness of their relationship in this thinly veiled depiction of the family.[29]

Lois felt that she "suffered from intense shyness" and also experienced the disadvantages of her position as the fourth child. With "three older ones to battle," she found herself "on the defensive most of the time." But she also admitted the advantages of being among strongly competitive siblings. As each learned to defend his or her own turf, "we learned a ready give-and-take," early and successful strategies for learning to be independent in her dealings with the world beyond the parsonage and Anna.[30]

Yet she was alert to what it meant to be a "P. K." or "preacher's kid," although these phrases were not hers. As the children of the Lutheran minister, "everyone looked up to us," Lois remembered. "We sensed that and tried to live up to it, although we often failed. . . . We had to keep our own counsel, not talk too much, above all, not judge others." Lois sensed that her own shyness was undoubtedly compounded by the necessity to remain somewhat apart because of the family's position in the community.[31]

In the quiet security of her Anna upbringing, Lois awoke to the first intimations of her attraction to literature and art, even though she had no way of predicting that these pleasures served as early signs of her career orientation. All the household experienced Christmases as "sheer magic," with the kitchen filled with the wonderful smells from Esther's

"The Glorious Fourth," 1901, an excellent example of one of R. C. H. Lenski's "artistic" photographs. Courtesy of Jeanine Covey Gutowski, Vivian Covey, and Michael Covey.

and Marietta's baking, a special program at the church where the Lenski children often had "pieces" to speak, and on Christmas morning, the joy of opening gifts. Beyond the dolls, hair ribbons, and other articles of clothing, "the important thing was *books*. We each had a pile and could hardly wait to start reading them. . . . We loved them and preferred them to all other gifts." Lois listed those she "grew up on," classics such as the *Little Women* series, by Louisa May Alcott; *The Five Little Peppers and How They Grew*, by Margaret Sidney; and *Rebecca of Sunnybrook Farm* and other books by Kate Douglas Wiggin, another of Lois's favorite authors. Although she regretted growing up "without benefit of *Alice in Wonderland*, *Treasure Island*, and *Huckleberry Finn* . . . our diet in books was a good one, considering how few books there were for children to read then."[32] Lois does not suggest that her parents objected to the classics that she missed; she simply was not exposed to them. Her childhood in the 1890s and early 1900s preceded by two decades the first surge in children's book publishing in this country. That initial wave included Lois's illustrative work.

Lois did not recognize sufficiently, even in her autobiography, how significantly her parents' own aesthetic interests nurtured her similar bent, long before she thought about "art" as art. R. C. H. took his photography very seriously and, "in addition to camera with tripod, acquired professional backdrops and props." He often arranged his young children in "artistic poses" on the brick back porch: Lois with her hair "flowing," unbound from tight braids, "smelling a lilac . . . Esther holding her violin at a precarious angle like a concert player . . . There was no end to his ingenuity and invention."[33] His arrangement of a variety of such tableaux of village life in a black-and-white format on paper impressed his middle daughter, even if she remained unaware of the ultimate impact this sense of layout and design would have on her life's work.

Lois enjoyed shadowing her mother when gardening and especially appreciated sharing in her mother's love of flowers. (Later, R. C. H. also became interested in raising flowers.) Mother and daughter became a team in planning, selecting, and executing garden beds for the Anna house.

> By the time I was eight, my mother and I studied the seed catalogs in the spring, made out orders for vegetable and flower seeds and gloated when they came. We both loved to watch a plant through its whole cycle of growth, from seed to bloom to seed again. We planted a vegetable garden, but our chief interest was in flowers. . . . The blooms on our beds of annuals and perennials were our pride and joy. While Esther and Miriam did the housework inside, Mama and I worked outside, busy with spade, rake, and hoe.[34]

Gardening remained a significant outlet for Lois throughout her life.

In emulating her mother's love of fashion and skills as a seamstress, Lois had begun making doll clothes at six, absorbed in creating in miniature what her mother was designing for the family. Lois loved mastering the techniques her mother taught her and exercising her creativity in designing. She decided that she would like to be a dressmaker when she grew up. Through this interest, she also inadvertently made her first foray into publishing. Marietta subscribed to a monthly magazine, *Woman's Home Companion*, which contained a children's page known as "Aunt Janet." Lois invented a workbasket for her sewing, "to be made of pieces of cardboard covered with cloth and fitted together, then tied with ribbon bows at the corners," and sent the instructions to Aunt Janet. When the magazine printed her directions and diagrams, Lois submitted a doll's nightgown she had created "with a lacy yoke and hemstitched hem." Aunt Janet rewarded her efforts with "a note of praise," a piece of fabric, and a doll's dress pattern.[35]

Lois had already demonstrated that she could dispense with her shyness when she was sharing something that she had created—another skill that she found necessary to ply repeatedly as a working illustrator and a beginning author seeking out publishers. When her third-grade teacher, Rose Foster, learned that she liked to draw, Rose gave her pictures of flowers from seed catalogs to copy, which Lois did in watercolor. A fresco artist (whom Lois did not name) came to Anna specifically to paint the church. He soon discovered Lois's talent and told R. C. H. that she needed a better box of watercolors than the beginner's set that she was using. R. C. H. gave him the money to provide Lois with a professional box of Windsor Newton watercolors that could "last a lifetime," and, indeed, she only had to replace the paints once. Under the fresco artist's temporary tutelage, Lois began copying covers of *Woman's Home Companion* and, once again, submitted them to Aunt Janet. One of these, a "charming painting" of the previous week's cover of a mother and child earned her a three-dollar prize. This was a "big moment" for Lois, especially when her father put his arm around her mother's shoulder and bragged, "Just think! Our Lois has won the three-dollar prize!"[36]

On the other hand, R. C. H.'s lack of enthusiasm could pierce her heart. Lois usually entered her paintings in the Shelby County Fair each fall, often winning prizes. One can sense the hurt she still felt when she wrote more than half a century later that her father would shake his head and tell her that her works "would be good, if they were only original." But R. C. H. was not an art teacher, and he did not know how to encourage Lois in that direction. She bemoaned the fact that she had no one to mentor her: "What a pity that no one told me to just draw all the things around me, to draw everything I saw, instead of copying other pictures. I had no idea 'how to be original' and it was many years before I learned. . . . All the pictures I drew or painted before I was fifteen were copies. I did not begin the study of art until I went to college." Knowing nothing of the history of art and never having visited a museum or art gallery, Lois was unaware of the venerable tradition of European artists who set up their easels or

This is the copy of the cover of *Mother's Home Companion* that garnered Lois her three dollar prize. Reprinted by permission of the Lois Lenski Covey Foundation and Burrell Covey, copyright by Lois Lenski. Courtesy of the Lois Lenski Collection, Western History Collection, University of Oklahoma Libraries, Norman.

sat with their sketchbooks in museums, learning to draw and paint by imitating the work of masters. In spite of the restrictions of her small-town childhood life, Lois concluded that she had gained "a love of people as well as of plants and growing things, and somehow in this perhaps unpromising soil, a seed was sown and nourished, the seed of creative life."[37]

What to make of the two chapters in *A Little Girl of Nineteen Hundred* that may be a wishful depiction of these early artistic endeavors? Although Lois makes no mention in *Journey* of Ella Brockway, her mother's friend from Springfield, "Miss Edna Bolivar of Smithfield" plays an important role in her interactions with "Flora," Lois's fictional version of herself in *A Little Girl*. In one chapter, beautiful and fashionable Miss Bolivar comes for a visit and gives Flora a doll. Flora refuses to accept it because one of the neighbor women had criticized her for being too old to play with dolls. In its stead, Miss Bolivar presents Flora with

> a wonderful box of water-color paints! . . . And then Miss Bolivar said there must be some water-color paper, too. So she bought a whole pad of it.
>
> The minute Flora saw that box of water-colors in the store, she made up her mind to be an artist! . . . Much nicer than getting married and spending your life washing dishes and other things you hate. It might be worth while growing up after all, if you could spend all your time doing something you liked.[38]

Flora finally shows Miss Bolivar her dolls and the lovely dresses she had made for them, and Miss Bolivar reassures the little girl by telling her, *"You're never too old to play with dolls, if you love them!* It must be true if Miss Bolivar said so. It must be true if Miss Bolivar and Mother both said so!"[39]

In a later chapter, Miss Bolivar invites Flora to come visit her in Smithfield, alone. Flora does so and has a wonderful time, sending enthusiastic letters back home describing her adventures. When she returns home,

> Mother told her how much they had enjoyed her letters. She said she was very proud of them. Not many girls of twelve could write so well.
>
> Flora's eyes sparkled. What a good idea! She wouldn't be a dressmaker and she wouldn't be an artist! Why hadn't she thought of it before? She'd be a writer! She'd write books! . . .
>
> She would write the True Story of Her Life. So many things to write about. . . . All the things that it was impossible to talk about.[40]

Was Ella Brockway the model for Miss Bolivar? Or was this Lois's lovely fantasy of an early precocious self who knew exactly what she wanted to do to satisfy her insatiable curiosity? Was there an unmarried and independent woman mentor who realized that marriage might be an impediment to creativity? Lois reported that Ella "went to France and brought Miriam and me little French boy dolls which we treasured. . . . She always dressed in the latest fashion and I looked up to her in awe and admiration." Lois's encounters with a real or imagined Miss Bolivar recur when many of the protagonists she creates have a "Miss Bolivar" in their lives as well.[41]

At elementary school, Lois was "always at the 'head of the class,' where my parents expected me to be." But high school in Anna proved to be below the ambitions of the Lenski parents.[42] The older two children, Esther and Gerhard, stayed with an aunt in Springfield to attend high school, and in 1908 Oscar and Lois transferred to Sidney to complete their secondary school education. They commuted on the trolley known as the Interurban Railway. Lois flourished in high school, where she produced her first written pieces—book reports, essays, and short stories. In Sidney, she also gained access to a public library and became an even more voracious reader, her old favorite authors giving way to new ones: Dickens, Thackeray, and Scott, but "Dickens above all with his vivid word pictures of real people, their trials and temptations, their sorrows and their joys. . . . There was no end to a young reader's happiness."[43] Lois had found her literary mentor, one whose sense of social justice she absorbed along with the characters and plots she admired. She, too, would seek to create those "vivid word pictures of real people" and add her own poignant illustrations for the youngsters who became her own readers.

By the time Lois graduated in 1911, R. C. H. was planning to relocate his family to Columbus to become a professor of classical languages and theology while earning his doctorate in divinity at his alma mater, Capital University. At the time, Capital University admitted no female students. The move to Columbus gave Lois the opportunity to matriculate at Ohio State University. The move to Columbus also meant that Lois was leaving her childhood. Her senior English teacher in Sidney, Frances Sharp, wrote a letter in which she told her promising former student, "I hope you will specialize in English in college, for I feel sure you will do some form of creative work." Twenty-five years later, Lois mailed her a copy of *Phebe Fairchild, Her Book*, the first of Lois's historical novels, which was also her first "chapter book" that was not autobiographical. With the publication of *Phebe Fairchild*, Lois believed that she had finally fulfilled her teacher's "prophecy."[44]

Lois returned to Anna only once, in 1961, fifty years after she left, and found that most of the town was unchanged. "Many stores and homes along the shady streets were the same, the people looked and talked the same, giving me a warm welcome." She contacted the Rev. F. J. Mittermaier, a former seminary student of her father's, who was then pastor of St. Jacob Evangelical Lutheran Church—the very building in Anna that he helped design and oversee being constructed in 1907. Rev. Mittermaier and his wife graciously invited Lois to visit them in the old parsonage, and she reported that although the exterior had been changed, "inside I had no trouble visualizing the lively activities of the Lenski family a half-century before. It was, in every sense, a joy to go home again, to re-live in memory the life of that little girl with flaxen braids who liked to draw pictures before she had learned how."[45]

CHAPTER 2

QUIETLY REBELLIOUS

ois's nostalgic account of her childhood, beginning as an extended letter to Stephen and expanding into the first chapter of *Journey into Childhood* over a quarter of a century later, is more than twice as long as any other chapter in her autobiography. She poured many delightful and telling anecdotes into the lovingly recalled experiences of growing up before she began to confront the inevitable conflicts between the practical route her parents had mapped for her and what she termed "the path of my destiny." Lois's account of her life beyond the age of seventeen, as described in *Journey into Childhood*, is singularly disappointing in its lack of satisfying details to support and augment the rudimentary chronology. Why? One can only speculate. That she recognized the appeal of these cherished childhood years is apparent from her dipping into them to write and illustrate *Skipping Village* and *A Girl of Nineteen Hundred*. When she began to narrate these years as a straight autobiography in 1941, she was not quite fifty years old, still filled with abundant creative vigor, and not yet the nationally acclaimed author-illustrator that she would become just a few years later. In contrast, Lois was at the end of her long, productive career and already in ill health in the late 1960s when she returned to her earlier notes and began to write her autobiography in earnest.[1] *Journey into Childhood* was published in 1972, and she died two years later. She could not invest the same intensity in the remaining chapters, not simply because she lacked the inclination and energy, but because she did not want to reveal too much detail about her personal life. As an extremely private individual who guarded her public image, Lois sought to concentrate primarily on reinforcing the professional profile already familiar in its broad outlines.

After dispensing with "Student Days," the second chapter in *Journey*, she divides the next three chapters—"The Twenties," "The Thirties," "The Forties and the Fifties"—into two sections, "Personal" and "Professional." Only the final chapter, "Later Years," less than ten pages in length, contains "Personal and Professional" as its sole subheading. Even though Lois worked in a studio at home, she kept these two spheres separate, and she chose to emphasize in her autobiography the *beginnings*, literally, the journey into the childhood of her public persona, the noted author and illustrator. In these early, relatively easy pre-collegiate years, she was a mostly dutiful and unspoiled daughter in an orderly small-town setting, the very environment that prepared her siblings for the prescribed roles that kept them close to the Lutheran church. But once the family moved to Columbus and Lois embarked on her undergraduate studies, she slowly began to realize that she had her own star to follow. She spent her college years, consciously or unconsciously, trying to resolve the opening gulf between parental expectations and her own hesitantly emerging sense of self. The experience of separation must have been difficult, especially for a gifted young woman bursting forth from the confines of such well-defined boundaries in the second decade of the twentieth century.

As the family was moving to Columbus and their furniture was being transported from Anna, the youngest members, Lois and Miriam, visited their aunt Ida in Lancaster. An anecdote from that visit reveals more about Lois's future than she could have imagined before her college career was even underway. A "little neighbor girl, only three years old" came daily to call at her aunt's, settling herself on the front porch at Lois's feet with her doll and a few toys. She had come to play and talk. This "unusually loquacious" child chose to share her thoughts unself-consciously. Lois responded by transcribing the "uninterrupted conversation" verbatim. That fall, in her freshman English class, Lois used the material she had documented for a theme she composed. She was astonished when "the professor read it aloud to the class and commended the author as a 'perspicacious observer.'"[2]

The Ohio State University lay across the city from the Lenski home adjacent to Capital University. When Lois began her freshman year in 1911, she enrolled in its College of Education—her parents' practical choice of study as "the most respectable profession for a woman." As an added benefit, the tuition of ten dollars per semester fit the family's budget; secondhand books could be purchased from the college bookstore; and Lois could continue living at home and commute to campus on the trolley. She studied during that full hour she traveled each way, but her social life was nonexistent. Marietta was not well and needed Lois's help with cooking and housework. Years later, Lois mentioned that one of her professors described her as quite the serious student, which was probably the case, since "there was no fun in my life at all at this time, and very little diversion."[3]

Lois followed her parents' wishes by majoring in education, but she selected art courses as electives, "venturing timidly into this unknown field" because she liked to draw. These electives were chiefly in design and lettering, and she was taught by one of the experts in the field at the time. Thomas E. French wrote textbooks on mechanical drawing, some of which remain in print today in revised and updated versions. Lois took both engineering drawing and lettering from him, acquiring the skills to "draw up house plans and specifications, complete enough for a contractor to build from." Understanding the language and terms of creating materials to meet specifications certainly proved useful in dealing with publishers. Lettering had a more direct application, since Lois hand-lettered all her own book jackets and title pages. She regretted that only in her senior year did she finally take a course in "figure-drawing from a costumed model," and had little chance to progress in the one area she felt she most needed.[4]

Tellingly, the most pleasurable activities as an undergraduate came not from Lois's interactions with other students—in her autobiography, she does not name even one college friend made during those years—but from her work with children. Even though she was preparing to teach English at the secondary level, Lois also studied German, which presented no difficulty after growing up surrounded by the language. On Saturday afternoons, she invited a group of neighborhood children to the Lenski home for refreshments and storytelling, translating French and German folktales in order to increase her repertoire. She worked on improving her own abilities to entertain and enthrall her young audiences and acquired Sara Cone Bryant's *How to Tell Stories to Children* and Linda E. Richards's *The*

Golden Windows. The tales in the latter she told "over and over again and loved them as much as the children did."[5]

Through her brother Gerhard, Lois learned about summer recreation employment at city playgrounds, and she was hired to teach crafts—principally sewing and paper cutting—and to assist the regular recreation teacher in leading "ring games, singing games, and folk-dancing," all of which Lois enjoyed immensely. During the winter, the summer instructors received training from the city recreational department, where they were given "concrete suggestions as to projects to be carried out with children." But that was not enough to satisfy Lois's intellectual curiosity about working most effectively with youngsters. Just as she researched and rehearsed for her informal Saturday storytelling sessions, she turned to the Columbus public library for books that might provide additional guidance. This search led her to the works of three of the most innovative European educators of the nineteenth and early twentieth centuries: the Swiss Johann Heinrich Pestalozzi (1746–1827), German Friedrich Froebel (1782–1852), and Italian Maria Montessori (1870–1952).[6]

Pestalozzi was the earliest of these revolutionary thinkers. He approached educating young learners in ways that stressed their capacity for independent thought and discovery through spontaneous play and direct interaction with their environments. Such a concept of fostering children's intellectual and emotional potential differed radically from the traditional approach to educating students through more direct, authoritarian teaching. Pestalozzi believed that education should be balanced, placing equal emphasis on "head, hands, and heart," which in twenty-first-century terms would be considered holistic development of the "inner dignity of each individual." Such an approach reflected Pestalozzi's commitment to social justice, because he believed education could improve society at all levels.[7]

Friedrich Froebel, whose father, like Lois's, was a minister, studied with Pestalozzi. Froebel believed that humans are "essentially productive and creative—fulfillment comes through developing these [attributes] in harmony with God and the world." His insight that the earliest years of a child's life were critical to intellectual development and that play therefore contributed to their understanding of the world led him to found the first kindergarten and to develop special basic toys or "gifts" that, through direct manipulation, could facilitate early learning.[8]

Maria Montessori emphasized the faith that an educator should have in the child's ability of self-revelation through work "in a favorable environment that will encourage the flowering of a child's natural gifts." She believed that a child's confidence grew through gaining mastery at his or her own pace, with the teacher's role as a mentor who encourages and facilitates that mastery. Like Pestalozzi and Froebel, Montessori's methodology had universal applicability, for she embraced education as a means of furthering "the interests of humanity at large and of civilization, and before such great forces we can recognize only one country—the entire world."[9]

All three educators championed the significance of early childhood in human development and therefore believed in educating the very young—of all classes of society—as a force for social justice. They also respected the inherent abilities of children's intellects and formed their philosophies in response to their direct observations and interactions with children. Their interrelated approaches reinforced Lois's natural predilection for observing and listening—absorbing all information—before creatively responding.

Although Lois never disclosed how the writings of these revolutionary educators may have influenced her, their ideas undoubtedly and ultimately shaped her own works for and about young children and her advice to parents, librarians, and teachers in articles and lectures. In "Let Your Child Draw; Don't Teach Him," which she wrote for *Better Homes and Gardens* in 1935, Lois described the way her own son, Stephen (then age six), had responded to the "inborn expression" of drawing. She believed that as soon as a child holds "a pencil, at 3 or even earlier, he will draw—and he will draw continuously if given encouragement. Drawing is the first creative power which appears." But she also argued that the aim is not to make the child an artist, but "simply to give him a facility in self-expression that will be of lasting value to him throughout life. . . . Let him draw what he will in his own way."[10] Such advice demonstrates that Lois had absorbed the principles espoused by Pestalozzi, Froebel, and Montessori and had applied them in her observations and work with children, including her own. She was also rebelling against the artistic sterility that she herself had experienced as a child. Lois felt that in copying pictures, only her imitative abilities had been encouraged. No one had helped free her young imaginative powers.

Lois openly credited the essential role children played in her own writing and illustrations: "I cannot create my books without the help of children. I go to them to observe, to listen, and to learn. Only with their help and inspiration do my stories and pictures grow and develop." She recognized that the child's perspective was essential. "Even in a picture book for the preschool child, where words and lines must be used with the strictest economy, I must somehow catch up with the very essence of his being, so that it shines through and wins his ready yet inarticulate accep-tance."[11] Surely the intellectual journey that began as a response to her summer employment became as instrumental as any of her coursework at Ohio State.

As a senior at Ohio State, Lois illustrated for several campus publica-tions and gained her first exposure to publishing when she was chosen art editor for the 1915 yearbook, the *Makio*. She produced charming, humor-ous, and highly stylized black-and-white, "full-page cartoonlike drawings for the headings of the different sections."[12] Was this experience positive enough to ignite the impulse to pursue dreams quite at odds with those of her education major? Or were the cumulative excursions into her art elec-tives responsible for giving her the backbone to buck parental expectations?

June 1915 proved to be a banner month for the Lenskis, with four degrees awarded to three family members: Lois, her father, and her brother Oscar. Lois received the bachelor of science in education, Oscar both the bachelor of arts at Capital and bachelor of architecture at Ohio State, and R. C. H. the doctor of divinity at Capital.

Marietta and R. C. H. anticipated that Lois would be applying for a position and, with her avid interest in art, perhaps become an art teacher. But Lois simply refused to accept the career that seemed inevitable. She received several good offers but rejected them all. Years later, she reflected on her fierce desire to pursue her own destiny.

It is remarkable that each time I evaded it [teaching school] and chose another path. Teaching would have brought me the contacts with children which I instinctively wanted and was looking for, but always another star loomed over the horizon, beckoning me on. I did not know what this star was or where it led, but I followed it blindly and with a sure faith.[13]

Louise Shepherd, one of Lois's art instructors and the only woman faculty member that she mentioned, had studied in New York City. She advised Lois to do the same. Lois found Shepherd's encouragement "the first step in finding my chosen work" and began to make plans to follow that dream, despite her father's "vigorous opposition." R. C. H. refused to help her financially, fearing for her personal safety as a young woman alone in a large city probably as much as he feared that her change in career choice would be both economically irresponsible and socially unacceptable. Lois understood his motive to protect her but resented her father's refusal to recognize her desire for additional training in art. R. C. H. simply felt that she needed to be self-supporting. Rather than cave in to the practical concerns that he raised, Lois enlisted the help of the head of the Ohio State Art Department, Charles Fabens Kelley, to plead her case to her father. Only after this visit did R. C. H. "give his reluctant consent." She remembered the internal turmoil of that decision, possibly the first time she had thwarted the will of her domineering father: "How I ever summoned up enough courage to make the break from home in the face of his disapproval, and embark into this adventure into the unknown, I do not know. I was sober-minded, timid, inexperienced, and practically never traveled at all. But something inside was urging me on and I had to listen to it."[14]

Although the decision must have been intensely emotionally wrenching, Lois was taking charge of her destiny. In spite of her inexperience, she had found the inner fortitude to marshal her own perseverance against her father's will and gain her independence. The strength she gained from this confrontation helped her face each new challenge. By standing up to her father, she realized that she had absorbed enough of R. C. H.'s mettle to make it on her own. Lois was beginning to abandon her timidity in earnest.

In October 1915 Lois followed the advice of Louise Shepherd, took her three hundred dollars in savings, and boarded the train to Manhattan. Once there, she headed straight for the Studio Club on East 62nd Street, the YWCA branch designated for "women students of art, music, and drama." With her limited funds, Lois was assigned to a "neighborhood house" in a brownstone on a side street. When she saw the tiny room, "7 × 11 feet" holding only "a narrow cot and one straight-back chair," she was "speechless." But it was a place to start. And she found the Studio Club "a wonderful anchorage" in the city where she interacted with other young independent, career-oriented women and appreciated the "opportunity to get needed help and advice."[15]

After getting settled in her room at the neighborhood house, Lois went to the Art Students' League and found herself on the steps amidst those assembling to register for courses. She immediately began talking with two other new arrivals, Mabel Pugh from Morrisville, North Carolina, and Agnes Lehman from Buffalo.[16] All three had just arrived in the city that very day and immediately bonded. In just minutes they became Lois's first significant peer relationships beyond her own siblings. She was finally entering her own social element. Although the three stayed in touch beyond their Art Students' League days, Mabel's friendship became a solid anchor throughout Lois's life. Just a few weeks later, the two moved into a more comfortable double room in another boarding house. Both were small-town young women who enjoyed discovering New York together. Lois described their "exploring and sketching in our free time, spending many hours on Orchard Street on the lower East Side, in what was called the 'pushcart section,' with teeming humanity overflowing streets and sidewalks." These sketching expeditions marked another turning point for Lois. All her previous artistic endeavors had been limited to the studio. Her excursions into the streets of the city brought new sights, smells, accents, and flavors. Lois also began recording her impressions in the diary she kept during her student years.

Charles Fabens Kelley had suggested that Lois study at the Art Students' League, a unique institution founded in 1875 "by and for artists." Quite the opposite of the large state university where Lois spent her undergraduate years, the league began as "a collection of studios, each autonomous and directed by the creative authority and counsel of the individual instructor, without interference from the administration," a structure that encouraged students to choose specific instructors with whom to study. From the beginning, many who studied at the league were women, and with courses funded solely by membership fees, studying at the Art Students' League was more affordable than other museum-connected art institutions. Kelley had even preselected the studio of Frank Vincent Du Mond for Lois. Like many of the faculty of the Art Students' League, Du Mond had also studied there and had developed a reputation as an excellent portrait and landscape painter and a masterful instructor. Lois found him "inspiring" but "very harsh" in his criticisms. She recalled her discomfort, "feeling his criticisms so keenly because I had started so far back and had so far to go. Trying to learn to draw under his tutelage was a hard struggle." Lois later studied under two other well-respected painters, F. Luis Mora and Kenneth Hayes Miller. Mora, the first Latino member of the National Academy of Design, was a prolific illustrator as well as a painter and portraitist, while Kenneth Hayes Miller enjoyed capturing contemporary urban scenes, especially women as consumers.[17] Like Du Mond, both Mora and Miller had studied at the league, and all three artists were collected by major American museums.[18] Lois surely found Miller's mastery of urban scenes exquisitely painted an ideal worth pursuing, both in subject matter and technique, and declared him her "preferred instructor." She made solid progress under his encouraging guidance.[19]

The aspiring artist from the Midwest found herself bombarded by initial impressions, and sketching and describing them helped her sort them out and make sense of them. Lois found "Bohemian life" thriving at the league, where "The girls wear their hair bobbed, mostly with a band around the forehead. The handsome young gents all have dainty little mustaches, swing sprightly canes, & toss their cigarettes nonchalantly into your soup (not mine however!) while sitting at the lunch table."[20] New York in 1915 was such an exhilarating city that Lois found other urban scenes equally visually alluring and soul-stirring as those she had witnessed on Orchard Street or at the league. At the opposite end of the spectrum from the pushcarts on the Lower East Side strolled the well-coiffed and well-dressed along Fifth Avenue:

> The latest rage in small boys' caps is tam-o-shanters, any color, with an appropriate motto on the front . . . and baby carriages are very faddy. Some have one very large wheel and one very small one, something like old bicycles—on both sides, of course. . . .
> *Ladies' skirts* are very short, the shorter the better; but the boots must be beautiful, long and laced, piped in white, or a color to match your suit, etc. Necks are closed up tight and high. The Jewish women are the most stylish of all. But the majority of people on 5th Avenue last Sunday were common ordinary ones.[21]

Lois may have been unaware that as she was absorbing her experiences and translating them into words and sketches, she was simultaneously training herself as a documentarian, capturing and preserving the scenes of the day. These ongoing exercises offered invaluable informal training that proved as significant to the development of her later career as any of the classes in which she had enrolled at the league.

By opening herself to the cultural smorgasbord that New York offered, Lois's appetite for adventure and risk-taking continued to grow. The Sunday morning after she arrived in Manhattan, she listened to a sermon at the legendary Broadway Tabernacle, a Congregational Church founded in 1836 that had boasted speakers such as Frederick Douglass and Sojourner Truth and early on advocated women's suffrage—a far cry from the orthodoxy of her father's faith. After the church service she and her friends walked over to Central Park to see the menagerie, where she most admired "the dignified lions." From there, they made what was Lois's first pilgrimage to the Metropolitan Museum of Art. "I was dead tired from having walked so far in the park, but I never felt it. I went on & on & the beautiful things went to my heart." Lois also was stirred for the first time by women's issues. On October 22 she joined others from the Studio Club who marched in or watched a suffragette parade, after which she reported: "The N.Y. women surely deserve the vote, merely for having braved this arctic weather which has descended upon us." As a member of the Art Students' League, Lois looked forward to attending lectures at no additional charge. They included presentations by early-twentieth-century American art lumi- naries, such as master illustrator Joseph Pennell, "a little man with white mustache & goattee [sic] (how on earth is that spelled anyhow?)," promi- nent portraitist Cecilia Beaux, and neoclassical sculptor Paul Manship. She also "listened in on art criticisms in the classes of George Bellows, Robert Henri, Gutzon Borglum, and George Luks (who painted & talked, too. He was wonderful, won everybody's hearts)."[22] The presidential portraits that comprise Mt. Rushmore constitute Borglum's most powerful legacy. Henri, Bellows, and Luks are three of the most famous artists of the so-called Ashcan School, former illustrators turned painters and enamored of por- traying the enormous variety of human endeavor—including depictions of working-class individuals and scenes—in the bustling city.[23] Did Mabel and Lois embark on their sketching ventures in Lower Manhattan inspired by these painters? Did the humanity the young women observed in the works of these stellar artists and in their talks shape these students' own ideas and interests? Lois doesn't refer to anything directly, but her own keen eyes and mind must have responded positively to such stimulation, or she would not have mentioned these artists and their lectures and critiques as she began assembling notes for her autobiography. Indeed, the young woman from Ohio and her friend from North Carolina were wading into deep cultural waters and loving it.

Lois had arrived in New York with very little money, and her "precious little bank account began to dwindle fast." She had to find ways to keep solvent, housed, and fed while she pursued her goal of becoming a professional artist. Instead of signing up for two classes each day, she enrolled in only one and then looked for work for the other half-day. The Art Students' League posted "want-ads" on a bulletin board, and Lois quickly realized that "other girls as hard-up as myself watched these advertisements like hawks. Through them, we got jobs to supplement our slender savings." During the four years that Lois spent in New York, she had to devote half that time to earning a living.[24]

Designing and decorating greeting cards allowed Lois to make artwork for a pittance, but she and her friends at the Art Students' League preferred the tedium of enhancing greeting cards to painting lampshades. They considered the latter not only the very lowest form of art-for-hire but also the work that paid the least. First, for Gorham's, Lois painted watercolors on "minute engravings" for a line of Christmas cards. This painstaking work originally paid thirty-five cents an hour, but later she "advanced" to fifty cents. Then she moved on to the Norcross Company, where she met and worked with Helen Sewell and Grace Paull who, like Lois, later became well-known and highly regarded illustrators of children's books. Unlike Helen and Grace, Lois started at the bottom of the heap. "*They* were designing the cards, mostly old-fashioned Christmas scenes"; Lois was allowed to do only the "hand-lettering of the message." Yet another greeting card company paid her a dollar for each original verse she submitted, something that she could do effortlessly. "I could jot down ten verses overnight, take them in, and come home with a check for ten dollars!" Every job reassured Lois that she could be self-supporting without succumbing to teaching, which would have sapped the energy that she needed to devote to her artwork. "If my first year in New York taught me anything," she reflected, "it made me realize how much creative work meant to me and how important it was to get more training. It was the beginning of a creative urge that was never to let me go."[25]

Lois returned to Columbus to help the family during the summer of 1916, and she and Miriam became friends with the Stellhorn sisters whose father also taught at Capital. The young women played tennis on the campus courts across the street from the Lenski house. This was Lois's first mention of participating in physical activity simply for the pleasure it offered. "I never had more fun in my life," she told Mabel. The evening routine began with an early supper, and then the young women played "till dark," getting "pointers" from several Capital students who watched them compete. After the games, "we go over to the drug store where the boys come in handy with their change. After that, we adjourn either to our house or to Stellhorn's where we spend the evening on the porch, Armbruster entertaining us with his mandolin, or else in the house where he delights us by breaking forth in song." Lois sounded atypically relaxed. "I don't know when I've enjoyed myself so much or found such a congenial crowd. It's an atmosphere of real friendship, a thing I didn't even catch a glimpse of in New York. For that reason, I shall hate to leave here in the fall." But she intended to make this her last summer at home. In order to pay for more Art League classes the following school year, Lois had spent the entire summer selling the flowers that her father had begun raising. Playing tennis and visiting with her friends in the evenings also led to the neglect of her artwork. Despite the diversion, her ambition had not dulled. "I can't afford to get so out of practice," she confessed to Mabel. The following summer, Lois wanted a job that would allow her more time for her artwork, but the summer spent out-of-doors with vigorous physical exercise and fresh air had filled her with an invincible enthusiasm that she took back to New York.[26]

In addition to the classes at the Art Students' League the previous winter, Lois and several of the other residents of the Studio Club attended a free night class under the auspices of the School of Industrial Art held in a public school on East 42nd Street. Lois, Mabel, and Agnes had all enrolled in an illustration class, where students were allowed to choose the subject matter and the medium in which they wanted to work. Arthur Sinclair Covey was the instructor, and Lois coolly reports in her autobiography that they all "got to know and like Mr. Covey."[27] Although she did not mention it, photographs from those years show him to be tall, slender, and stately, with a chiseled face, high forehead, serious demeanor, and—like Lois herself— slightly twinkling eyes that hinted at an underlying sense of quiet humor.

Arthur Sinclair Covey had already achieved recognition as a skilled illustrator and muralist when Lois and her friends entered his class. Born

I am working on the drawings now." Published as the *Children's Frieze Book*, the "something-to-do-book" allowed children "to color the drawings, cut them out and mount them on the wall as a frieze. A continuous landscape held the drawings together." Lois ultimately received $100 for her efforts, but as soon as she was commissioned, she was ready to declare children's books her "specialty." Evidently, she had been experimenting with the idea before she began her night school studies. She also accepted a position as a crafts counselor at Camp Tahoma, a girl's camp in Pike, New Hampshire, from mid-June to the beginning of September, teaching arts and crafts. Lois deemed the summer work "very healthful and refreshing," with "fifty dollars in my pocket to take back to town with me."[33]

The following autumn found Lois back in Arthur's class, and he generously offered to make her his assistant. The department store Lord & Taylor had commissioned a set of murals for their Christmas toy display, which, coincidentally, also included nursery rhymes among "many others, dolls, toys and games, Eugene Field poems, and fairy-tale characters. Also to be done were some romantic landscapes with castles and moats, backgrounds for fairy-tale characters and episodes from Gulliver's Visit to Lilliput." Lois collaborated in executing the designs. She summed up the teamwork:

> Not being keen on children, & it being a rush order, he got me to help & used my designs almost entirely. I did all the drawing, while he followed up with the big flat washes, then we both refined. It was lots of fun, but very hard physical labor, from crawling up step-ladders to sitting on the floor & jumping up & running back to see the effect. . . . Mr. C. says they look *fine* since they are up. I must get down to see them.

Lois also felt like she was hitting her stride with her own illustrations. Platt and Munk was impressed with the work that she was currently executing, "a series of 10 color plates for Grimms' fairy tales," and told her to anticipate doing a similar series for Andersen's. Perhaps the most startling event of the season occurred when Lois found herself sitting in church beside John D. Rockefeller Jr. "Can you beat that?" she wrote Mabel. "I nearly dropped dead. He looks just like his pictures, tho not so feeble as they make him look. It was pure accident that I even got into the church." Lois was expanding her horizons by "visiting all sorts of churches

& hearing various new ideas—Unitarian, Ethical Culturalism & even Anarchism. I actually heard Emma Goldman! Heard Billy Sunday twice, but didn't hit the sawdust trail."[34] Another bonus of 1917 was being able to see her brother, Gerhard, who was serving as a chaplain for the navy and stationed at Brooklyn Navy Yard "awaiting sailing orders between his many trips across the ocean to France on troopships." The two of them shared many "literary and artistic interests," enjoyed each other's company, and "established a lasting friendship and respect for each other" as they attended concerts and opera together. Lois also admitted, "Knowing that I was living on a shoestring, Gerhard often slipped a ten- or twenty-dollar bill in my purse for which I was most grateful."

But for Lois, the high points of 1917 started to vanish in the spring of the following year, and from there cascaded downward except for occasional patches of brightness, sparked mainly by Arthur's presence in her life. In April, Arthur had to give up teaching night school when he began taking classes in camouflage held in New Jersey. Lois told Mabel that she hadn't returned to the School of Industrial Art since, because the substitutes "don't know a blessed thing." About the same time, Lois received an attractive offer to teach at the Brearley School, a prestigious private school catering to the likes of the grandchildren of the same John D. Rockefeller whom she had sat beside in church. The part-time position she was offered as assistant in the art department would have provided her with sufficient salary to rent a studio near the school, but she "turned it down! Just like that . . . !!! Filthy lucre has no lure for me, & that was the chief advantage in it . . . in spite of Mr. Covey's & everybody else's advice to take it by all means. But since I turned it down, I haven't had a single regret, so I think that's a good sign."[35] Lois's parents would have wept at their daughter's impractical idealism. And she herself later admitted that if she had "been able to foresee the dark days that lay ahead," she would have decided otherwise.

Later that spring, Lois inadvertently started a small fire in her Brooklyn apartment, destroying only some of the furnishings but making it uninhabitable after her return from her job as a summer camp counselor. Nothing had been repaired in her absence. She moved in to a friend's studio back in the city but found, to her "utter dismay," that when she went to visit publishers, restrictions on paper usage caused by World War I meant that her "prospective income vanished in smoke," which left her feeling that she "nearly vanished" in response. She could not afford the rent and finally managed to beg a room for temporary lodgings at the Studio Club. After two weeks there, she reported that Arthur "came to my rescue with a nice job," and through another friend, "another fell into my lap, so things began to look a little more cheerful." Come fall, Lois did not return to the Art Students' League. The relationship with Arthur was also shifting. Although Lois limited the discussion of her personal life in her autobiography, she discreetly mentioned that on Armistice Day, "Mr. Covey and I walked over into the cheering crowds on Fifth Avenue, celebrating the event." Even though the war had ended, prospects in publishing remained scarce.[36] Almost like an errant knight, Arthur rode in to rescue Lois once more, with another Lord & Taylor toy department Christmas commission in which she could assist him. She again was exhilarated by the experience, both professionally and personally:

> I painted fifty feet of the panorama all by myself! I worked right along with Mr. Covey through it all—planning original compositions, stretching those enormous canvases, drawing in with charcoal and then painting! It was certainly a valuable experience. Mr. Covey let me paint all the children! He has been awfully good to me and is now giving me as much credit for the finished product as he is keeping for himself. We have come to be very good friends. I can hardly imagine him as he used to be at night school.[37]

Arthur and Lois worked mornings and evenings, and to make extra money (so much for the proud disdain of "filthy lucre"), she also took a part-time job as a sales clerk at a small gift shop. That full schedule, demanding physical work from early morning to late at night, proved too much for her health, coinciding as it did with one of the major waves of the Spanish flu that struck the nation in the fall of 1918. By December, Lois succumbed to the disease. She was fortunate to be taken to New York Hospital, where she "occupied the last empty bed in a busy ward." After her release from the hospital, old friends from Ohio, the Reverend F. H. Meyer and his family, welcomed her into their home where they cared for her "like one of the family." In spite of their excellent ministrations, not only did Lois relapse, she contracted diphtheria, which slowed her recovery. That she recovered when 675,000 fellow citizens died in the pandemic is remarkable, but the illness initiated her "lifelong battle for good health."[38]

As she recovered, professional recognition cheered her up. The National Academy of Design accepted *The Fire Escape*, one of her oil paintings (very likely Ashcan School inspired) for their annual show. Gerhard, visiting New York from Newport News, also admired the work. Lois was also thrilled to see several of her Platt and Munk books for sale at Brentano's. Both Lois-the-artist and Lois-the-illustrator took pride in these achievements, which gave her spirits a boost but delivered no similar boost to her finances. Lois's hospitalization expenses and rent still needed to be paid.[39]

By March, Lois had sufficiently recovered and found part-time employment with a greeting card publisher, tediously "lettering verses and making designs." Fortunately, she confided to Mabel, "Here comes our beloved Mr. Covey again," who offered her additional hours converting some Christmas holiday department store displays into illustrated tales from *The Arabian Nights*, with Santa Claus transformed into Sinbad the Sailor. Mabel had won a prestigious Cresson fellowship from the Pennsylvania Academy to study in Europe. Not to be outdone by Mabel's windfall, Lois found that she could pay her bills and bank her savings as she planned *her* first visit to Europe, which she hoped would coincide with Mabel's travel plans.[40]

That summer, Lois did not return to her arts and crafts position at camp. Arthur invited her to join him on-site in Morristown, New York, for two months to work on murals for yet another Lord & Taylor commission, this time for the "Infants' Wear" department. Arthur's friend and fellow artist, Charles Chapman, gave Arthur permission to use the barn on his family's ancestral home as a studio to prepare these murals. Lois told Mabel that she hated to give up the camp position, but "had to choose what I thot [*sic*] was best for my work, & that is again assisting Mr. Covey. . . . I am doing all the murals by myself . . . am working 7 hrs. a day on the Pied Piper of Hamelin." After completing the large Pied Piper panel, Lois worked on a series of smaller panels depicting aspects of a child's day.

Arthur was sharing housekeeping expenses with Charles Chapman's mother, who lived on the homestead. His children were also on the scene for the summer, the first time Lois spent any time with them. She was so busy working, however, that she rarely saw them. Adding to the stimulation of the summer residency, Arthur introduced her to some of his friends, "real artists" who "motored up to Morristown," among them "wildlife artist

Charles Livingston Bull and his wife" and cartoonist and illustrator Peter Newell, best remembered for his innovative and perennially popular books for children, including *The Hole Book* (1908), *The Slant Book* (1910), and *The Rocket Book* (1912). He spent several weeks working with Arthur and Lois. She found him "kindly and loveable. It does one's heart good just to think of him."[41]

Two seemingly divergent subplots had probably begun to take root earlier that spring and ripened over the summer months. Lois and Arthur were working ever more closely; she was getting to know his children and meeting his friends; and she was planning to go abroad. Were these completely separate simultaneous occurrences, or was the development of one affecting the evolution of the other? Lois conveys very little in the letters she saved or in *Journey into Childhood*,[42] so very likely her growth as an independent artist and her attraction to the possibilities of a more intimate, romantic relationship with Arthur Covey may have given her reason to want to sequester herself abroad. Crossing the Atlantic would give her the necessary distance and perspective to contemplate how any major decision might affect her future career or her personal happiness.

Lois returned to the Art Students' League in late fall to take life drawing with Boardman Robinson, an École des Beaux Arts–trained artist and outstanding teacher. She reported, "I'm more serious than ever in my life before."[43] By February 1920, her plans to study abroad had begun to coalesce, and she hoped Mabel's had as well. "I want to go to London long enough to try out the children's book field there. If successful, I would probably make London my headquarters, tho I should want a year or more in Paris." Six months later, Lois had firmed up her departure date, sailing for London in October. She explained to Mabel that, as much as she wanted to get to Paris, she thought starting in London was more practical, "to get used to a foreign country without the change of languages . . . knowing as little French as I do." Then, too, if Lois were able to get work in London, she thought she might "lengthen my stay indefinitely . . . & get in as much travel in France & Italy as I can afford."[44]

By late November, Lois had found a studio ("a lovely place, all furnished with wonderful old-fashioned furniture . . . so homey and cozy, I feel as if I had lived here for years") and begun classes at the Westminster School of Art, studying with painter Walter Bayes, who was also the school's principal. Lois was disappointed in the quality of the European art educational experience, however, as were some of her friends who had chosen to study in Paris. Too few "advanced people" were enrolled. "The war kept people out for 4 yrs., you see, & that makes a gap among students. . . . Mr. Bayes has a curious idea about painting which doesn't interest me much; but he's quite harmless & lets you do much as you please."[45]

But if art classes disappointed Lois, the city of London did not. She had just begun exploring museums in late November, reporting enthusiastically, "the South Kensington is full of all kinds of applied art and also has the largest art library in the world." On Thanksgiving, Lois celebrated by touring the National Gallery, where she had her "first real visit with the Florentine painters." Overjoyed, she declared, "It's marvelous, stupendous. I don't know when I've been so thrilled." She found London "wonderfully fascinating, like a city of dreams." As she stood on the steps of the National Gallery overlooking Trafalgar Square, "it seems like fairyland, with its mists and sparkling light. There's a magic in the atmosphere that's hard to describe, a sort of old-world air, especially when all the bells are chiming."[46]

Lois probably chose London not simply because navigating a major European capital would be easier in English, but because London had become *the* center of children's literature illustration and publishing in the pre–World War I era. While publishing for a youth audience in the United States was still in its infancy and would not begin to take off until later in the 1920s, British author-illustrators and illustrators such as Kate Greenaway, Beatrix Potter, Edward Lear, and L. Leslie Brooke had won the allegiance of parents, librarians, teachers, and children on both sides of the Atlantic. As Barbara Bader summarized in her authoritative study, *American Picturebooks from Noah's Ark to The Beast Within* (1976), "We [Americans] were accustomed . . . to looking abroad for the best literature, the best music, the best art. Not until the close of World War I, a time of national assertiveness, did the cry go up, why can't we have picturebooks like theirs? By then it was too late; the Europeans had so far outdistanced us in color printing that, whatever the will, there was no way, not for another fifteen years."[47]

But American "minders" were keen on catching up. Even before Lois's arrival in London, public libraries in the United States extended their services to children. Then in the summer of 1919, the first Children's Book Week took place, largely the result of a collaboration of Franklin K. Mathiews, the chief librarian of the Boy Scouts of America; Frederic G.

Melcher, co-editor of *Publishers Weekly;* the New York Public Library's first director of work with children, the already influential Anne Carroll Moore; and Louise Seaman, whom Macmillan Publishing Company had recently appointed director of "a new editorial department to be devoted to children's books. . . . Macmillan's Department of Books for Boys and Girls was the first of its kind anywhere in the world."[48] The publishing world across the pond would be ready for Lois's return.

Not surprisingly then, Lois's most significant news from London involved publishing.

> I went to a publisher the other day, and much to my surprise, was practically given a book to do before I'd been there ten minutes, & it's no less a publisher than John Lane Co., the Bodley Head. I was so astounded, I could hardly believe it. . . . I've submitted the first pencil sketches & they have been approved both by John Lane & the author & I have orders to go ahead. So I'm very much pleased, for I hope this will be a start towards making other publishers take a little notice of me. At least it is a chance for me to prove whether I can really do anything or not. The book is a set of short stories, fairy tales of a crazy fantastic sort, but rather well suited to my particular style (!) of drawing.[49]

Lois was describing drafts for *The Green-Faced Toad,* by Vera B. Birch, for which she told her sister, Esther, "I'm laying myself out to do my level best, for any future work will depend on my success with this." After the sketches, she used "a line drawing technique in colored inks, which came out very attractively," for the eight color illustrations, title page, and cover,[50] and the book was published the following year. Lois's stylized and charming full-page, pencil-thin, ink line drawings—partially filled with colored inks—depict fantastical medieval scenes dominated by whimsical figures, sporting beautifully detailed costumes. The costumes and flavor reflect and carry forward late-nineteenth-century European illustrative traditions, particularly the work by Randolph Caldecott, Walter Crane, and the French favorite, Maurice Boutet de Monvel.[51] Even if the style was derivative, the illustrations for *The Green-Faced Toad* also retain the unembellished and sure-handed line and flavor of the humorous drawings that Lois provided as the art editor for the *Makio* at Ohio State. Her more skillful and imaginative mastery of the entire page demonstrates how much she had progressed since devoting herself full-time to artwork over the past five years. She later sent a copy of *The Green-Faced Toad* to Alice Robinson, her former design instructor at Ohio State who had encouraged her to go to New York. Alice responded that "for design and originality and attractiveness, [the book] places you without question in the front rank of children's illustrators. The page is so very much more decorative with the colored inks than with the usual heavy colored plates." Alice added, wistfully, that she appreciated Lois's "journey into another world . . . a world I have always been interested in and had a longing for, but never had the courage to attempt to enter."[52]

The Green-Faced Toad marked only the first commission from John Lane. Not long after its publication, Lois had already begun drawings for Kenneth Grahame's *The Golden Age*, followed by illustrations for Grahame's *Dream Days*, both written many years before his classic *Wind in the Willows*. She took pride in her "good start in this illustrating business," but that success did little to ameliorate her extreme loneliness. Although Lois sounded very upbeat in December when she wrote Mabel, "I've made more friends here already in two months than I ever made in 2 yrs. in New York," she nevertheless gave up her lovely studio to move to Bedford House, run by the YWCA, because she needed more companionship. When Lois penned her autobiography many decades later, she expressed distinctly opposite impressions. She remembered the other London art students as "unapproachable, with one or two exceptions." Arthur had given her introductions to his deceased wife's relatives there, whom Lois had "called upon and found kind," but she never found "longed-for companionship." London's winter weather and her need to curb her spending (very likely further than she should have to ensure a healthy and substantial diet) undoubtedly combined to contribute to her becoming so run down that she visited a doctor. He pronounced her anemic and prescribed a tonic. To add to her personal misery, Lois had spent the Christmas holidays alone, as she had at Thanksgiving. She compensated by working at the National Gallery as European art students did, copying "in oils" a sketch by one of her favorite artists at the time, Puvis de Chavannes.[53]

But the joy of work was simply not fulfilling enough to take the place of warm human friendship, and Lois began planning spring travel. She still intended to stay situated in London, as she told Mabel, "long enough to

Illustration from *The Green-Faced Toad*. Reprinted by permission of the Lois Lenski Covey Foundation and Burrell Covey, copyright by Lois Lenski. Courtesy of Illinois State University's Special Collections, Milner Library.

profit by it. That is, get enough books out, to have enough of a reputation when I return, so that I won't have to begin at the beginning again with N.Y. publishers. In other words, I want the N.Y. publishers to take me on without any questions." With her sudden and welcome professional success matched by her desire to explore other European art capitals, especially Florence and Paris, Lois had yet another option to think about, one that she (seemingly very reluctantly) introduced to her dearest friend, Mabel: "Then there's just another possibility—of my being called home & not having the chance to stay for another winter—for various reasons. I hope not, for I'd die unhappy if I had to go back without seeing Paris & Italy. But I can't tell yet, and I don't want you to count on me too definitely—until I am absolutely sure."[54]

Lois only partially accomplished half of these conflicting goals. An older woman and artist who befriended Lois now wanted to travel with her to Italy the following month. Lois complied willingly, since she was afraid to travel on the European continent alone. But before leaving London, Lois told Mabel that these travel plans meant that she would not be staying in Europe long enough to join Mabel in France the following autumn. Not only did Lois lack sufficient means,

> Then, too, there are other things at home, which are making my stay much shorter than I once thought it would be—things are pulling me back in spite of myself. I can't explain very well now, but will be able to do so later, & then you'll be sure to understand. It's just this—there are two people inside of me pulling in opposite directions & the Lois who wants to be independent & live abroad for years & be a wonderful artist sometimes is squelched entirely by another very different Lois. . . . I came to Europe for other reasons than just to see pictures—and I'm going back again without having seen half of what I really want to see. . . . My whole world has been topsy-turvy for over a year now & sometimes I don't know whether I'm coming or going. . . . Just remember, Mabel, that I'd have loved to go with you, but my path seems to lie in a different direction, though I tried my best to make it join yours.[55]

For all her indirection in skirting the issue, Lois's developing relationship with Arthur had at least partially motivated her London sojourn and travel to Italy. She needed to come to terms with the kind of future she wanted. She certainly had made up her mind before witnessing the architectural and artistic marvels that Italy held in store.[56] Her oblique confession to Mabel preceded the three months in Italy, the final chapter of her European adventure. Lois sailed back to New York in mid-May on the S.S. *Providence*, and on June 8, 1921, two weeks after her return, married Arthur in the Bronx, New York.[57]

CHAPTER 3

FINDING TIME TO CREATE

arried! Now twenty-seven, Lois wondered how marriage to Arthur might affect her career. Having decided that love must supplant art as her primary vocation at this point in life, she remained determined to move forward as an artist. Even before she had taken such a "fatal step,"[1] she held no illusion that what she sought to achieve would be simple. Lois had expressed such hopes explicitly in a letter to her sister Esther from Rome earlier that spring, acknowledging that she wanted "to prove that a woman (or at least this one woman) can do two jobs at once!!! . . . I know I am taking on the hardest job that any woman can possibly take on, but I believe all my sacrifices will have equal recompense." She truly imagined herself faithfully relieving Arthur of "a multitude of details which have been keeping his mind off his work," as she took on the immediate twin responsibilities of wife and stepmother. Of course, Lois still planned to "go on with my work much the same." Perhaps she unconsciously chose her father, R. C. H., as her role model rather than her mother, who had given up her career when she married. Women in the United States had won suffrage just the summer before, and few middle-class American women at the time envisioned balancing marriage and a profession. Lois insightfully recognized the strength of her creative impulse as much as she emotionally required a husband, home, and family. Her experiences of living and working alone in New York and abroad were exhilarating artistically and rewarding professionally but, ultimately, lonely.[2]

Now that both her sisters were already married with children of their own, did Lois believe that marrying Arthur was her one chance at love? She knew him well, undoubtedly loved him, and felt she could remedy his untenable situation as a single parent, yet she did not intend that the commitment would replace or eliminate her artistic ambitions. As she considered her future, she had poignantly confessed to Esther:

> I've come to believe that if there is some one who really cares, then nothing else matters—anything can happen; sorrow and trouble only deepen real love. But when you are alone and nobody cares— then everything matters and life is not worth living. I know more of that than you think, and that is why I cannot let love pass me by when it has actually come to me.[3]

Arthur was forty-three at the time of their marriage, and Lois still primly referred to him as "Mr. Covey" in her letters and in her autobiography. Lois had not told Mabel about her upcoming marriage before the ceremony took place, and then apologized to her friend. "Everything seemed to be happening at once," the bride explained, "a telegram from Gerhard, & later meeting him at the train, then the excitement of collecting our party in the auto & driving up to the church, etc. etc." That is the only description of the wedding day that Lois recorded. Since Gerhard was a Lutheran minister like his father, he may have performed the ceremony. The newlyweds took time to be alone while Arthur's children—Margaret, now twelve, and Laird, four—were spending summer visits with loving adults elsewhere. Lois and Arthur rented a cottage in Rockport, Maine, where they could sketch as well as learn how to live with each other before adding the children to the mix, undoubtedly a practical decision. Their cottage "on a little neck of land on one side of the fishing harbor . . . surrounded by numerous picturesque fishing shacks" provided pictures "in every direction," and she hoped "to devote a great deal of concentrated effort to really producing something." But Lois felt that her artistic endeavors that summer were unfulfilling, and she complained that the results were less than she had anticipated.[4] Marrying her mentor may have already begun proving more problematic

Lois and her stepchildren, Margaret and Laird, about 1921. Courtesy of Jeanine Covey Gutowski, Vivian Covey, and Michael Covey.

than she had imagined. She found herself measuring her own productive capabilities against her husband's—and possibly against what she may have known about the artistic ability of his first wife, Molly—while assuming the unfamiliar role as wife, and somehow finding herself lacking. And she had not yet experienced mothering Margaret and Laird, even though she admitted that, as she considered marrying Arthur, "the presence of the children was, indeed, one of its main attractions."[5]

By August, however, reality set in when the children arrived in Rockport, and Arthur left to find an appropriate home for the family outside of New York City. Lois hoped that he could secure a place with enough space within and grounds surrounding so the children would have "a place to stretch their legs." And Arthur chose just such a house to rent at 971 Split Rock Road in Pelham Manor, New York, about fifteen miles northeast of Manhattan. Lois was pleased with the "gay nineties" house, which she deemed "the second fantastic house" to call home. Like the former Victorian parsonage in Anna, the rambling Lenski-Covey residence would prove "difficult to care for." Lois reveled in its gracious spaces, nevertheless, because they offered ample room for the entire family to spread out. While Arthur claimed the living room as his studio and devoted the adjoining sunroom to his etching press, upstairs Lois had a studio ("a room of my own," she called it) with a sewing alcove.[6] Initially, the trick was finding the time to get *into* the studio.

Writing her autobiography over forty years later, Lois looked back on the early years of her marriage and recognized that attempts to balance family obligations against her own self-realization reflected the massive changes in women's lives that the post–World War I world revealed:

> When I was a young woman and an art student, in the years before 1920, there was considerable agitation and discussion about women's rights, and the whole question of career versus home. The question has never been settled, and is ever new with any woman who tries it. . . . Something has to give somewhere, as I quickly learned from experience. It may be true that a woman can have her cake and eat it too, but she does not accomplish both without a struggle, and usually one side suffers if the other succeeds.[7]

Although reared to become a dutiful young woman and subservient wife, Lois served in the vanguard of single young American women who moved into professional careers of their own. Remaining far from bohemian in behavior and outlook, she had still managed to make a living and grab what she could afford of an art education, including making an extended trip abroad and gaining her first "real" books to illustrate. Lois returned to the United States to embrace the mantle of marriage and family at the very moment when the whole field of children's book publishing—especially of picture book publishing—was in the process of taking off on this side of the Atlantic. Most of the "minders" in children's literature that Leonard Marcus identified were women, described by historian Jacalyn Eddy as "bookwomen." These first-generation professionals helped define "the specific economic and cultural niche of the modern children's book industry between 1919 and 1939 . . . as part of the advance guard to ensure that children received what they regarded as the best reading material possible."[8] Lois was returning to American publishing at a turning point, and, most significantly, she was returning as an illustrator who had published in London.

The devastation that World War I had caused in Europe stimulated America's ascendancy in many fields—radio, recording, the rise of Hollywood, the burgeoning automobile and garment industries, among countless others. Women who could afford to do so were asserting more independence by learning to drive automobiles because they, like the Coveys, relocated to suburban neighborhoods to give their children fresh air and more recreational space. With electrical appliances making household duties more manageable, affluent women could increasingly focus their maternal energies on providing their offspring with every benefit.

The simultaneous emergence of a fairly broad-based economic boom, greater freedom for women, and more attention paid to early childhood coincided with a rise in interest in child development. Arnold Gesell's *The Preschool Child from the Standpoint of Public Hygiene and Education* (1923) and *The Mental Growth of the Preschool Child* (1925), intersecting with a more widespread blossoming of child-centered education, typified these impulses. The ideas of Pestalozzi and Froebel were no longer revolutionary in the latter years of the nineteenth and early years of the twentieth century when Maria Montessori began enunciating the principles of her methodology in Italy. But in the United States at that time, it was the University of Chicago's pragmatist philosopher, John Dewey, who made great headway in his arguments for child-centered pedagogy based on his studies and observations of child development. Through such writings as *School and Society* (1899) and

The Child and the School (1902) and his Lab School at the University of Chicago (which opened in 1897), he became the father of what became known as progressive education. Lois cited Dewey's contemporary and fellow pragmatist philosopher, William James, as being one of those whose thinking had most influenced her own approach to children.[9] Historian Anita Clair Fellman writes that the "profound concern for children's reading habits" reflected "contemporary child-rearing philosophies," which made "children's interests a prominent factor in experts' selection of good juvenile literature." As Leonard Marcus succinctly points out in his comprehensive study of the development of American children's literature, *Minders of Make Believe*, "Implicit in their work was the suggestion that children's books, as distinct from other types of literature, might be understood, evaluated, and perhaps even written and illustrated within a developmental framework." Fellman emphasizes that "the goal was not to force adult likes on children but to ascertain 'scientifically' children's literary interests at various stages of their young lives and to stimulate those interests in wholesome ways."[10]

Lois took note, and she spent the next five decades working to actualize such understanding by creating a wide range of illustrated books that targeted specific developmental needs of young readers. More immediately, during the 1910s and '20s in New York City, the energetic Lucy Sprague Mitchell began applying progressive principles directly under the auspices of the Bureau of Educational Experiments—that she founded originally at 69 Bank Street and which ultimately became Bank Street College of Education—where educators were introduced to progressive principles in their classrooms. Ultimately such efforts led to the Bank Street School for Children. Mitchell and the teacher trainees at Bank Street benefited from observing the children in their midst. As Marcus writes, "in the best Dewey-James empirical way," they learned "directly from children and from each other. Mitchell and her colleagues rarely spent time with the children without notebooks in hand. . . . Mitchell sifted through the 'language data' collected from the children's 'spontaneous utterances'" to identify "developmental patterns and considered the implications of her findings for children's literature at every level." With the publication in 1921 of her *Here and Now Story Book*, Mitchell pioneered in generating specifically age-appropriate and reality-based stories for preschoolers. She—and Lois in the decade that followed—felt that young children did not need fairy tales to enchant them. To a preschooler the everyday world itself *is* enchantment.

Nearly simultaneously with the establishment of the Progressive Education Association in 1919 came the enunciation of its seven principles, which included ideas that echoed those early-nineteenth-century romanticists, Jean-Jacques Rousseau and Pestalozzi, such as allowing children the freedom to develop naturally, with the teacher as guide to the pupil's ultimate independence as a thinker.[11]

More financially self-sufficient and forward-thinking parents not only welcomed schools catering to the developmental aptitudes of their children but wanted to ensure that their home environments supported their offspring's healthy growth. Who could advise them about the best books available? During this particularly fertile period in rethinking education for the young, American publishers and public libraries both began to cater to the specific needs of their juvenile readers. Public libraries were simultaneously investing in special and separate children's reading rooms and hiring librarians to direct them. Librarians assumed the role of advising parents and teachers about suitable books for young readers, a concern that only grew throughout the decade. *The Bookman* had already introduced the best-seller list to the American public and, in 1918, engaged New York Public Library's Anne Carroll Moore to "contribute a regular column on children's books." She "wasted little time in highlighting the need for a new set of publishing arrangements to ensure that the exploding demand for good children's books would be met." The nation's largest publisher, Macmillan Publishing Company, set a precedent by hiring an editor to head the newly established Department of Books for Boys and Girls. Louise Seaman was a Vassar graduate who had taught at a progressive school in Connecticut before seeking a position in publishing. Marcus puts this move into perspective: "It was thus that in 1919 the editing of children's books joined school teaching, library service to children, and missionary work in the sisterhood of modern-day 'mothering' professions."[12]

Upon marrying Arthur, Lois instantly became stepmother to twelve-year-old Margaret and four-year-old Laird, both of whom she found "interesting, unpredictable, congenial, and companionable." Margaret (called "Peter" by her parents since early childhood) was "beautiful, intelligent, healthy, and talented . . . very gifted." As the apple of her father's eye, Margaret could do no wrong; Arthur sided with her during any dispute with her stepmother, making Lois's role that much more difficult. Lois believed that Margaret had been "greatly indulged" by both parents, and had become "over-emotional" and "subject to temper tantrums." According to Margaret's oldest son, Alan Chisholm, Arthur kept a photograph of Molly on his dresser until the day he died. This visual reminder further reinforced Margaret's perception that her own mother had achieved "sainthood" and that Lois was something of an "imposter." As Lois reflected in her first draft of *Journey into Childhood,* Arthur and Molly should have recognized that Margaret needed "psychiatric help from early childhood." Lois respected the independence and self-reliance that Margaret demonstrated and wanted her to understand that, as stepmother, Lois had no intention of "supplanting" her birth mother. Although Arthur decided that Laird should call Lois "Mother," because she was "the only mother he ever knew," Margaret always called her "Lois." That Lois was the stepmother *and* the disciplinarian did not help matters, either. According to Alan, Margaret and Lois maintained a "civil," but not warm, relationship, and Margaret's children called Lois "Aunt Lois," or "Lo-lo," but not grandmother.[13]

Laird required a completely different kind of mothering. He was, of course, not a perfect child, never having known his mother, and in the care of many different babysitters since birth. By the time Lois became his stepmother, Laird had already achieved a reputation for temper tantrums, several of which she had witnessed before marrying Arthur. But Lois felt that Laird was young enough to accept her as a mother and recalled, "From the moment he came into the house after I was there, all his tantrums ceased. He was always open to reason and suggestion, and I never, even in later years, had a discipline problem with him."[14]

Although she loved Margaret and Laird and felt "they loved me from the start,"[15] she had to learn to be a mother as she simultaneously concentrated on pursuing her career as an artist or illustrator—she had not yet chosen one profession over the other. As she began to sort out how to manage the roles that competed for her time and energy, she could not have predicted that the children's books that she would ultimately create would actually serve as her own entrée into a "mothering profession," as parents, librarians, teachers, and other educators turned to her for advice.

Even before her marriage, Lois understood that the children's loss of their mother and their father's shouldering "an impossible load" as the surviving parent and breadwinner presented challenges that she anticipated meeting. Loving Arthur as she did, she "wanted to make a happy home for him, and give the children love and a kind of contentment and security they had never enjoyed." Full of idealism, Lois was primarily motivated by her "desire to be worthy of my husband's love." But it did not take long to realize that the sixteen years' difference between their ages created generationally antagonistic approaches to child-rearing. She identified Arthur's method as "pressure and force" when persuasion failed, the kind of discipline that only inspired rebellion and worsened the situation. Since her undergraduate years working with children, Lois had utilized the progressive principles she had studied and applied them as a playground recreation leader and then as a summer camp crafts counselor. She therefore perceived herself as more understanding and more willing to consider the source of the children's issues. Unfortunately, she found it difficult to gain Arthur's respect for her more modern viewpoint, claiming, "It was years before he learned to trust me and stop interfering."[16]

In her "desire to be worthy" of Arthur's love, Lois tried to achieve what would later be termed "supermom" status by meeting her high self-expectations on all fronts: sewing all the children's clothing, cooking, housekeeping, and entertaining his many friends. She had reassured her sister Esther before marrying Arthur, "The last thing he wants is for me to give up my work, and of course, whether I have to give it up or not will depend entirely on him. But I have the greatest faith in him as well as the greatest love, so what else matters."[17] Very early in their marriage, however, when Lois complained that she had no time for her own creative work, she was shocked by his reply:

> "Your job is the home and the children. They come first."
> "But what about my work?"
> "That's up to you. . . . You'll have to find time for it."

Lois later recognized that Arthur's lack of sympathy gave her all the determination she could muster "to hold fast" to and nurture her own creative endeavors. "His words, in putting the responsibility up to me, in offering me no aid in my struggle, helped me to realize that I was truly possessed by this creative demon and *could* not and *would* not give it up."[18]

Near the end of her life as she penned her autobiography, Lois realized that she had entered the world of children's publishing at an opportune time, what children's literature scholar Anne Scott MacLeod called "halcyon years" in children's publishing, when "trained librarians, editors, and reviewers, experts with wide experience of children's books, dominated the field." When she returned from London in 1921, May Massee was the only children's editor she knew, but within the next couple of years, she had also become acquainted with Louise Seaman and Helen Dean Fish. "By 1925, their numbers had increased and soon all the major publishers had special departments with special editors for their children's books. . . . I came to know all the early editors because I illustrated books for most of them."[19]

Lois invested her hard-earned savings in household help (when available) and gladly gave up as much housekeeping as she could avoid or postpone. Then she escaped to her studio ("sanctuary") where she locked the door behind her, "turning a deaf ear to doorbell, telephone, delivery man or outside interruption." Real joy, her "beloved work," awaited her, and there she found "solace" for her spirit. From her Art Students' League days, Lois was used to calling on publishers without the aid of an agent, and she never acquired an intermediary to provide her with commissions but kept making the rounds herself.

As she began her second decade creating illustrations and books for children, Lois's career hinged on her commitment to realism for young readers at different developmental stages. But during the 1920s, she accommodated herself to the current publishing trends in children's literature in which fairy tales, folktales, and historical fiction topped the lists of popular children's books.[20] She illustrated story and poetry anthologies—*Chimney Corner Stories* and *Chimney Corner Fairy Tales* (both 1926) and *Fireside Poems* (1930)—collected by Veronica S. Hutchison and published by Minton, Balch, and Company and Padraic Colum's *The Peep Show Man* (1926) for Macmillan. In her European travels, Lois had loved the patterning of medieval tapestries and had drawn "figures in Medieval costumes . . . for my own enjoyment." These experiences undergirded her illustrations for two projects for Dodd Mead, *A Book of Princess Stories* (1927) and *A Book of Enchantment* (1928), compiled by Kathleen Adams and Elizabeth Atchinson. These two projects allowed her "love of the Medieval . . . full sway." Lois mentioned that Arthur admired and collected Persian prints, and through their visits together to the Metropolitan Museum's Persian rooms, she, too, became obsessed with Persian design and was able to utilize it in illustrations for Alan Lake Chidsey's *Rustam, Lion of Persia* (1930), published by Minton Balch.[21]

Lois's lovely, but hardly distinguished, early illustrations—with their castles, excessive attention to costume, decorative landscape elements, repetitive motifs, shallow perspective or space, all to be "read" as tableaux—while charming, indicate little about the consistent and extremely distinctive elements of her more mature style. Although at this point in her still-early career she probably thought of herself as an easel artist, she demonstrated her sense of design in her arts-and-crafts-like sense of composition. The accent is definitely on the decorative. Faces reveal little emotional or dramatic content and do not yet fully capture the signature expressions that later came to be read instantly as "Lenskiesque." Over the decade, she began to show more self-confidence. Her forceful and more defined black-outlined figures already move toward a simplification of design that even her youngest readers would come to recognize immediately and love.

The first picture books that reveal the emergence of Lois's deft sense of humor for her youngest readers are *Jack Horner's Pie: A Book of Nursery Rhymes* (1927), which she "selected and arranged," and *Alphabet People* (1928), an ABC book with original verses, both published by Harper's and designed by Arthur Rushmore. *Jack Horner's Pie* received outstanding reviews. According to the *New York Times*, "All the old nursery favorites are here in this bright and alluring book of yellow and shaded green . . . with pages upon pages of pictures in gay colors. . . . Even the smallest tots will enjoy picking out the various characters." And *Booklist* echoed the theme by remarking that "the delightful illustrations in line and flat color are childlike in conception . . . revealing the characters surrounded by just the right amount of minute and interesting detail." Writing for *Publishers Weekly* in 1930, Josiah Titzell praised Lois's illustrations in "sympathy with the form and the audience for whom her books are intended." He recognized her "honest love of order and beauty, a true feeling for pattern, and above all . . . a sense of humor that allows much unspoken comment—a comment that is never cruel." Evidently Titzell had spoken to publishers in preparation for his review, because he also mentioned that Lois demanded perfection in the printing of her work: "When you admire the printed color in her illustrations, publishers will tell you with a quiet respect that Miss Lenski keeps calling for proofs until she has the color she originally asked for." He also understood her no-nonsense personality: "She is quiet and direct . . . always amiable without going in for affability . . . far from being a

Lois often used some kind of grid in her early illustrations like this one from her first book, *Jack Horner's Pie: Lois Lenski's Mother Goose*, 1927. Reprinted by permission of the Lois Lenski Covey Foundation and Burrell Covey, copyright by Lois Lenski. Courtesy of the Lois Lenski Papers, Special Collections, Butler Library, Buffalo State College.

publicity shark, for she is a serious artist and interested in her work rather than in herself."[22]

By far Lois's most significant commission as an illustrator came at the end of the decade when Arnold Munk, her old friend and the owner at Platt and Munk, asked her to illustrate the original version of *The Little Engine That Could* (1930), by Watty Piper, Arnold Munk's pen name. Lois capably incorporated several techniques for variety: colorful endpapers and several full-color illustrations scattered within, line drawings and repeating motifs in silhouette. The overall effect is fresh and charming, and this illustrated version remained in print for nearly a quarter of a century; in 1954 the publisher revised and updated the book. In the online *Print Magazine* (2012), graphic designer J. J. Sedelmaier compared the two versions, claiming that "the 1930 version kicks the 1954 version's ass! I love the simplicity of the design, the flat primary colors, and the printing in the earlier version. . . . I get a much richer experience from the journey I take with the 1930 version of the story . . . but putting the two side by side makes me appreciate Lois Lenski's version more." As an interesting sideline, cultural historian Lawrence Levine saw publication of *The Little Engine That Could* in 1930 and its essential message of hard work and perseverance ("I think I can! I think I can!") as an illustration of the "political philosophy of the Hoover administration in dealing with the Depression."[23]

Lois-as-artist versus Lois-as-illustrator struggled for primacy during these early years of her career. Each was vying for her limited studio hours. Sometimes, the artist seemed to be calling. In December 1921, for example, Lois won the Adolph Grant Prize of fifty dollars and high honors for her sketch entitled "New England Town" in the New Rochelle Art Association's show at the New Rochelle Public Library, just north of Pelham Manor. According to a local newspaper article, she had bested over one hundred entries by thirty-one competing artists, "and among these were her own husband, Arthur Covey, with two entries, under whom his wife studied and through whom she gained repute." She often shared her pride with Mabel:

> I sold my largest watercolor, the one called "The Golden Age" at the Pennsylvania Watercolor show for $150.00!!! I never was so astonished in my life. Now if you had not told me that my watercolors were good enough to exhibit, I would not have dreamed of exhibiting them & would not have sold this one. . . .

"Possessed" by her "creative demon," Lois realized she had to keep making art, as she is here, illustrating at her desk at Pelham Manor, about 1925. Courtesy of Jeanine Covey Gutowski, Vivian Covey, and Michael Covey.

> I was lucky enough to have five accepted for the N.Y. watercolor show now at the Fine Arts Gallery—so I'm beginning to think I am a real water colorist & have been missing my calling heretofore.[24]

Yet in the next sentence, she confesses that she hasn't been doing any watercolors "lately." While managing her full-time job as wife and mother, actively building a reputation as an illustrator just as she was beginning to exhibit as a watercolorist, Lois continued to assist Arthur with seasonal mural commissions, working "on a real thousand dollar job for my hubby for Lord & Taylor's Infants' Wear Dept. Two huge panels 6 × 10 ft., & 7 smaller ones about 5½ ft. square." She was also trying to squeeze in time to improve her skills, taking Saturday classes at the Art Student's League. Lois still maintained that she "needed work on the human figure more than anything," but she also spent more time sketching outdoors, becoming increasingly self-assured in work that would amplify her reputation in galleries and in print.[25]

In the late spring of 1924, Lois wrote Mabel what must have been a long-overdue letter, packed with news that hinted at the forces tugging at her from different directions and how she responded to each of them. First, she talked about her family life, mentioning that her mother had died Easter night. Lois tried to justify why she had not returned to Columbus for the funeral. She had spent time earlier that spring helping deal with her mother's declining health, and very likely felt guilty for choosing not to travel to Ohio twice in such a short period. Now, as she described the situation to Mabel, Lois couldn't help thinking that her mother, just sixty, "should have had ten or even twenty more happy years." Still, it seems strange that Lois did not insist upon returning for the burial. When Mabel's mother died the following year, Lois's sympathies also spoke of her longings: "I feel more vividly than ever the beauty and strength of our relationship. It seems to me that all that there is of good or worth in me came from her. She stands for the highest and best in my life." Moving on to her own nuclear family, Lois shared her pride in Arthur's landing a big job, "the best he has ever had," working on a series of murals for the Kohler Company in Wisconsin ("all industrial subjects which he likes best of all").[26] And Laird, now seven, had become "the joy of [her] life!"[27]

Apart from the strain of loss and the typical issues of family life, Lois's hard work was paying off. The *New York Times Sunday Magazine* had mentioned a group of watercolors that she had exhibited in the city, and these paintings were currently in Chicago at the annual International Watercolor Exhibit sponsored by the National Watercolor Society. She had heard that two had sold. Despite such good news, Lois lacked self-confidence in herself as an artist, perhaps because she understood that it was one thing to get into shows and obtain positive reviews and quite another to succeed financially. Fortunately, the reputation she had gained illustrating in London had given her "immediate entrée to publishers here," with "prospects for work . . . very good." Already she had "2 or 3 prospective books . . . looming up." Ever practical and pragmatic, Lois began to come to terms with her predicament. She told Mabel, "Since I can't seem to make a real fine-art artist out of myself, I might as well content myself with being an illustrator, so [I] am going after the publishers as hard as I am able." More happily, Lois mentioned that

Frederick A. Stokes was "considering publishing one of my own with my own illustrations." No wonder Lois periodically became totally depleted and needed "absolute rest & quiet" for a "terrible aching back."[28]

Lois's business relationship with Stokes began even before she first visited the publisher, when she discovered just how valuable her association with John Lane in London proved to be.

> In 1921, Mr. Dominick of Stokes, on his annual book hunt in London, had found a book called *The Green-Faced Toad*. No one could tell him much about the illustrator, but he bought an edition for the American market largely on account of the illustrations. Not until he returned to America did he learn that the artist was neither Russian nor English, but a native of Ohio. All the people at Stokes were surprised when this illustrator walked into their office one day, unannounced!

She felt that *The Green-Faced Toad* association probably privileged her presentation to the Stokes children's editor, Helen Dean Fish, who "paid particular attention" to her. Two years later, Lois mocked up a dummy of a book of verses that she called *A Child's Town* and took it to Fish, who promptly rejected the book, explaining that poetry did not sell well. Instead of turning Lois away, Fish suggested, "Write a story about your childhood—in prose." Unbeknownst to editor and illustrator, that casual suggestion launched Lois's career as an author, and she "went into action at once," working "hard to turn my verses into prose, elaborating the ideas with remembered incidents of the various escapades of the Lenski family, and to make a story of it." Lois simply could not bear to delete all her verses, however, so she "sneaked a few of them in, between the chapters."[29] Fish saw the first draft and dealt out a heaping dose of helpful criticism plus enough encouragement to motivate the novice author to persist.

At last, in February 1926, Lois proclaimed proudly to Mabel:

> My big news is that I am now an author! Have just signed a contract with Stokes, to publish a book which I have written & will illustrate, called "A Child's Town." It will not be out until next January. . . . You will have to be my agent in N.C., & sell as many as you can as I will get a royalty on each copy sold, & I hope that the book will

make me rich. If it is a success, Stokes have made me promise to let them publish my "second volume"—So I may have to be a writer in spite of myself.[30]

In the meantime, she and Mabel had long been planning a sketching holiday. The year before, Arthur and his brother went to Europe in June and did not return until September. With Margaret away at Camp Tahoma, the very camp in Pike, New Hampshire, where Lois had been in charge of handicrafts, she thought she would have more time for her own artwork. She learned to drive and bought an "overland coupe" to traipse about the countryside, and admitted that she intended "to make enough sketches that would sell to pay for my car." However, commissions for illustrations and family visits usurped her best intentions. With autumn and Arthur's return, she had more success, "sketching my head off (mostly in pencil) . . . to collect a lot of material to work on during the winter." Lois admitted that Arthur "feels rather guilty . . . about my staying at home while he went gallivantin' all summer, so has suggested to me that I take a sketching trip sometime this winter—to a warmer climate incidentally! . . . If you are staying down south this winter, how would it be if I came to N.C. & visited you for a while?"[31]

When Arthur took his extended European trip without her and the children, Lois once again realized that she could not depend on him to support her professional ambitions. Marriage anchored her to family and home, but it could not have been the marriage of artistic minds working together that she might have hoped for or imagined. They were husband and wife, but unless she was assisting him with his mural commissions, their union as partners-in-art left much to be desired. Whether she chose to forge her career as a fine artist, an illustrator, or an author-illustrator, she knew she would have to shape her artistic future by and for herself.

Although Lois and Mabel did not venture far beyond Mabel's hometown during her visit to North Carolina, Lois enjoyed the break from domestic responsibilities, the chance to do more *plein air* sketches, and the opportunity to share ideas with an old and dear friend. This initial visit to a different region of the United States proved to be a journey of discovery, where Lois remembered, "I saw my first mule, my first gray-haired Negro, my first red clay soil. . . . I enjoyed hot biscuits and fried chicken for breakfast." Relaxed and refreshed, she also gained "much needed weight" after her first exposure to southern cooking. Afterward, she thanked Mabel for her "hospitality and constant kindness . . . with sunshine & warmth & sketching in the bargain." During the visit in Mabel's old-fashioned home, she found time and energy to sketch "all the things I grew up with and loved to draw so much—oil lamps, footstools . . . chenille table cover with tassels"—sketches that later became details in illustrations for *Skipping Village.* The two friends continued to meet periodically for such sketching ventures in other parts of the country, which were a welcome change from the isolation of family life and working alone.[32]

Stokes changed the title of Lois's first book of completely original material from *A Child's Town* to *Skipping Village* in the fall of 1926, and it was published the following spring, dedicated to the memory of her mother, whom Lois regretted not living to see her daughter's first book published. Lois was undoubtedly surprised by her father's enthusiastic response:

> You know I meant to write to you at once if not sooner. And now look! Well, be comforted—when I opened the big package & drew out the book, I sat right down and *devoured* it! Does that satisfy you? I dropped everything & went through the "Skipping Village" without skipping one thing. I think the book is very excellent. It is one fine piece of work, story & pictures. You tell things well, exceedingly well. Your chapters are neat & tell a story. And the pictures are certainly fine. You have the peony bush in the front yard of the parsonage, but you left out the roses on the opposite side. I just love to look at that old swing under the apple tree, it seems so like old times.
>
> You use your poetic license, that's your privilege, but do you know that reality is stranger than fiction! Don't be afraid, when you write again, to stick closer to the facts. You couldn't get anything funnier than Pet running away with Gerhard in the spring wagon. . . . Do let me encourage you to recall & retell the real things—they will turn out to be the best. I don't mean this in criticism at all. I only felt that you were a bit timid about the realities, & I don't want you to be.[33]

That R. C. H. took great pride in his daughter's work must have been an irony that Lois savored, probably chuckling internally as she mentioned, "he forgot that he had ever objected to my going to New York to study, and in later years, even took credit for it." Old Ohio friends told her that he shared each new publication that Lois sent with everyone he met as he boasted about her achievements. Surely, he recognized in Lois's powerful incentive to produce the same compulsion that he experienced as he translated from the Greek to write a twelve-volume commentary on the New Testament.[34] Lois must have been especially thrilled to hear from her English teacher at Sidney High School, Frances Sharp, who had encouraged her creative writing and hoped she would major in English in college:

> The whole book seems well constructed, the spirit of childhood well brought out. The page balance is good, the rhymes clever and appropriate. The pictures are delightful. . . . A teacher's results are so indirect that we can't show much for our work—but I have many good friends scattered around the country from the students I have taught—of many I am very proud. I can be proud of knowing them even though I have no claim on their achievements. Of none am I prouder than I am of you. Your success has been so merited—no tricks or luck about it! I surely hope that your writing may continue, and meet the recognition it deserves—if for no other reason, just to prove to the publishers that you can do more than one thing.[35]

Lois, however, remained ambivalent, recalling, "I was now an author, but I did not take it very seriously. I was still determined to be a painter." While the thrill of publication and the warm acceptance and endorsement of her father must have filled her with pride, Arthur's expectations and her desire to gain his complete appreciation may have figured in her failure to commit fully to being satisfied as an author-illustrator. After all, Arthur had started out his career as an illustrator for *Harper's* and other late-nineteenth-century periodicals, and he had worked hard to become one of the nation's leading muralists.[36] Lois, too, may have seen easel painting as her "higher calling," and she still wanted to ascend its heights. Yet the promise of a second book lay ahead. She remembered her father's advice to be less "timid about realities" and began to apply it to the writing and illustrating of *A Little Girl of Nineteen Hundred*,[37] published the following year.

Both books received coverage in *The Saturday Review of Literature* soon after publication. Titling her review "An Unusual Book," Marian C. Dodd glowingly commented that in *Skipping Village*, Lois's "pictures in this charming book are as constant and spontaneous an expression of her thought as are the chapters and paragraphs in which normally one would expect to find it embedded. . . . In the world of child literature we seem to have here a new ideal—pictures and text in equal value." The latter statement speaks as much to the history of American children's book publishing in this takeoff decade as it does to Lois's accomplishment. Dodd adds that "the text is one of delightful simplicity," presenting "a pleasant and interesting realism" of village life "through its round of months with their routine of characteristic homely happenings. . . . That is all of the book— no plot, no thrills." But she felt that what Lois wrote contains "the real stuff of life," and that children would enjoy the "high spots of the village blocks on the delightful map within the book cover" as well as the other illustrations sprinkled generously throughout the book. The reviewer also enjoyed those little rhymes that Lois had "sneaked" in, feeling that they "complete the very full measure of this unusual book, whose quaint and attractive jacket is an appropriate sign-post for what waits within."[38] One of those rhymes, "People," in particular, caught fire and was reproduced in numerous anthologies. Frugal, and already demonstrating a keen sense of scrupulous handling of all her own professional interests without an agent, Lois retained the rights and responded to the many requests for reprinting "People," and she noted the compensation received from each publisher. Lois's illustrated collection of her own poetry, *The Life I Live*, contained a longer version of the poem. Here is the way it appeared in *Skipping Village:*

> Tall people, short people,
>   Thin people, fat,
> Lady so dainty
>   Wearing a hat.
> Straight people, dumpy people,
>   Man dressed in brown;
> Baby in a buggy,
>   —These make a Town![39]

When *A Little Girl of Nineteen Hundred* was released in 1928, reviewers felt that it did not live up to *Skipping Village.* "This ought to be a much more charming story for children than it is," began the unsigned reviewer for *The Saturday Review,* who concluded by wondering "whether the audience for which it is written will not find it a slow moving chronicle of a pompous and somewhat stuffy decade." Mark Graham Bonner, writing for the *New York Times Book Review* the following month, echoed those sentiments, pointedly stressing that *A Little Girl of Nineteen Hundred* "would be a very good book for some little girl to give to her mother, for it takes up all those pleasures her mother knew when she was young," but "this material could have been put into more interesting shape."[40]

Actually, Lois had not yet figured out the demographics of her audience. Once she began writing her own picture books, she immediately created exactly the right combination of illustration and text to meet the needs of preschoolers. But she had a more difficult time learning to write a chapter book well suited and age-appropriate for an older group of youngsters. Years later, Lois acknowledged that her first efforts at authoring a chapter book were less than perfect, that her father's critique had been right on target—and well-taken.

> *Skipping Village* & *A Little Girl of 1900* are just surface stories of my childhood. Because they were my very first books, I had not the courage to use the real material that was there. After they were pub'd, *my father* read them with great interest, & pride, but commented sagely: "you have only touched the surface. Why didn't you really tell it all?"
>
> If I were to rewrite them today, they would be made much richer & more honest. I tried to "fictionalize" them too much. Editor's influence entered in. I was a beginner & did not know any better.[41]

After the positive reception to *Skipping Village*, receiving less than enthusiastic endorsement for *A Little Girl of Nineteen Hundred* must have been disappointing. A large part of the problem was the look and feel of the second volume. Stokes invested more heavily in the production of *Skipping Village*—with larger format, larger font, more leading between lines, a multicolor and very attractive dust jacket, and illustrated endpapers— which added a great deal to the book's charm and character. The writing of *A Little Girl of Nineteen Hundred* has much the same appeal as the first volume—and a much more satisfying, truly delightful final chapter—but the book's design qualities pale by comparison. And as Lois later confessed, as a newly minted author, she still had a lot to learn.

In addition to the mixed reviews following the publication of *A Little Girl of Nineteen Hundred*, the year 1928 presented other challenges as well as blessings. Lois and Arthur had to face their most difficult time as parents. At the end of April, Margaret, who had been so successful as an art student at Yale, suffered a nervous breakdown, had to drop out of school temporarily, and probably needed several months to recover. Her collapse was sudden and "completely unexpected," and the strain on both her parents "dreadful." This was the first of the mental and physical health difficulties that Margaret was to suffer, although she finished Yale, became a successful portrait painter, married, and had three sons. Unfortunately, only after her death at fifty-five from a brain tumor—just two years after her father's death—did family members wonder if there may have been some association between her earlier problems and her later demise.[42] On the other hand, Lois had news at the opposite end of the emotional spectrum to share with Mabel in late December:

> I have also been busy getting ready to have a little holiday in the hospital in March! This will be a real surprise for you! So don't faint! I'm going to have a baby all my own at last & it's very thrilling! I decided I needed a more genuine inspiration for my work, so this will be *it*! Also, thought I'd better get busy & get it over with before it's too late. Of course, the chee-ild will be the greatest artist that ever lived!! Have been feeling perfectly wonderful & going ahead with everything just as per usual. The only thing is that I'm not specially beautiful to look at any more.[43]

Married at twenty-seven and a stepmother for over seven years, Lois was embarking on biological motherhood at thirty-five, at the time an age considered rather late for having a first child. She was surely overjoyed about the anticipated arrival of this prayed-for and dreamed-of bundle of "more genuine inspiration."[44] At the same time, she had no way of imagining how the arrival of a new baby would bring new life to her work.

CHAPTER 4

THE BIRTH AND GROWTH OF MR. SMALL

Two major changes—the Covey family's relocation and the birth of Lois and Arthur's baby—transformed Lois's life and work, awakening creative impulses that ultimately brought her renown and commercial success in the midst of the Great Depression. Her role as an illustrator and author-illustrator grew as the demand for Arthur's work inevitably fell when the stock market crashed, and companies could not supply enough work for their employees, much less hire a muralist to enliven the walls of their workplaces. A traditionalist in many ways and sensitive to her husband's need to be perceived as head of household, Lois never commented directly on how becoming the majority breadwinner may have affected her relationship with Arthur. While she worked long hours, she worked at *home*, an arrangement that protected the illusion of the era's socially stable gender roles. As the decade unfolded, however, and Lois committed herself to a career that proved rewarding, she gained more confidence in her talents. Constantly defining and refining her chosen path, Lois moved in two complementary directions, nearly simultaneously—writing for the very young and for the reader approaching adolescence. While her move to New England would provide the impetus to research and write historical fiction, giving birth and mothering an infant and toddler stimulated her creation of original picture books.

About a month before she was expected to deliver, Lois gave birth to a son, Stephen, on February 8, 1929, in the New Rochelle Hospital. In late January, when her doctor had discovered "some complications" in her condition, he had Lois hospitalized for treatment and rest. She had recovered enough to return home but stayed there only five days when, as she told Mabel, "a hurry call brought me back again." Tiny Stephen weighed less than four pounds at birth. He had to remain in the hospital when Lois went home ten days later. Stephen was still there at the end of the month, "making a good account of himself by gaining an ounce each day," while Lois was still confined to the house. She complained, "It was very hard to leave him behind when I came home, & I have the queerest feeling now, as if it was all a mistake or a dream or something & I never had a baby at all." Lois had only seen her son three times, all before leaving the hospital, and now realized, "I don't even know what he looks like." She longed for the day when she would first be well enough to visit him at the hospital.[1] This long delay in mother-child bonding seems especially onerous and outrageous today, when mothers are encouraged to get up and get moving as soon as possible. Even premature babies who need longer hospitalizations can be visited regularly. Stephen was finally able to come home from the hospital the last week of April, when he was just shy of three months old. Had Lois been able to spend any time with him before then? There's no evidence that she visited the hospital, but relieved to have him home at last, she happily reported that he had been gaining weight steadily ever since.[2]

With Arthur's large industrial mural commissions from the Kohler Company in Kohler, Wisconsin, and the Norton Company in Worcester, Massachusetts, later in the decade, the Coveys saved enough to begin looking for a farm of their own. The August before Stephen's birth, they purchased 113 acres of "woodlot, meadow land, and pasture" near the village of Harwinton, Connecticut, six miles east of Torrington. They moved to their new home in early June, just over a month after Stephen left the hospital. Lois reported that in the midst of the chaos of packing and moving, the "perfect angel" slept most of the time. Dubbing their eighteenth-century New England farm Greenacres, "because of its wide expanse of meadow," the Coveys "loved it from the beginning."[3] The house and setting showed great potential, but it had been abandoned five years before the family moved in. They knew they would be living there during extensive renovation without indoor plumbing, electricity, or gas—all with a new baby!

Illustration of Greenacres from a Christmas card Lois designed not long after the Coveys moved to Connecticut. Reprinted by permission of the Lois Lenski Covey Foundation and Burrell Covey, copyright by Lois Lenski. Courtesy of the Lois Lenski Papers, Special Collections, Butler Library, Buffalo State College.

Lois described her first trip to the local doctor when Stephen was four months old. The baby had already endured a couple of "rounds of bronchitis," and entering the office, she felt that the doctor judged her to be "a greenhorn, rightly," and then "tried to impress upon me the importance of giving my baby the proper care." Overwhelmed by the amount of specific advice and admonitions, Lois began to take notes in her ever-present notebook, but to no avail. She felt ever more anxious, frustrated, and incompetent. "Confronted for the first time with all these new and strange duties," she felt that "life seemed suddenly too short to accomplish it all." Lois wrote the dialogue in a first draft of *Journey into Childhood:*

> "How can one human being do it all, doctor? I won't have time!"
> He looked at me coldly.
> "Madam, do you want to make a man out of that puny little baby?"
> "Why, yes, of course!" I murmured feebly.
> "Well, then!"

The doctor mentioned another client, "Mrs. So-and-So, that *other* mother, who did everything she was told and whose baby was perfect!" Because the doctor insisted on bringing this woman up as an example each time Lois visited with Stephen, she finally decided that the woman was "a legend and never existed." Lois purged her anger by writing a humorous article that she entitled "The Legend of Mrs. Sprightly," eventually published in *Parents' Magazine*. As Lois described her, Mrs. Sprightly "has become a veritable American myth, an imaginary figure of heroic proportions, worthy of being in the same class with Paul Bunyan. . . . She is a composite invention of all the baby-rearing, child-guiding, mother-educating forces in America today . . . hung up before the eyes of the modern American mother to urge her on to unobtainable goals." *Parents' Magazine* served as the perfect vehicle for Lois's satire, because the periodical functioned as part of the essential superstructure of advice for the striving mothers of the day. Of course, Lois did not believe that the doctor would ever see or read the article, but she hoped that it "gave comfort to other younger greenhorn mothers faced with problems similar to my own. The best thing about it all was that through all my difficulties, I managed to keep my sense of humor. The article proves that!"[4] At least Lois felt that she maintained her sense of humor *in print*, although there is no record of how she may have expressed herself at home. Mrs. Sprightly introduced Lois to a new audience—parents. And in the 1930s, she continued to write articles for the popular press aimed at parents.[5]

Taking care of a premature newborn proved difficult at Greenacres, without the conveniences of ready-to-eat baby food or the presence of pasteurized milk. A neighboring farmer brought the raw milk, which had to be kept at the correct temperature on their "temperamental" stove. Diapers had to be washed daily without a washing machine. And because Stephen weighed so little, the doctor insisted on a 2:00 A.M. feeding. Never sleeping more than four hours in a row, Lois was exhausted. Although she believed that the rustic living at Greenacres reeked of the "dark ages," Lois was experiencing such deprivations in 1929 and 1930, "in a country village in Connecticut, a hundred miles north of New York."[6] And it goes without saying that, given the gendered expectations of households at this time, all these duties were considered "woman's work." Arthur would not have felt that he had to help with such chores.

Stephen caught up to a normal weight by his first birthday, and Lois reported, "Soon he was an active small boy running all over the place and furnishing all of us much joy and delight." She shared a sweet anecdote about Stephen's first glimpse of the small crèche under the family Christmas tree his third Christmas. When he knelt down to look at the small nativity scene, he turned to Lois to tell her, "The baby Jesus is cold." Mother and son found a small piece of wool cloth to cover the little Jesus, and only then was Stephen satisfied and able to look at his toys. Ever the observer, Lois was struck by the limited extent of the small world that Stephen was seeking to master at play. Inspired by the direct simplicity of his needs, she thought that "it could be told in a few pictures." As a result, she decided to create picture books. Although intrigued by Stephen's play, she was less than happy when his need for activity interfered with her work. In August 1932 Lois shared her excitement about recent work with Mabel: "Doing big charcoal landscapes & having the time of my life! Also painting in oils . . . with results . . . so surprising to me that I'm as thrilled as I can be & enjoying every moment, & can hardly sleep at night for excitement!" Then, confessing that she "must not complain," Lois could not help herself:

> The only fly in the ointment is that I have to have young Stephen at my elbow or under my feet or round about all the time, & perhaps by the end of the summer he will have learned to let me alone, but I doubt it! You see Peter's [Lois's pet name for her stepdaughter, Margaret] gone to Fontainebleau, & England to visit relatives for the summer. Laird is home & 15 yrs. old now, a terrible age, & he is no good for S. at all, scolds him all the time & gets him crying, & my present maid isn't interested in him & is too busy besides, so there's nothing else for me but to have him with me, & he is at a bothersome age.[7]

Lois channeled some of her frustration with a toddler into her first picture book, *The Little Family* (1932), which she created for Stephen.[8] Published by Doubleday, Doran, and Company in child-friendly size, five-by-six inches, the book was perfect for small hands. The slightly more horizontal format, with simple black-line drawings, filled in with pastel washes—yellow, pink, green, soft turquoise, and Caucasian flesh tones—presented a simple day of Father, Mother, Sister, Brother, Dog, and Cat. Marjorie Smith Olson, who grew up on her family's farm opposite Lois's studio at Greenacres, remembers that she posed for Lois when she was a young girl. Lois would telephone Marjorie's mother and request that her daughter wear a blouse of a certain color, so that Lois could capture the image just as she wanted it for her illustration. Marjorie found sitting for those sessions really "boring." She was the model for the daughter in *The Little Family*, the only full-color picture book that Lois created during the 1930s.[9] It was a little story for a young child, dedicated opposite the title page simply: "The Book was Made for S. C., age 3." On the last page, after the children tell their parents goodnight in the living room (no drawings of real hugs, kisses or getting tucked into bed or having a book read to the children), there's a little illustration of the sun setting behind the house, with the words "and that's all."[10] Those three simple, somehow reassuring, words later become part of Lois's signature closure of the Mr. Small books. And reassurance in the midst of the Great Depression with the New Deal not yet underway delivered a boon to young and old alike. In December 1932 editor Dorothy Bryan wrote to Lois, "I thought you might be interested to know that THE LITTLE FAMILY is bowling along as happily as the real little family journeyed on their picnic. We have sold nearly 2500 copies so far, which is not bad for these dull days." In a handwritten postscript, Bryan added: "Just found it on the recommended list of the Child Study Association of America! Exclusive!!"[11]

According to Anne Scott MacLeod, the timing of the publication of *The Little Family* fit perfectly within the trend of American publishing. During the takeoff 1920s, few "family stories" appeared, but in the 1930s the focus shifted entirely: children's literature became less sentimental and romantic.

> Where 1920s authors tended to look toward the future, putting achievement, social mobility, and material affluence at the center of their stories, 1930s authors turned their attention from future to present, and from status in society to relationships within families. The characteristic children's book of the 1930s was the family story, in which relations between children and parents, children and children, and children and community constituted the plot, while childhood furnished the major theme.[12]

That reassurance of staying closer to home in spirit outlasted the Great Depression. Two decades later, Miriam Sieber Lind wrote her "story of one family's adventures with one author's books," describing how she and her children discovered the works of Lois Lenski. As the young mother of a two-year-old and his newborn brother, she received a copy of *The Little Family* as a baby gift. After repeated readings of the book to the older brother within the first two days of its presence, she reported, "By the end of the second grueling day, though the boy had memorized the book word for word, the request was forthcoming—'Read, Mommy, please!' Thus was *The Little Family* tested and approved by the most reliable of critics—the child. . . . And so Lois Lenski became our friend. During the following decade, four more toddling Readers literally cut their teeth on *The Little Family*, two additional copies of which were needed, each to replace the one going before."[13]

Although Lucy Sprague Mitchell advocated for developmentally appropriate literature in *The Here and Now Story Book* a decade earlier, *The Little Family* was among the first books written purposefully targeting the very young. In her masterwork, *American Picturebooks* (1976), Barbara Bader assured readers it was "no coincidence" that Lenski's book for S. C., age three, was small in size, hand-lettered, "cast in the present tense," and without a plot. This formulation fit a young child's brief attention span, in which he or she has "little sense of sequence, of the order in which events occur. Lenski's hand lettering complements and enhances the book's design—a harmony with the drawing that machine type lacks, an individual character and warmth, and in little books particularly, a concordant intimacy, the sense of a private communication." In summary,

> The Littles are a model family saved from stuffiness by the prosaic sorts of things they do and the laconic matter-of-fact text. Similarly, what is chaste about the pictures is offset by their compact cheerfulness and certain small, light touches—the steam corkscrewing up from Mrs. Little's washbasin, Mr. Little's flapping shoelace, the flying grass-clippings. . . . As compositions, they have order, definition, above all equipoise; as illustrations, they come alive.[14]

Less than a decade later, Bader revised her glowing description, perhaps because she noticed that the Littles' rigid gender roles were, by the 1980s, perceived as hopelessly outmoded (just as they already were when she wrote *American Picturebooks*). In her 1985 article, she pointed out that although Lois was obviously a working mother, "We can safely say that *The Little Family* was an unconscious reflection of certain social conventions—a model or abstraction of family life; its realism lay in the very depiction of a father leaving for work and a mother keeping house."[15] That critique never really bothered those who kept purchasing *The Little Family* and the children who wanted it read and reread. They kept the little volume a well-loved, if now quaint and politically incorrect, classic. A reviewer in 2008 posted on the Amazon.com website that he found it "a sweet little book about a family going through their normal daily routines. It was written in 1932, a much more innocent time, but the daily tasks are basically the same—they're just accomplished differently. My son (age almost three) loves this book and asks to read it several times a week. I think it is very relaxing and comforting."[16]

Because of the immediate success of *The Little Family*, the book's editor, Dorothy Bryan, asked Lois, "Have you worked out very definite plans for another book like this? . . . Every place that I talk about the book parents fall upon it with joy because there is so little offered for very young children in the book world."[17] Lois may not have had anything already in the works, but by the time Stephen turned four the following year, he had very defined personal preferences. "Automobiles were his major interest, with other vehicles secondary—the train, the tractor, the airplane, the fire engine, the sailboat. His interest in these was not passive, but active." Stephen and his friends "*never* personified an automobile or a train. They never imagined a face on the front, they never made it talk like an adult or run away, or move of its own volition." Lois loved watching Stephen and his friends playing their favorite game, "Auto . . . with invention and imagination." Whether they were using "wagon, tricycle, or scooter, it was always an imaginary automobile, and they pumped up tires, poured water in the radiator and were continually getting stuck in the mud. . . . They played this game with variations, day in and day out, never tiring of it. Always the boy identified himself not with the vehicle, but with the driver of the car. He was never a passenger in a vehicle; he was the driver. He wanted to know what made the vehicle go. He wanted to make it go himself." Realizing that their play probably reflected a "fundamental interest of small boys," Lois created *The Little Auto* (1934), the first of the Mr. Small books, later commenting, "Stephen loved every word and every picture." In *The Little Auto* and the Mr.

Stephen Covey, already comfortable drawing like his parents, 1935. Courtesy of Jeanine Covey Gutowski, Vivian Covey, and Michael Covey.

Small books that followed, she emphasized that the reader "becomes Mr. Small and enjoys his experiences vicariously as the driver, the engineer, the pilot, the farmer, the captain, the fireman, the cowboy and the father. . . . There is some unseen bond between him and Mr. Small, which I myself cannot explain."[18]

Although Lois wrote and illustrated several less memorable picture books during the decade,[19] *The Little Auto* established Lois's inimitable picture-book style: black-and-white illustrations with enough gray tones (and a single accent color wash) to give the paper-doll-like figures more dimensional substance, background reduced to only the elements a young child would want to see included, streamlined in look and in focus. May Hill Arbuthnot, mid-twentieth-century advocate for children's literature, wrote that Lois's line drawings were "sparing of details but get the maximum characterization, action, and drollery into the fewest lines." Mr. Small was rendered with crayon that gives him (and his devices) "a pleasant rotundity and depth." Arbuthnot appreciated the significance of Lois's artistry: "There is a blandness about the Small clan that is amusing to adults but properly grave to children."[20] Creating Mr. Small presented Lois with the first inkling of how she could turn this character's adventures into an even more significant—financially as well as stylistically—series of books with Mr. Small assuming the subsequent roles mentioned above. Stephen, of course, *is* Mr. Small.[21] As Lois explained, "Because Stephen was four at the time, I drew the main character in the proportions of a four-year-old; but I called him Mr. Small, because Stephen always played he was a man. The book shows Mr. Small, Stephen in disguise, doing all the things to the little auto that Stephen had seen his daddy do to our family car. . . . I told the story with the fewest possible words & illustrated it with the simplest possible drawings."[22]

The manuscript did not meet with immediate success. Lois mentioned one "eminent but short-sighted" editor who "hardly glanced thru my dummy & handed it back to me, saying: 'There is no story.'" On the other hand, Lois took pride in the book's being "daringly accepted by another," Grace Allen Hogarth at Oxford University Press. Hogarth remembered Lois's coming to her office with a "perfectly designed and executed picture book with color carefully separated to save cost." When Lois told her that she had made it for her son who was about two at the time, Hogarth was amazed "because we did not believe then that two-year-olds should be given books." Lois argued that, on the contrary, children could be taught to "love books and treat them with respect." Hogarth was less persuaded by the argument than "the beautiful economy of the book. . . . I could see . . . without too much arithmetic, that we might well be able to publish it for seventy-five cents, and that was a depression price." Economical as the book was in style and in price, "critics were very severe," a reaction, Hogarth believed, of the "stern and unrelenting realism" of the Depression years. Lois remembered the decade differently. She thought that *The Little Auto* "was a little ahead of its time" when a book about an automobile was an innovation and a great risk: sales for the first year or two seemed to bear this out. The book made not a ripple. Nobody noticed it." Hogarth realized "as a young and untried publisher, I was frightened; but I did not have long to wait before I saw how right Lois Lenski had been and how truly she was a pioneer."[23]

Lois's delving into picture books emerged primarily from her thoughtful observations of Stephen and his friends. She recognized that although the very young child cannot read words, that same child could "read pictures," poring over them with unrelenting—even if not long-sustained—focus. The young child

> can, in fact, draw pictures of his own and other people's activities, several years before his conscious mind can be taught to read printed words. So his understanding of pictures comes very early, often before the age of one year. In the preschool years, he looks at the picture of a child in action and understands what he is doing. As he looks at a series of pictures of successive actions, the whole story unfolds—he needs no words. Each picture is an exciting experience, a happening in itself. The thought stimulated by one picture carries into the next. He loves to turn the pages.
>
> This is why the picture book came into being. . . . If words are also used, they merely reinforce the pictures. Often, when the words are not right, the child will disregard them, look at the pictures and make up his own story.[24]

When the slow-starting Mr. Small began to pick up speed, Lois found other personae and adventures for the little man: *The Little Sail Boat* (1937), *The Little Airplane* (1938), *The Little Train* (1940), *The Little Farm* (1942), *The Little Fire Engine* (1946), *Cowboy Small* (1949), *Papa Small* (1951), all originally published by Oxford University Press. *Policeman Small* followed in 1961, published by Henry Z. Walck. Once president of Oxford, Walck acquired the children's book division in 1958. "By the time one generation of small boys had gotten their hands on it, refusing to let it go, copies were selling by the thousands," Lois took pride in noting.[25] Why?

Barbara Bader tried to find the answer. Although she considered Lois "in no sense a major talent, either as an artist or writer," she postulated that the secret to Mr. Small's success "may be the combination . . . of directness, purposeful activity, and individuality. Mr. Small is the little man who can, the doer—whether as sailor, engineer, pilot, or cowboy. Then he is Papa: not an authority figure, not even an exalted personage—but everybody's dad. . . . Probably he became 'Papa' as a parallel to 'Pilot' . . . and so on. . . . So the books can be at once documents—social or vocational microcosms—and timeless mini-dramas, with personalities of their own."[26] That the Mr. Small books lack plots is a great advantage: young children can more easily project themselves into the book world and create their own sequences and outcomes without needing to encounter a countervailing adult worldview. Even Bader admitted that Mr. Small, "always a little stiff, a little unreal," is truly "no-man, the better to be everyman."[27]

In their overview of children's literature, Charlotte Huck and Doris A. Young had a slightly different take on the impact of Mr. Small in his various guises. They understood that small children wanted real information to satisfy their curiosity about the world they inhabited. "They want answers to their questions," these authors explained, "but not complex answers. Lois Lenski's books satisfy children without overwhelming them." Happily and conveniently, Mr. Small never ages, attracting legions of young, principally male, readers in each generation. Lois claimed that Stephen actively participated in developing the series, "supervising every detail or word and picture." When she was working on *The Little Train*, Stephen was already ten years old. Neither mother nor son had ever been inside the cab of a steam engine, and both were anxious to see how the equipment worked. Lois persuaded an engineer to allow them to ride as guests in the cab from Torrington to nearby Winsted. While the train waited at Winsted before its return run, Lois interviewed the engineer. Many years later in a short, undated memoir, Stephen recalled the event "vividly," remembering how his mother "made sketches of the inside of the cab, and while we waited for the train to turn around at the end of the line, she drew exterior views of the engine, the coal car, and the passenger coaches."[28]

Being the son of working parents, Stephen spent much time on his own as a young boy. Of course, he was unaware that growing up as the child of working artists was different from the way the way his peers were raised. Lois recalled that when he was about four or five, he rushed home from visiting one of his friends in the neighborhood to announce, excitedly, "'Lewis's mother *can't draw!'* . . . He saw his own mother making pictures every day and had assumed that all mothers did the same." Marjorie Smith Olson recalls that her family's farmhouse directly across Harmony Hill Road was one of Stephen's favorite destinations, since Marjorie had three brothers, and one was just about the same age as Stephen. When he was somewhat older and visiting, Stephen started using all kinds of swear words. Marjorie's father told him, in no uncertain terms, that he could not talk like that in the Smith home. Stephen replied that since he was not allowed to use those words at home, he thought he would try them out at the Smiths![29]

By the time of that incident, Stephen was too old to be a reliable critic of picture books. Just as Marjorie Flack, a contemporary children's author and illustrator, submitted a draft of a story to two different school groups for their appraisal, so Lois arranged several visits to Horace Mann School in New York City to meet with classes of five-year-olds and first-graders. She wanted to see how they felt about a mocked-up draft of *The Little Train*.[30] One student teacher described the students' reactions: "While the story was being read the children expressed their interest by imitating the various sounds: whistle, bells, and brakes. Many anticipated parts of the story such as the turn table [*sic*] and the tunnel—thus adding to their interest and enjoyment."[31] One of the first-grade teachers wrote a longer summary to let Lois know how much the students enjoyed taking an active role in the development of *The Little Train*. She included one child's pointed critique who felt strongly that "the sound of the bell at the crossing is wrong. He thinks it should be, not Ding-a-ling-ling! Ding-a-ling-ling! but rather, should be Ding-ding-ding-ding-ding-ding-ding etc. That more or less bears out my own experience of country grade crossings." The teacher closed the letter by telling the author, "I can't say enough in tribute to the effect on the children of your presence and personality. It was a rare experience, and one of which I think most of them have some real appreciation. Please don't forget us when you embark on your next book at our level, will you?" Lois paid close attention. In the published version of *The Little Train*, the text reads, "The little train comes to a crossing. The bell begins to ring. Ding, ding, ding, ding."[32]

Although the text is minimal and the drawings are greatly simplified and highly stylized, Lois insisted that all details included be as accurate as possible. She told Emma Celeste Thibodaux, an early elementary school teacher in rural Louisiana who became one of her most significant friends, correspondents, and informants:

I'm working on plans for a Fire Engine book now for my famous Mr. Small. . . . Children & teachers & librarians & booksellers all over the country have been demanding a fire-engine book for him for 4 or 5 years! And so I spent part of this winter in Fla., visiting the firehouse & talking to firemen, & studying up in some Fireman's Manuals they loaned me, so now I think I can qualify for Fire Chief any day!

Lois took the model book or "dummy" to the teachers at Horace Mann and shared it with groups of four- and six-year-olds. She was thrilled to witness "their intense absorption," especially that of one four-year-old boy. After the session, Lois met the child's mother, who told Lois that her son was a real fan of Mr. Small, and "always spoke of Lois Lenski as if he knew her, as he would speak of a friend, & that he *never* mentioned the names of the authors of *any* of his other books! And was she thrilled to have him actually see me & hear me tell all about the new Fire Engine book!" Lois took time to talk to the youngster individually, somewhat amazed to find that little boys derive such joy from her depiction of the simple things that they love. Having witnessed that response repeatedly, Lois felt she had to get every detail right.

> So I feel a heavy responsibility in my efforts to get the Fire Engine book just right—not too scary—but healthfully exciting & building up a feeling of confidence in the power of the fireman & the fire engine which can be relied on, in times of danger—& pictures accordingly—until it meets their entire *satisfaction*—It won't be published till after the war, perhaps *well after,* when there's *plenty of paper,* for it will have to be a huge edition, to meet the demands of the boys who grew up with the first Mr. Small [who] are grown men now! But Mr. Small stays forever young![33]

Robert Lawson, winner of the 1941 Caldecott Award, reiterated this sentiment in his acceptance speech for *They Were Strong and Good:* "No one can possibly tell what tiny detail of a drawing or what seemingly trivial phrase in a story will be the spark that sets off a great flash in the mind of some child, a flash that will leave a glow there until the day he dies."[34]

And as Josiah Titzell had earlier noted, Lois demanded perfection not simply in her transmittal of factual information in simple terms, in interpretation and illustration, but in reproduction. By the mid 1940s, Eunice Blake had taken over Hogarth's position at Oxford University Press, and was Lois's editor. The press was planning an initial printing of one hundred thousand copies of *The Little Fire Engine,* and with wartime shortages still in effect, needed to raise the price of this new and longer Mr. Small book to one dollar. Although Lois always insisted that the books be affordable, and therefore accessible as possible, she understood and acquiesced. But she demanded "the right red for the fire engine," since she found the samples she had received completely unsuitable. She was enclosing another sample, suggesting that Eunice "give only half of it to the printer this time, and keep the other half safe somewhere" for comparison. "There is no reason (unless he is color-blind)," she complained, "why he cannot match this red exactly. If and when he does, it will improve the general effect tremendously, because it is what I call a 'singing red.' He just MUST match it EXACTLY!!!" Then, too, Lois wanted only the "snappiest black." The sample pages did not meet any of her expectations: the pale grays so poor in register that "a good bit of the drawing gets lost—the eyes of the people, for instance." Lois realized that she had never provided drawings for the endpapers, but now she had a "brilliant suggestion"—printing the endpaper that same "singing red." She told Eunice, "I'm sure all the millions of children who have red for their favorite color will be entranced by it; as well as many grown-ups. I assume you are printing the jacket design on white cloth for the cover. When you open the book, you will then be confronted by this nice red endpaper. Will that not be a nice solution?" Eunice replied, "THE LITTLE FIRE ENGINE is being done over with the proper red and I have impressed the printer with the necessity of making the black good and black."[35]

Two decades later, Lois's "Literary Scrapbook, 1950–1968," contains an undated press release from the Henry Z. Walck Company, complete with photos of Thomas Trieschman, age three and a half, and his mother, as they received two hundred dollars' worth of books (sixty-eight books) from the Walck Company. Mrs. Trieschman had purchased the two millionth copy of a Lois Lenski book published by Walck—*The Little Fireman!*[36]

Cowboy Small was by far the most anticipated book in the series. Cowboys gained widespread currency during the 1930s, celebrated in songs on recordings and radio and with Hollywood's singing cowboys. As a prototypically American cultural icon, the cowboy's heroic and fearless ability to survive on the frontier reassured a public filled with Depression-fed anxieties.[37] Cowboy images and paraphernalia were also popular with children, and the fascination only grew in the 1950s when singing cowboys moved from Saturday matinees to television. That Mr. Small should become Cowboy Small could not have happened at a more opportune moment. Lois actually double-dipped while researching one of her regional books for upper-elementary-aged readers, *Texas Tomboy*. Through librarian friends in

West Texas, Lois was introduced to former librarian-turned-ranchwoman, Mary Davis Coupe. Mary lived on a ranch outside of Eldorado, and in the spring of 1948, Lois visited her and her ranch foreman, Bob Whitley, to learn about the real work of cowboys—and cattlewomen. *Cowboy Small* was published the following year, with *Texas Tomboy* released in 1950.[38] In August after her visit, Lois told Mary about Eunice Blake's reaction to the first rough sketches:

> The editor was ecstatic over them! She & others in her office had been "guessing" what Mr. Small would do next, and no one had thought of "cowboy" at all. She predicts the book "will sweep the country!" So I've got to make it as correct as possible. Otherwise this vast army of would-be 5-yr-old cowboys all over the country will rise up to point out my mistakes and say "the book is no good!" I've been having a terrible time with his rope-throwing. Why didn't I have sense enough to take a few lessons from Bob while I was at the ranch, so I would know what curve it takes when it goes through the air?[39]

Lois and Mary corresponded over questions about the way the lasso ought to be drawn. Mary provided diagrams to help with the visuals, and offered suggestions such as: "The line from the hand of cowboy to the loop should be straight, because the weight of the loop pulls the rope out of roper's hand." Lois was also concerned about portraying the cows properly. Mary sent her many copies of *The Cattleman* magazine, with cheerful support: "I am sure that Cowboy Small should have Lenski cows, but can't they be Herefords too! You were drawing them with personality when you were here. The markings will adapt themselves wonderfully to the two-color scheme of your book. I think they will *just have* to be Lenski Herefords." Bob laughed when Lois wanted to know if Cowboy Small should say "whoa" and "giddap." He then replied, "No! . . . you don't gen'nely have to talk to a cow horse about things like that; you kick him with the spur when you want him to go, and pull up on the reins when you want him to stop." Still, Cowboy Small says, "Giddap" and "Whoa," since Lois's little boy fans would be disappointed if they couldn't "holler" like cowboys they had seen on the silver screen. Afraid that her original illustrations might get damaged or lost in the mail, Lois traced some to send for Bob and Mary's approval.

Original illustration of Cowboy Small taking good care of his horse, Cactus. Reprinted by permission of the Lois Lenski Covey Foundation and Burrell Covey, copyright by Lois Lenski. Courtesy of the Lois Lenski Papers, Special Collections, Butler Library, Buffalo State College.

"Put the bridle reins in Cowboy Small's left hand" (where reins are typically held when one is mounted on a western saddle), Bob responded, because "I think this is important because he is greeting his friends and yours" (on the title page). The endpapers are particularly charming, with one page devoted to Cowboy Small's horse, "Cactus," surrounded by the equipment—with names for each, such as "Branding Iron," "Lariat or Lasso." The other endpaper shows Cowboy Small dressed as a typical little boy with t-shirt and blue jeans, encircled by chaps, ten-gallon hat, spurs, and other necessary accessories.[40]

While in West Texas, Lois visited schools around Eldorado to talk with teachers and young students. Expressing her concern for social equity, she wanted to ensure that Mary distributed multiple copies of her books to both rural Anglo and Mexican schools to express her appreciation. Lois was quite explicit in her request:

> I think the pre-school books will be very useful in the Mexican schools where the children are so backward in reading English, as they have a limited number of words per page. When I watched these children take books out of the bookmobile, $\%_{10}$ of them checked out readers & primers because they couldn't read the picture books carried by the bookmobile. I wished then that the bookmobile had a set of my pre-school & Mr. Small books, as I felt they would meet the needs of the children better than any others.[41]

As a footnote to this initial request, the Spanish translation of *Cowboy Small*, *Vaquero Pequeño*, appeared in 1961, translated by Donald Worcester in bilingual format, with both Spanish and English text on each page. *Cowboy Small* was also translated into many other languages—Portuguese, Arabic, Afrikaans, Danish, and Burmese—each edition similarly formatted. Buffalo, New York, elementary teacher Marie Ram wrote an article entitled "Mr. Small—Ambassador," in which she declared: "Since 1953, the United States Information Agency (USIA) has been distributing these beloved books by Lois Lenski to libraries and information centers throughout the world."[42]

Two years after the publication of *Cowboy Small*, *Papa Small* made his debut. In many ways, this domestic story mirrored *The Little Family* by depicting a family going about its weekly (rather than daily) routine. Only, as Barbara Bader adroitly pointed out, family life is less narrowly gender-defined. Papa Small shares more of the responsibilities (grocery shopping, cooking Sunday dinner, helping with household chores)—reflective of changes in American society toward less formality, with "the family arrangement . . . casual and practical."[43] The most significant change is in the expression of family love. Instead of the children stiffly bidding their parents goodnight in the living room as they did in *The Little Family*, Papa Small is holding brother, sister, and baby in his lap and reading them a bedtime story as Mama Small turns down the covers on their beds. "'Good night, Papa Small. Good night, Mama Small.' And that's all about the small Smalls."[44]

May Hill Arbuthnot claims that the "great virtue" of Lois's Mr. Small books is the "honest" and "unadorned simplicity" of the writing. Arbuthnot succinctly analyzes the gift that Lois bestowed to young and curious-about-the-way-things-work children. Her "straightforward narrative" is written

> so that a young child can understand every detail of something
> that is really complicated. Nothing important is omitted; nothing
> trivial or extraneous is included. It is more fact than fiction,
> more information than story. Yet Mr. Small is a real person to the
> young reader. Undoubtedly, the child identifies himself with the
> competent Mr. Small. Perils lie on all sides of Mr. Small, but with
> masterly presence of mind he always does the right thing. "That's
> just what *I* do when *I* drive," commented a four-year-old.[45]

Lois's favorite Mr. Small story involved a little boy from New Haven, who worried his mother with his obsessive love of *The Little Auto*. He even slept with the book at night. His mother reminded him that "'Mr. Small is just an imaginary character. He was made up by a lady called Lois Lenski.' But the boy would have none of it. 'Mother,' he said, 'that's not true. Mr. Small is real. He eats and sleeps with me. Mr. Small tells me things!'"[46]

The success of the Mr. Small series spawned two others, also issuing from Lois's relationships with family members: the Davy series and the Debbie series, inspired by grandchildren. Lois was such a productive author and illustrator that her series did not follow each other sequentially but overlapped. She was still in the midst of the Small series—and others—when stepdaughter Margaret's ongoing mental health concerns were again temporarily debilitating, and her two sons, Alan (seven) and David (three), spent the summer of 1944 with their grandparents. The boys spent additional time with them later that year and the following summer. Lois decided that David was even better in helping her understand the world from a child's point of view. The Davy series differs from Mr. Small in that Davy grows from a toddler to a little boy in subsequent stories, and Lois's sure-handed line drawings typically reveal more than the simple accompanying text. Lois claimed that by the time she and Davy had completed their third summer together, she had "made notes or dummies for six picture books, all inspired by his companionship," and she treasured the memories of the "richness" of that relationship. Alan recalled that during that first difficult summer of 1944, after breakfast was eaten and the breakfast dishes washed and kitchen swept, Lois daily set out for her studio with David, who played in a special area set aside for him nearby. Arthur retreated to his studio, and Alan claimed he simply "shadowed" his Uncle Stephen, who was then fourteen. Exasperated by Alan's constant proximity, Stephen turned to him one morning and commanded, "Occupy yourself," echoing a message he must have heard Lois repeat when she needed to work.[47]

Lois really considered her picture books "sheer indulgence" that she did "for the fun of it." Except for Margaret, whom Lois did not get to know as a toddler, all of Lois's experiences as stepmother, mother, or grandmother were relationships with boys for many years until Stephen married and had three children—the middle and youngest were both daughters. Finally, she could build a series around a little girl, and thus the Debbie books were created.[48] Lois worked diligently to make sure that "all the illustrations are done from the child's eye view—not an adult 'eye level.' Only portions of adults are shown, never the full figures. The child's eye-level is 2½ or 3 ft. off the floor." She felt this perspective was essential in creating situations where "the child changes places with these characters, becomes them outwardly and inwardly—which is the true basis for understanding in all human relations,"[49] a concept that gained more currency in the regional books she developed for middle-level readers in the 1940s.

Looking at the evolution of only some of Lois's picture book series—and not her individual picture books, many of which also became classics—has taken us from the 1930s through the 1960s. In the years before *The Little Family* had become a nursery favorite and a year before the publication of *The Little Auto* and Mr. Small's ascension to celebrity status, however, their creator and her husband were finding it difficult to earn money. During the spring of 1933, for example, Lois wrote Mabel, "I am racking my brains to find a new market for my work, as books seem to be absolutely dead." That her books could not command sufficient anticipated income in such straitened times did not keep Lois from creating them. But writing "The Legend of Mrs. Sprightly" had given her the courage to try producing articles on a wide variety of subjects: "gardening, baby-raising, child-training, keeping house, managing a maid & also my life experiences! Now the question is where can I sell?" No wonder that Lois landed in the hospital in Torrington "for an indefinite stay" due to complete exhaustion within months of her asking Mabel's advice about marketing her work. Home from college for the summer and obviously stable at the time, Margaret capably assumed household duties, allowing Lois the chance to recoup adequately. And some of the ideas she had floated in her earlier letter to Mabel actually began "to bear fruit." In addition to selling "Mrs. Sprightly" to *Parents' Magazine*, Lois secured work in *McCall's*, *Condé Nast*, and *House Beautiful*, relieved that she had not "cast my bread upon the waters in vain. And at least I'll be able to pay part of my doctor & hospital bills!"[50] The real bread-and-butter commissions were for illustrations, however, in magazines for a general audience, for other children's authors, and especially for children's periodicals, such as *Child Life* and *Story Parade*.[51]

During the Great Depression, Arthur received commissions for only a handful of murals. The first, *Washington Taking Command of the Army*, was displayed at the National Gallery in Washington, D.C., along with murals by other known American mural painters in 1932 to mark the bicentennial of George Washington's birth. He also painted two sets of post office murals in Connecticut for the New Deal Works Progress Administration (WPA) and one for the Anderson, South Carolina, Post Office. His other commissions were also government-related: for the New York World's Fair and for the La Guardia Airport, both at the end of the 1930s. Arthur competed to win the commissions, worked hard to execute them, and evidently took pride in his excellent work. Still, spread over the decade, these projects did not bring in much needed income.[52] There is no record of his producing or selling smaller works during this period.

No wonder Lois was trying her hand at so many potentially income-producing ventures. She simultaneously raised and canned vegetables from her garden and worked hard to be a strong and supportive mother. Even as a woman endowed with prodigious ambitions and energies, she still strained to manage. Knowing the larger context of Lois's personal and professional life as a working mother of a baby and toddler and two other growing children, one can appreciate more fully how the "sheer indulgence" of creating picture books gave her such pleasure.

CHAPTER 5

IMMERSED IN HISTORY

With the Covey family's relocation to Greenacres in Harwinton, Connecticut, Lois got her first taste of living in an authentic early American house in a New England village. Although she had earlier in her life experienced the region as a camp counselor in New Hampshire over a few successive summers, settling into a not-yet-renovated home stimulated her imagination even more than her desire to make it more comfortable. The house and its surroundings whetted her appetite to know and understand the history of its inhabitants, her neighbors along Harmony Hill Road, and the larger story of the countryside and region where she and Arthur were sinking roots. Lois's belief in the power of the local environment—topographical, economic, social, historical, cultural—in shaping individuals undoubtedly quickened her interest in integrating and synthesizing these large unseen forces in her work.

Pouring her energies into rendering the abandoned farmhouse and its neglected outbuildings and fields into a compound that could simultaneously serve as home for the family and workspaces for the two resident artists also provoked her natural curiosity. Just as she had devoted many pages at the beginning of her autobiography to describe the marvelous Victorian parsonage in Anna, Ohio, Lois wanted to make Greenacres come alive for her readers by sharing the history of its inhabitants. She carried the primacy of scene-setting into the historical fiction that she began to develop while she was producing her delightful picture books, writing occasional pieces, and illustrating for other authors; that is, honing the craft of "making do" during hard times.

At the beginning of the 1930s, Lois had almost instantly and effortlessly mastered creating picture books for the very young. In sharp contrast, mid-decade, she spent several years groping for the right narrative, words, and images to enliven the realistic historical chapter books she created for upper elementary and middle school readers. As she wrestled with acquiring the basic building blocks of historical literacy, she ultimately found her voice and expanded her repertoire as an illustrator to accompany this more fully realized sense of herself as an author. Indeed, Lois was at last ready to commit to this career path, and to pursue it intently.

The Coveys learned that they were only the third family to occupy Greenacres, even though it had been built nearly a century and a half earlier. Lois described the house itself as a "plain, sedate, white New England mansion" typical of the late eighteenth century. The term "mansion" today suggests perhaps a somewhat grander house than this large but compact two-story, five-bedroom farmhouse built by Jonathan Balch and known as "the old Balch homestead."

The layout of the house mirrors that of neighboring houses from that period, with its low ceilings, small entryway, four fireplaces, and three sets of tight, steep staircases, the first encountered immediately facing the front door. North and south parlors flank the entry, and the large original kitchen with an enormous shallow hearth—the original crane and pot hooks that once held large cooking pots still in place when Lois and Arthur first visited—conveys to all that this area forms the heart of the house. The Coveys used this gracious space as their dining room, with a large round oak table in the center of the room, surrounded by Windsor chairs.

When tearing off the wallpaper in the north parlor, Lois and Arthur were thrilled to find original paneling (complete with homemade wooden nails). Because the wide pine floor planks of the large room directly above showed little wear, Lois assumed that it must have been a ballroom, used only occasionally. Behind the kitchen were two small end rooms. When the Coveys remodeled, they transformed these spaces into a study, a porch, and a pantry. The latter had contained milk and cheese pans when Greenacres had served as the farm for some members of the second family, the Drakes.

On the north, Lois and Arthur had their new kitchen built and connected with the large toolshed, which they made into a garage and utility room. These spaces led directly to the old clock shop belonging to the last of the Balch family members. The shop became Arthur's studio.[1] Although the front door was narrow, a wide "coffin door" to the exterior in the south parlor indicated that the original owners understood that such a door would be necessary for the periodic visitations of death that residents would face.

In the attic, Jonathan Balch had carved his name into one of the huge hand-hewn beams that support the roof, the marks still visible over two hundred years later. In 1954 Lois told a teacher friend about the property and pointed out that Shelton Balch had begun to build a New England stone wall "8 ft. broad at base . . . every stone pulled by ox-team, but he did not live to finish it." Balch had also jigsawed fanciful little animals on the eaves of Arthur's studio. With such abundant evidence of the previous owners' lives, it is easy to see why Lois was so intrigued to learn—and to imagine—more about what it might have been like to reside in the house when it belonged to the Balches and the Drakes.[2]

The Coveys' interest in purchasing a late-eighteenth-century farmhouse in a remote New England village reflected a passion for Americana that had begun sweeping the country in the 1920s. As Michael Kammen points out in *Mystic Chords of Memory*, the affection for recognizing and celebrating American history and culture exhibited itself in widely diverse ways. In an era when automobile travel had already sparked the creation of better roads, historic markers made their appearance along highways. Indeed, some highways "were constructed or proposed for the exclusive purpose of facilitating nationalism and tourism," with the Jefferson Memorial Road an even earlier example (1902) of a three-mile corridor promoted to connect Monticello with the University of Virginia. Artists like Thomas Hart Benton felt that one needed to travel, as he did, "the back countries of America" to search out authentic American subject matter, while individuals and families of immense wealth—such as Henry Ford, John D. Rockefeller, Jr., and Henry Francis Du Pont—amassed collections of Americana that became cultural tourism institutions and destinations by the following decade: the Henry Ford Museum and Greenfield Village in Dearborn, Michigan; Colonial Williamsburg, Virginia; and Winterthur in Wilmington, Delaware, respectively.[3]

An awareness of the necessity for preserving historic structures emerged earlier in the twentieth century in some places, such as Litchfield, Connecticut—less than ten miles from Harwinton—which, Kammen noted, "became the first town in America to remodel its historic architecture and landscape comprehensively in the colonial style. . . . By 1930 . . . Litchfield had quietly become New England's Williamsburg—sans admission fees, sans hostesses in costume, sans p.r." Restoring structures and designating historic places manifested one aspect of the preservationist spirit. Collecting primary resources that revealed the substance of the everyday life of American regions represented another. New England figured prominently as the repository of our cherished roots, with Colonial Revival architecture the most popular style in American history, especially dominant during the 1920s and 1930s.[4]

According to architectural historian Richard Gary Wilson, the Colonial Revival house "developed very early in American history and . . . evolved into being one of the identifying features of American culture. . . . American architecture is in many ways a history of the single-family house and how architects have seen and reformed it." Lois caught the fever of this fascination, especially, in Wilson's words, "the Colonial Revival's emphasis on home, hearth, and the image of family," which "offered a respite from the strain of change, whether in the nineteenth, twentieth, or twenty-first century."[5] Intrigued by the authenticity that Greenacres offered, she sought source material to deepen her understanding of the ways in which youngsters living there might have spent their lives in the first decades of the nineteenth century.

Lois felt that her birth and upbringing in Ohio contained "little to remind one of the past," since the settlement of that part of the country was a nineteenth-century story. But being in New England with "history on all sides" awakened a whole new consciousness of the past. "Every town, every crossroads, every cemetery, every old house was filled with stories and traditions . . . which were still living, being handed down from one generation to the next. . . . One could only understand the present by delving into the past." Some of Lois's neighbors had lived in their homes and on their families' land for several generations, and she enjoyed hearing them talk about their ancestors who had helped build Harwinton, a stagecoach stop along the Hartford–Litchfield road from the mid-1700s until the railroad supplanted stage travel more than a century later.[6]

Lois created this engaging, American Regionalist–inspired lithograph called *Farm by the Road* in 1932. Courtesy of the Lois Lenski Papers, Special Collections, Butler Library, Buffalo State College.

She began haunting antiques shops and auctions, collecting memorabilia and artifacts to help her get a more tactile and tangible feel for the past, as so many Americans of that era were doing. At one country auction, she purchased an "armful of books," among them *Scenes from the Country*, a small book in green paper covers inscribed "in a stilted hand, in faded ink: Kate Daniels Her Book—October 1825—from her Cousins in Litchfield." And then the quotation:

> This is a preshious Book, indeed,
> Happy the Child who Loves to Read.[7]

That one inscription formed a turning point. Lois became obsessed with the need to learn more about the rich and relatively long social history of her neighbors. She found that research, not simply studying the past, "but living it and feeling it," proved a completely different orientation from the history she had abhorred as a grade school student, with its emphasis on the memorization of names, dates, and battles that made the past seem distant and irretrievable. Lois discovered that approaching the past "from the human standpoint" made it "absorbing and very much alive." Her fascination with New England as the American past writ large occurred within a major cultural phenomenon in children's literature that Gary Schmidt has identified. "Mid-century children's literature would simultaneously posit America as a pioneer nation and America as democratic experiment, the first a story of rugged independence and self-reliance, the second a story of interdependencies, social tolerance, and cooperation. . . . [A] distinctly American children's literature was often the story of America itself, and often the story into which child readers were engrafted, usually through an assumed identification with a national culture."[8]

Because of Lois's interest in writing and illustrating principally for children, the evidence she encountered convinced her that youngsters of the early 1800s "did not live lives of their own"—at least in the sense that people in the twentieth century would recognize. The self-sufficient home of the 1820s was "a busy plant" where adults felt the need to train children for their future roles as adults but took no time listening to their needs or dreams. The past had no glorious or rosy glow for the youngsters who might have lived in Greenacres, but "thrown upon their own initiative, they developed inner resources of strength and vigor which enabled them to withstand the rigors of their harsh training and environment." Lois decided that young readers in the 1930s needed to learn about this radically different social universe where children were to be seen and not heard. With the phrase "Kate Daniels Her Book" very likely repeating in her mind, Lois began to research *Phebe Fairchild Her Book* in earnest. She single-mindedly went about constructing in words a realistic world for her first historical protagonist who lived in Greenacres, at least briefly.[9]

Not trained as a historian or as an anthropologist, she nonetheless possessed a lusty capacity for consulting and/or acquiring every shred of primary material that she could find that would shed light on the *reality*, not the romance, of life in the 1830s.

> What was family life like then? . . . I had to find out. I studied local
> town and church records; I visited historical societies and museums
> in the area. I studied old newspapers, letters, and diaries. . . . Not

many children wrote them, but those who did were often articulate. Here the child speaks in his own words across the gap of time. . . . He gives us a vivid picture of his activities, especially the large amount of work he did and the small amount of pleasure he enjoyed.[10]

In the diary of eleven-year-old Zeloda Barrett of New Hartford, for example, Lois found brief entries: "Attended school. Weather pleasant. Evening, knit," or "I spun today. . . . I have spun 2 skeins a day every day for 3 weeks past," or "I made 18 dozen candles and washed." These and other small tidbits, written in a child's hand, sensitized Lois to the world of children a century earlier, which she in no way sugarcoated. Hard work, poor diet, and untreatable communicable diseases resulted in high childhood mortality. "It is not surprising that the old cemeteries are filled with tiny headstones on children's graves," she noted, "mute testimony to the hardships of their lives." Lois "loved all these details which made the past different from the present." She also felt that the child inhabiting that past "was no different, had still the same loves and hates, the same desires and frustrations, the same stoicism and courage, and the same joys and sorrows as the child living today."[11]

Fulfilling an assignment to provide "decorations" for a book by another author may have initiated the research in documentary sources that ultimately served Lois's historical fiction. She illustrated the introductory essays that May Lamberton Becker wrote for the collection of stories she edited, *Golden Tales of New England* (1931). Becker selected authors, mostly from the nineteenth century, who ranged from regional local color writers such as Sarah Orne Jewett to more literary national figures, such as Nathaniel Hawthorne, Harriet Beecher Stowe, Louisa May Alcott, and Henry David Thoreau. *Golden Tales of New England* and other regional collections compiled by this prolific editor were aimed at a general audience of readers—not children—another example of the overall cultural interest in Americana from this period. Becker opened this volume by stating

The preface to this collection will be found scattered through its pages, in the introductory notes to the stories [each with its Lenski "decoration"]. In other words, there will be seventeen curtain-raisers and no overture. All there will be at this point is a statement of purpose: to bring back—living, breathing, talking—some part of an America that has ceased to be, but only in the sense that it has disappeared from our everyday experience to become part of our national consciousness.[12]

Each selection conveys its locale through its distinctive dialect, an element that clearly impressed Becker, one that she realized was in danger of disappearing under the onslaught of the radio with its "mail-order catalogue of speech." She believed that this collection might help stem the tide.[13]

Lois may have taken a cue from Becker in helping the characters in *Phebe Fairchild* speak like New Englanders of the 1830s—in a rich New England dialect. She trusted that her readers would adapt and *listen to,* as well as read, the characters' conversations as they themselves would have spoken. Ten-year-old Phebe may also have been inspired by Phoebe Preble, the child for whom the wooden doll, Hitty, was carved in Rachel Field's Newbery Award–winning book, *Hitty: Her First Hundred Years* (1930).[14] Although Field's work is pure fantasy—a doll writing her memoirs—the details of Hitty's exploits reveal the author's meticulous scholarship. Every detail of the doll's clothing and furnishings, her surroundings, her sensibilities, the quotidian life of the humans and animals with whom she comes in contact (whether on land or sea), and even her rather prim voice demonstrate Field's virtuosity as someone who has steeped herself in the sources. Both Field's Phoebe and Lois's Phebe have sea-captain fathers. Hitty, Phoebe, and Phoebe's mother, Kate, sail on the whaling vessel *Diana-Kate* with Captain Preble. Phebe Fairchild, on the other hand, is sent off to stay with her father's strict Puritan family in rural Connecticut while her mother accompanies Captain Fairchild on the *Phebe Ann* (with ships named after the characters in both cases). Yet the fathers' occupation in both books provides a useful arc that contains the subsequent unfolding of the narrative. Even the names of the two titles have a similar ring, with or without the colon separating the names of the leading protagonists from the rest of the title.[15]

Lois became engrossed in establishing historical accuracy. Like Field, everything had to be exact to be convincing: "the right style of clothing . . . the right kind of furniture in houses of the right architecture built in the period described" as well as her characters' "manners, speech, and customs." She wrote that she *had* to give those populating Phebe's rural Connecticut "cornbread to eat and homespun clothing to wear, in the days before facto-ries." Her foreword unambiguously states, "This story is an attempt to picture a cross-section of New England life in 1830. The setting is a small town in the northwestern part of Connecticut." She chose that date because it was a time of "transition between the home industry period and the beginning of small manufactures." The opening of the Farmington Canal, for example, generates the following dialogue between two of Phebe's relatives:

> "Bill Johnson's got no use for the canal," said Uncle Jothan. "He vows it is going to be ruination for the wagoners. . . . It'll hurt their house-to-house business if the canals bring prosperous stores to every small town. Of course, it will take all the freight. All the towns in western Connecticut will soon be making use of it. . . ."
>
> "I'm all for progress, Jothan," said Great-aunt Pettifer. "Times are bound to change. Ox-carts have been out of style for some time."
>
> "Yes, you're right. They say that the canal will revolutionize the clock business. Better transportation means greater local prosperity."[16]

Lois is devoted to such incidents. The subplot of Phebe's clinging to her father's farewell gift of *Mother Goose*, a beloved book meant simply for pure enjoyment rather than instruction—to the horror of his extended rural family—tells us more about Lois's compulsion to provide a complete "cross-section of New England life in 1830" than to tell a compelling story. Details like these, though accurate and fascinating to Lois in the midst of her own discovery of primary historical research, are far beyond the range of her young readers. But then, one wonders, had she actually determined who those readers might be?

Helen Dean Fish, Lois's editor at Stokes, expressed her reservations in October 1935, when Lois mailed her the original manuscript that became *Phebe Fairchild*. Fish initially told Lois that she believed it to be "the start of a successful story for little girls," and thought that Stokes would be interested in publishing it. Fish suggested that Lois needed more of a plot: "Period background in itself, or just developed in incidents, does not make a very strong book or have as much appeal to the children as a plot with action that carries the interest straight along."[17] Lois resisted these initial editorial suggestions, but six months later, Fish more specifically reprimanded her.

I am enthusiastic about the story you are eventually to bring out of this fine material, but I've got to say what I feel pretty sure you must have suspected yourself: that I think it needs a lot of pulling together, a good deal of cutting and a clearer plot outline—a story that never forgets its center Phebe. . . . I do think it is a little girls' story and that it will be a mistake to over-emphasize the period background for its own sake, in the hope of making an older book of it. . . .

I am afraid this manuscript needs the benefits of time to help you in seeing the essentials of a well-connected story about Phebe's visit, so that all that does not really contribute . . . may be eliminated.[18]

Lois must have replied immediately, because less than a week later, Fish wrote again to tell her that she was going to spend the day on "New England Tapestry," Lois's working title for the Phebe saga. Fish countered with her strong belief that "the book will be far more successful as 'Phebe Fairchild: Her Book,'" and that "all episodes not directly concerned with Phebe should be eliminated, but that the child could naturally be brought into almost every episode and interest in the story." Although grateful for her editor's suggestions, Lois still wondered if the more generalized title, "New England Tapestry," might underscore the fact that "Children were unimportant in those days, an inconspicuous part of a busy adult world, and it is their real place in that actual environment which I have tried to stress in my story." Not only did she remain too attached to the evidence she had encountered and overly absorbed to have sufficient perspective, she found it difficult to fictionalize it in a way that would appeal to young readers, as her editor was trying to help her understand. Fish replied even more firmly: "We feel here that the title 'New England Tapestry' has very little appeal for the boy and girl and also that it isn't a mistake to label the book as a story of primary interest for girls. After all, you can't sit on two stools. It is a story about a little girl and no matter what the title, probably most boys would be a little disappointed to receive it as a Christmas or birthday present instead of a book definitely centered in a boy character and boy interests."[19]

A children's librarian who read the foreword told Fish that it "would put the children off" because it was "quite definitely over their heads. If it is *their* book, there should be nothing in it out of reach, especially at the very start." Lois remained on the defensive. She argued that the foreword was "not intended for children, but for the two types of adult reader—those who read the book for their own pleasure, and those who control children's reading—parents, teachers, librarians, educators, bookshop directors, etc." Lois concurred that the child reader's "only interest in the book is in the story," but she argued that a "straightforward statement of facts" regarding her sources in the foreword would "distinguish" *Phebe* "from previous imaginary books." She and her editor finally reached a compromise. The foreword remained, set off in italics, to alert any child "worth his salt" that these pages are for adult eyes only, a convention Lois maintained throughout all her historical and regional works. Here is Lois's first proclamation of her intent to create *realistic* fiction, a position she would continue to defend, define, and refine over the course of her career.[20]

When arguing for appropriate compensation, Lois had previously stated that she believed the book to be "the best thing I have done and am capable of doing at this time." She was confident that *Phebe* would be "a contribution of lasting value" for which she anticipated "a generous reception." Part of the problem with her unwillingness to focus on a particular audience is that she believed that her book would appeal to adults as well as children. Might she have hoped that *Phebe Fairchild* would match the appeal of *Oliver Twist* or *David Copperfield*? Lois chastised her editor for misrepresenting the book in her marginal "write-ups" as "a story—'of Phebe who travels alone by stagecoach from New Haven to spend a year with her country cousins.'" Lois felt that this honest yet prosaic synopsis "makes it sound like the most ordinary and dull story imaginable." Instead, she believed that Phebe's copy of *Mother Goose* and the controversy it engendered was the key to the book's conflict between the more sophisticated urban life of Phebe's home and the life of her father's rural relatives.[21] But why would any children care about or be able to discern the historical significance of *Mother Goose* from reading *Phebe Fairchild*? Lois's stubbornness demonstrates how much she still needed to learn about writing historical chapter books.

With her editor's insistence and persistence, the author finally complied with sufficient revisions to make *Phebe Fairchild Her Book* a more successful first attempt at historical fiction than one might expect, given Lois's defensiveness and resistance to reworking her initial draft. She had correctly predicted that the illustrations would charm the reader. Her pen-and-ink drawings indicate that she had steeped herself in the children's literature of the early nineteenth century,[22] which her small images replicate in feeling. All the drawings of Aunt Betsy's and Uncle Jothan's country home are of

Greenacres, including the large kitchen hearth where Phebe first encounters her grandmother and Aunt Hannah busily knitting. Lois undoubtedly was remembering Zeloda Barrett's diary, which dutifully noted how often she had to knit, something that Phebe must master as well, as Aunt Hannah instructed: "Hold the needles just so, put the worsted round this needle and stick the other through the loop. Then bring the wool just right between them and hook it through. There, ye've done a stitch. Land sakes, you're awkward as a cow! Fancy a girl o' your age not knowing how to knit! Seems as if I could knit before I could talk." The illustration on the page shows Aunt Hannah at her loom with her protégée at her side, concentrating on her yarn and needles. "Aunt Hannah's voice went on and on. Phebe tried harder . . . [she] harbored a wicked presentiment that she was going to hate it as long as she lived, and like those ignorant and unuseful people whom Aunt Hannah so often mentioned, go down in misery to the grave."[23] Image and text work well together here, but the proportion of illustration to text is meager; the font is fairly small with minimal leading, which would discourage most readers of Phebe's age. Even the two examples cited indicate that the writing makes no concessions to a twentieth-century child's reading vocabulary in 312 densely packed pages. *Mother Goose* wins in the end, even converting stern old Aunt Hannah, who had earlier taken the "wicked book" from Phebe. On the final page, Aunt Hannah returns the book to the departing child:

> "Do you *like* Mother Goose, Aunt Hannah?" she asked. "Do you like Mother Goose?"
> "Like her?" cried Aunt Hannah, with the tears rolling down her face. "How can I help it? Here, take the book, child. If you left it here, 'twould be the ruination of your poor ole Aunt Hannah!"[24]

But the last-minute triumph would still elude the understanding of young readers, who would wonder why adults or even children their age would find Mother Goose endlessly amusing.

Fish's suggestions and Lois's compromises ultimately worked, and *Phebe Fairchild* won solid reviews, including one from May Lamberton Becker, writing for the *New York Herald Tribune:*

> Miss Lenski's story of ten-year-old Phebe from New Haven spending the year 1830 with her father's folks in the Connecticut

country . . . is more than a pleasant tale of a child's ups and downs in hard living and no place to wear pretty clothes. It is the nearest to a complete reconstruction of child life in this place and period that has been offered to children so young. . . .

The reliability of its incidents distinguishes the book: its determination to be faithful to the time and show its differences between what one might call the coastal and the inland points of view. These differences began early in New England. . . . A child may not get this from the story, but the liveliness of the plot is kept up by it, and a reading child will find a lovable little heroine, homely incidents, and a happy ending. . . . The many quaint little pictures are at every point in the text, true, tidy, and funny.[25]

Anne T. Eaton concurred, in her review in the *New York Times:* This is "a book that girls from 10 to 12 will enjoy and one that adults interested in the history of books for children should on no account miss."[26] *Phebe Fairchild* was even selected as a Newbery Honor Book for the year 1937, but adulation did not hold up over time. Nearly a half-century later, Marilyn Leathers Solt appraised the book in *Newbery and Caldecott Medal and Honor Books: An Annotated Bibliography:*

It appears that the author, absorbed in the study of her period, simply could not bring herself to omit interesting data, with the result that there is a plethora of facts, submerging the imaginative content of the story in an accumulation of irrelevant details. This may be the reason the author failed to create the living and memorable characters that appear in some of her later books. None of the children, not even Phebe, is a very real child. The adults are more memorable than the children, perhaps because they live for us in relation to their eccentricities.[27]

Lois had made a giant step forward from writing the light, semi-autobiographical *Skipping Village* and *A Girl of Nineteen Hundred* to attempting historically accurate fiction. She still needed to find her voice and to match that to the interests and reading abilities of her readers, increasing her use of illustrations to propel the narrative forward.

Nonetheless, Lois felt flushed with the joy of having completed her first major book in the summer of 1936, and then caught Mabel up on recent events. The letter in the archival collection at the University of Oklahoma is missing the first page, and Lois penciled in the date on page 2. One can only wonder what Lois chose to conceal from posterity, but with the first extant paragraph on the second page, one certainly senses her priorities, comforts, and discomforts with domestic and family affairs:

> I did not finish my book until June 15th & was pretty worn out at the end, & my Dr. recommended a *complete rest*. Instead of that I had to plunge into housework, Laird home, my family to cook for, all eat like woodchoppers, the work wore me to a frazzle in no time—Nothing wrecks me as quick as housework! I had to give up everything else—speech-making, gardening, art—in order to have the strength to cook 3 meals a day. I stuck it out till end of July, then found a young high school girl from the neighborhood to help & have been able to get some rest since then. She had been here only a few days when I got word of my father's sudden death (heart attack) in Columbus, so I had to go out there & stay several weeks as there were a lot of things to be attended to—Just got back day before yesterday, worn out again from the ordeal.

Lois began her next paragraph with, "It seems it never rains, but it pours," as she complained about a forthcoming visit from one of Arthur's brothers and his family, who were due to arrive from California and were staying a month. She confessed that they were "perfect strangers to me, not interested in any of the things I am, so I don't relish the prospect much. But it can't be helped."[28]

About a decade later, Lois shared her management techniques in an essay, "Professional and Domestic Life," in which she created an annotated listing of the methods that she devised to maintain her rigorous work schedule: "1-Industry; 2-Determination; 3-Ability to plan and organize; 4-A willingness to make sacrifices; 5-A definite purpose in life." Under "Industry," she explained that no one simply dashes off a book for children. "Each of my longer books for older children represents at least a year of work . . . and this means eight hours a day, six days a week for that period." She noted, under "Determination," that "the management of my home and the children put continuous obstacles in the way of my professional work," and "only by exercising a steady determination not to let other things crowd out my work" did she struggle to advance her professional career. Coping with this delicate balance led to her third category, "Ability to plan and organize." By simplifying household tasks, she could conserve her "time and energy" that were "too precious to be wasted." For example, she canned the summer fruits of her garden to have healthy food readily available during other times of the year and reserved "the best hours of the day for my studio work" by doing domestic chores in the evenings after dinner.

Lois recognized that having a studio near, but not *in* the house, was also mandatory. She kept no telephone there, so that she could be completely undisturbed between 9:00 and 12:30 and again from 1:30 to 5:30 each day. Revealingly, she commented: "My family has been trained from the early days of marriage to respect my work and to consider it important. They are accustomed to my absences from the house, and cooperate in every way. I am quite sure they never feel neglected. My son, although trained not to disturb me when I am working, has always had access to my studio at any time for any purpose." One only has to recall fourteen-year-old Stephen's comment to his young nephew, "Occupy yourself," to form a clear picture of the Covey family's household discipline and routine. They may also have been trained not to interpret Lois's work as in any way neglecting *them*.

But Lois and Arthur could become so focused in their own work that they failed to respond to the world primarily as parents. A hurricane hit their area of New England in 1938, but Arthur and his assistant were so engaged in his studio that they "never noticed that the wind was blowing harder than usual . . . tearing down trees and bending others over to touch the ground. Mr. Covey completely forgot to drive down to the little one-room country school which Stephen, then age nine, was attending, to bring him home through the storm." Meanwhile, Lois was a frightened "captive" in her studio, "fully expecting the little building to be blown over any minute and go bouncing across the fields like a tumbleweed." She tried repeatedly to open the door, but the wind's strength prevented her from doing so. Late that afternoon after the wind subsided, she finally made it back to the house, where she found Stephen safely at home. "A kind neighbor, transporting his own children, had brought him right to our house door. When it was all over, Mr. Covey asked, 'Was it a hurricane?'" Years later, Stephen remembered getting home and discovering that "my mother and father were so absorbed in their studios that they had no idea that there was a storm, much less a hurricane! My father was working on a commission of the Contemporary Arts Building, for the 1939 World's Fair, and my mother was working on one of her historical stories, OCEAN BORN MARY [*sic*]."[29]

When Lois discussed the fourth category in her list of management techniques, "a willingness to make sacrifices," she noted giving up "many forms of recreation that other women consider essential, such as attending luncheons or club meetings." But she failed to mention that she had no interest in the kinds of events "sacrificed"; they were simply activities from which her career path conveniently helped her steer clear. By 1946, the date penciled on the essay, Lois felt that her life had reached the fifth point she had outlined: "definite purpose." She had achieved sufficient recognition to be able to claim that she had "been endowed with a special instinctive understanding of children and with unusual creative gifts," and that her work had become "a sacred trust." Her "responsibility toward the children of this country" motivated her to give them her all.[30] And give she did. The only children who may have felt slightly left out of the equation were those under her own roof.

In all fairness to Lois, her position was unenviable: an older husband with fixed ideas of gender roles, who took no interest in her work even as he must have reluctantly accepted that she was bringing in the lion's share of the household income; a complicated set of competing demands from stepchildren and their progeny and a son who seemed more like an older cousin to his nephews; and her own lingering or recurring health issues that sapped her strength. She was working when few educated, married women maintained separate careers, and living in a remote village, she had no local network of support. Perhaps that is one reason she kept up a formidable correspondence with friends and editors (and in the decades that followed, with fans, teachers, librarians, and other educational professionals).

After the publication of *Phebe Fairchild* in the fall of 1936, Lois enthusiastically told Mabel that she planned on a busy winter, since she was "embarking on a new historical book—and you've no idea how this sort of work has changed my whole existence."

> I have to do so much research, over so long a period of time, that I seem to be veritably living in the past—only now & then do I come up to the present—for a little air! If I go anywhere this winter, it

will have to be to N.Y. to work in the library there or to Hartford or Worcester to work in their Historical Societies—or to all three! It's a great life—but I've had such a splendid reception on "Phebe Fairchild" that I think it will be worthwhile.

This "splendid reception" may have been enough to inspire Lois's readiness to completely desert earlier ambitions to be an artist. In her very next sentence, she confessed, "To tell the truth I'm getting a little off of easel pictures, as nobody ever buys them anyway [this statement made in the heart of the Great Depression], so what's the use? I've a good market for my books, so it looks more sensible to put my time & energy in them. At least that's the way I feel at the moment."[31]

Yet the prospect of leaving painting behind had, just the previous year, remained out of the question. In 1935 Lois even had the outbuilding south of the house that had once served as the Balch coffin shop renovated to serve as her studio. Part of the renovation included a fourteen-foot addition with a north skylight providing optimal light for painting. When the addition was completed, however, Lois found little time to paint. The building of the studio took place after Lois experienced her "first serious illness," which Stephen identified, years later, as pernicious anemia. Of course, Lois had suffered from serious illnesses before—especially the membranous croup of her childhood and the flu during the epidemic of 1918—but she may have meant that pernicious anemia, which was not fully understood until a couple of decades later, affected her energy level and strength for the rest of her life. She simply no longer had "the physical energy to stand to paint." But writing was sedentary, and she could easily keep up with it "propped up to a desk with pillows at my back." *Phebe Fairchild* conveniently had taken hold of her imagination at about the same time, which facilitated the complete transition from artist to author.[32]

Writing had financial as well as physical benefits, but Lois retrospectively framed her acceptance of her role as author somewhat differently. She recalled that she felt the "uselessness" of painting when there was no market, although she fails to link that statement to the economics of hard times. Having experienced the joy of knowing that the books she wrote and illustrated were *useful*, that they reached and could be enjoyed by thousands of children, she recognized as a "legitimate purpose." Lois linked her vocation as an author to her undergraduate major in education: "While I early gave up the idea of being a teacher I have remained one at heart, and instead of reaching a small group in a classroom, the influence of a book upon many children has been unfathomable." Did her father's death in any way lead her, perhaps unconsciously, to accept the mantle of his sense of righteous purpose? For the first time, she expressed her belief in the spiritual dimensions of this choice:

> In the early days my ideas were few, hard to arrive at, unsure. Now they came on wings, they were legion—if only one had health and strength and wisdom enough to put them down on paper. Always through the ecstasy there ran a deep humility. This power is not of one's own making, how clearly we saw that. This creativity is a Higher Power working through us. That alone can account for its persistence, for the fact that it pursues us so relentlessly and will not let us go. . . .
>
> A lame and halting idea suddenly takes on wings and soars of itself, with no conscious volition of mind. . . . How often do entire scenes enact themselves more vividly and meaningfully than we had ever intended. And so the use of our gifts becomes not a selfish pleasure, but the holding of a sacred trust.[33]

Lois's spiritual sensibilities in no way inhibited her intensely practical side. In the same letter to Mabel in which she had explained her "conversion" to author, Lois asked her friend for a small favor. Mabel was teaching art at her undergraduate alma mater, Peace College, in Raleigh, North Carolina, and Lois complimented her on being "such a good publicity agent for me in the South. . . . See that the bookstore sells plenty of copies of 'Phebe Fairchild' won't you? You don't want an exhibit of originals, do you? Have sent some to Hollins College, Va., with copies of the books, too, to sell."[34]

Lois may have resisted promoting *Phebe Fairchild* as a book for girls, but once *Phebe* had achieved success, Lois created a succession of historical books—*A-Going to the Westward* (1937), *Bound Girl of Cobble Hill* (1938), *Ocean-Born Mary* (1939), *Blueberry Corners* (1940), *Indian Captive* (1941), and *Puritan Adventure* (1944)—with girls as the main protagonists.[35] Being pigeonholed as an author of "girl books" no longer seemed to bother her as she created a set of windows into a buried past, describing the realistically difficult lives of young females born into a society that tightly circumscribed their potential for self-fulfillment. Given these constraints, her protagonists learned to deal with the obstacles and trials in their paths and thereby achieved the necessary agency to gain self-worth and dignity. Megan E. VanderHart discussed the protagonists' strengths when she wrote her master's thesis, "In Pursuit of Womanhood: How Lois Lenski's Little Girls Learn to Change Their World":

> Her heroines were raised as submissive but not subordinate, and as daughters, not sons. By allowing her heroines to be active little girls in their historical context, respectful of their elders while asking questions and taking initiative, Lenski's little girls both changed their world and entered the beginning of womanhood. . . . Lenski does not bring her girls to the cusp of marriage. . . . Instead, they remain young girls, endowed with strong character, but without the complications of adolescence.[36]

The books themselves exhibit their own strengths and weaknesses, as Lois struggled to create fully realized and credible protagonists to make her historically accurate narratives engaging. She still found it difficult to resist crowding in every delectable detail.

Unfortunately, *A-Going to the Westward*, which immediately followed *Phebe Fairchild*, proved to be the most problematic, very likely because Lois had such a personal stake in the research. She dedicated the book to "Mary Willis Heltzel and Philip Heltzel, My great great-grandparents, who with their eight children, emigrated from York County, Pennsylvania, and settled in Hamilton Township, Franklin County, Ohio, in the year 1808." Lois crafted the narrative to demonstrate how "three distinct types, the Yankee from Connecticut, the Pennsylvania Dutchman from eastern Pennsylvania and Kentucky southerner," settled the then-frontier of central Ohio. She sought to convey the way these "people of different languages, religions and ways of life mingled on the road and in the wilderness, where they made their homes side by side." Indeed, she argued, "These are the people who made America."[37] The commingling and community-building of these three groups settling in the wilderness seem to be a sufficient subplot for the narrative. But Lois wanted the chapter development to mimic the structure of John Bunyan's *Pilgrim's Progress*, a venerable seventeenth-century classic that, in the nineteenth century, populated many household bookshelves along with the family Bible. In *Pilgrim's Progress*, the protagonist, Christian, leaves home alone to journey to the Celestial City, dealing with all kinds of obstacles (as well as help) along the way. Helen Dean Fish tried to disabuse Lois of the "suitability of the 'plot'" that she "superimposed on [her] fine foundational material. It seemed to me artificial, not especially convincing and, most serious of all, not very interesting for readers of the teen age. . . . We can by no means take for granted that younger readers know 'Pilgrim's Progress' and will appreciate this analogy unaided." Fish had even asked three readers to evaluate the original manuscript (all of whom had been enthusiastic about *Phebe Fairchild*), and they concurred that this quite artificial device would be ineffective, make little sense, and be of little interest to young readers. Lois revised her work in other ways that Fish suggested yet must have insisted that Bunyan's work remain to reinforce the narrative, hinted at by the use of italicized quotations in a very small font under the title of each chapter.

Her brother Gerhard questioned another troubling aspect of the manuscript:

> You have given yourself a tremendous problem. You are trying to combine fiction and narrative and imagination with a certain literal exactness and historical accuracy. . . . To write for the fiction reader you need a breezy, swift-moving style, easy to read and follow. To write for the historical students you need accuracy, references, detail, etc. It seems to me you are aiming to please both sets of readers—which, in my poor judgment, is something like using one bullet with the hope of bagging two birds.[38]

Perhaps Lois was trying to differentiate the Ohio-bound pioneers from those going to western New York in another children's book that had been published in 1932. Helen Fuller Orton's *The Treasure in the Little Trunk* was a popular chapter book about a Vermont family that, like many New Englanders in the 1820s, sought better land and traveled by covered wagon to "The Genesee Country." Not only was the narrative similar in basic outline, *The Treasure in the Little Trunk* was yet another example of the Americana surge. Lois had just finished reading it to Stephen when she was corresponding with Helen Dean Fish about issues concerning her forthcoming *A-Going to the Westward*. She and Stephen both felt "the lack of

A group of backwoods women entered the Bartlett family's floating store on the Ohio River in Belville, West Virginia. Their "protruding sunbonnets . . . overshadowed their smoking pipes," in this illustration for page 261 in *A-Going to the Westward*, 1937. Reprinted by permission of the Lois Lenski Covey Foundation and Burrell Covey, copyright by Lois Lenski. Courtesy of the Lois Lenski Papers, Special Collections, Butler Library, Buffalo State College.

a map keenly" in Orton's tale, because it would have been helpful to have a visual reference for the family's arduous journey. By designing a map for the endpapers with "all important points marked clearly," Lois intended to make the longer, more complicated route in *A-Going to the Westward* a visual plus for her readers.[39]

Once published, the book received some positive reviews—particularly in praise of the research undergone, but the *Library Journal* review presented the most honest appraisal of *A-Going to the Westward:* "Miss Lenski seems to have omitted no significant detail in presenting the many angles of her story. . . . The various types of pioneers and their diverse viewpoints are well conceived and painstakingly drawn, yet she has . . . somehow missed the real spark of life and adventure . . . [in] a succession of hardships borne with fortitude, but without zest."[40]

Lois must have taken these criticisms to heart. She handled the narrative of *Bound Girl of Cobble Hill* with more assurance, even though another reviewer had commented, "It is in her settings and backgrounds that Miss Lenski excels, rather than in her characterization. Mindwell Gibbs is Miss Lenski's most successfully realized heroine, but even she is not entirely convincing and the other characters of the story never come to life."[41] In look and feel, Lois's first three works of historical fiction have much in common: cinnamon-colored cloth covers, densely packed text, each running nearly or over three hundred pages, relatively few illustrations, and none larger than half a page. Phebe is the least complicated character, Betsey the most incidental, and Mindwell the most interesting. The latter survives the terrifying fate of being "bound out" as an indentured servant because she was an orphan.

With *Ocean-Born Mary*, both story and presentation ascend in appeal. Although the book is the largest of her historical novels at 385 pages, Lois allows more room for her black-and-white ink drawings, including a frontispiece and four full-page illustrations. These bear less resemblance to the winsome woodcut-like features of the earlier works but are more appealing in their openness and ability to more fully complement the narrative and propel the plot development. Lois broke from her typical outline by using an afterword instead of a foreword, as she explains that ocean-born Mary was a real person, born at sea when her family was emigrating from Ireland to New England in 1720. According to "tradition," shortly after her birth, pirates captured the ship on which the family was traveling. The pirates did not harm the passengers and allowed them to proceed on their journey. Perhaps moved by having found a newborn aboard, the pirate captain "obtained a promise" from the baby's mother "that she would name Mary, for his wife. . . . This signal deliverance from the pirates was commemorated during a generation by the annual observance of a day of thanksgiving by the people of Londonderry [New Hampshire]." No evidence suggests that ocean-born Mary ever lived in Portsmouth (Strawberry Banks in the book), New Hampshire, but Lois situated the twelve-year-old protagonist in this seaport town for about a year and a half. There, Mary helped her ailing aunt with her household. This environment also allowed her to have further encounters—completely fictional as well—with the daring pirate captain, Philip Babb, who named her. The dangers in maintaining this relationship provide the book's central drama, even though Lois still had difficulty culling historical detail and minor characters that too often obscure, rather than enhance, the plot.[42]

By the time she wrote *Blueberry Corners*, Lois realized how to reach young readers. She created illustrations more nearly equal to the text in value. This proportionate balance of illustration-to-text remained a key to the success of the subsequent regional series that Lois began writing during the World War II years. In creating the setting of *Blueberry Corners*, Lois once again chose her own village, dedicating the book "To the Town of Harwinton, Connecticut where the biggest blueberries grow in 1940 just as they did one hundred years ago in 1840." Both font and illustrations have increased in size, making the book more accessible to younger readers. The arrival of the first train in the Naugatuck Valley in 1849 was one of the double-page, mural-like spreads that Lois included, an event she heard about from her ninety-six-year-old neighbor, Sara Goodwin, who as a child of seven had witnessed the event. Sara had told the story "with real dramatic fervor," awakening Lois's passion for oral history, or what later would become her signature "getting books from life," which figured so meaningfully in the creation of her regionals. The author called *Blueberry Corners* a "happy book," and even the shorter foreword without italicized text alerts the reader that this is a book meant to be savored by a younger audience.[43]

Lois also included a delightful local historical anecdote in chapter 8, "A Tree of Apples." The character, "Aunty Ruth," was based on the life of Ruth Mansfield Hodges (1779–1863), a widow, whose farm was located near the one-room school. The widow designated one of the trees in her apple orchard to the schoolchildren to enjoy as their own, a tree that would provide them with all the apples their hearts desired. Lois inserted the incident after a scene where schoolboys had shaken an apple tree and stolen its fruit. The irate farmer then threatened to have the schoolmarm fired for her lack of control:

"The sun will be shining tomorrow," said Aunt Ruth cheerfully, "and all the boys will have to stay at home and work. As for the apple fights, I'll tell you what I'll do. Do you see that tree down there by the fence? That's a Seek-no-Further apple tree and it's loaded with apples. I'll give that tree to the 5th district school children."

"Give them the tree?" asked Miss Belinda, puzzled.

"Yes!" said Aunty Ruth, her eyes snapping. "For their very own! There will be apples enough to last them a long, long time!"[44]

The travails of *Bound Girl* had given way to something much easier to digest.

Apples also figured in Lois's domestic life in the 1930s, since Greenacres had several apple orchards on the property, which, as Lois said, "caught my husband's eye." With the onset of the Great Depression not long after the Coveys had acquired the Harwinton property, Arthur had joked that if he and Lois could not sustain their family as artists, they could "get rich by selling apples from our big apple orchards on the streets of New York." Although the Coveys avoided that particular scenario, Arthur *did* become something of an apple impresario. "He advertised his apple crop in the local newspaper, selling the apples tree by tree, making friends of many Italian and Polish families from Torrington, who came out year after year to pick. He loved to boast that the apples paid the taxes every year."[45] But he left the real hustling to his industrious and much younger wife.

While Lois was hustling to publish both picture books and historical fiction during the 1930s and into the 1940s, she was still very much engaged in illustrating for other children's authors. Prominent among them was Maud Hart Lovelace, whose Betsy-Tacy series became an immediate success and a subsequent classic, and Lois's sensitively envisioned and executed inked illustrations perfectly complement the first four of the charming autobiographically based stories. The first book, *Betsy-Tacy*, was published the same year as *Blueberry Corners*, with illustrations very much akin in spirit and style (although the eras depicted were a half-century apart). *Betsy-Tacy and Tib* followed in 1941, and *Betsy and Tacy Go Over the Big Hill* and *Betsy and Tacy Go Downtown* were published in 1942 and 1943 respectively. Although Lois worked extensively from photographs and even traveled to Mankato, Minnesota, to get the feel for the setting of the Lovelace books, she and Maud were born a year apart, and the scenes she depicted were not that far from those of Anna that she illustrated in *Skipping Village* and *A Little Girl of Nineteen Hundred*. What had changed was Lois's style. The characters in *Blueberry Corners* became much more important than the background, a stylistic development that had been emerging throughout the 1930s. In the Betsy-Tacy series, the illustrations consume even more of individual pages, and they are also slightly more open in rendering. Lois applied what she had learned in these books to her next, most important, and enduring historical book. The settings are lovely, but the characters now reign supreme. Perhaps the popularity of the Lovelace books also may have "prepped" a larger audience of youngsters to look for more Lenski illustrations and therefore seeded readers of her own well-received books, such as *Indian Captive* and the regionals, that followed in the 1940s and 1950s.[46] In her autobiography, Lois mentions her initial illustrations of the 1920s. But why, one wonders, did she never mention the subsequent works she drew for other authors, even if they were landmark books like *The Little Engine That Could* and the Betsy-Tacy series?

While Lois was in the midst of publicizing *Bound Girl* at Book Week in Cleveland, Ohio, in 1938, she met with Elrick B. Davis, literary editor of the *Cleveland Press*. Familiar with her other historical books, he suggested that she do a volume on Indians, treating them sympathetically. He felt strongly that they had been "unjustly presented" in the literature available for children, and she could write something to remedy the situation. The following spring while she was doing research at the American Antiquarian Society in Worcester, Massachusetts—probably for *Ocean-Born Mary*—she spoke with librarian R. W. G. Vail. He told her that if she were looking for an Indian project, "I know just the story for you—Mary Jemison, who was captured by the Indians and lived in New York State." The idea of the young captive captivated Lois, and she began intensive research for her timeless and enthralling *Indian Captive*. Vail put Lois in touch with Dr. A. G. Parker, director of the Rochester Museum of Arts and Sciences, who told Lois about the wrongs done in past depictions of the Iroquois confederacy, which included the Seneca Nation, Mary's captors. Lois wanted "to do justice to the actual facts of Mary's capture, to make a good story, and to present the theme of conflict between the Indian way of life and the white way of life, with the former winning," since "Mary Jemison had several opportunities during her long life, to return to the whites, but, of her own choice, stayed with Indians."[47]

For the first time, Lois moved beyond her comfort zone of writing about white Americans from northern European backgrounds. In spite of the difficulties they encountered, these Euro-American experiences became part of our accepted American heritage repertoire. On the other hand, writing about an American Indian community and trying to present a balanced—and, ultimately, positive—view of that particular culture from the Indians' perspective presented a greater challenge. To gird herself appropriately for the task, Lois assembled a team of experts with whom she could confer. In addition to Vail and Dr. Parker, she sought help from the archaeologists and museum staff at the Museum of Natural History and the Buffalo Museum of Natural Science. Dr. Parker gave Lois access to his institution's collections and gave her room in the staff studio in which to work while she was in Rochester. Although she intended to stay only a few days, she spent two weeks there, examining Indian drawings and artifacts, which she felt "contained more of the essence of Indian action and spirit than any illustrations in books." Dr. Parker also agreed to review critically Lois's manuscript and to provide an introduction to *Indian Captive*. He praised her "detailed studies of the Indian way of looking at things and her painstaking effort to find out the exact type of implements, utensils and methods of producing them." He contrasted her research with that of authors who "ignored this basic necessity . . . filling in the gaps with pre-conceived knowledge or basing it upon modern adaptations of European practice."

A visit with Dr. Parker to the Tonawanda Indian Reservation in western New York, the home of one band of the Seneca Nation, gave Lois the opportunity to observe craftspeople "working at the same crafts as their ancestors, the old methods having been revived as a WPA project." Her research fortuitously intersected with a federal program of historic preservation, an example of the serendipity of her writing at this particular juncture in American history. At the Tonawanda Reservation, Lois met Jesse Corn Planter, an artist whose watercolors of "a vanished way of life" helped mightily with her own depictions.[48]

In October 1940 Lois made a visit to Letchworth Park along the Genesee River in northwestern New York, where the region's connection to the lifeways of the Seneca Indians is well documented, including a restored Seneca Council House and Mary Jemison's grave. She had hired a driver to take her the fifty miles from Rochester. West of Portageville, they stopped on a bridge above the Genesee River. "The place was quiet. I could imagine the river full of Senecas: I could watch them land at the carrying place, and take their canoes on their backs." A little further along "at the brink of the Upper Falls," Lois "jumped out and over a four-foot stone wall" to get as close as she could to take in the scene:

The day was made just for me. It was a perfect day in late autumn, the month of falling leaves, the exact time of year that Mary Jemison first came. . . .

I could not help feeling, as I gazed entranced at the double rainbow, and back again to the great rush of falling waters, how great a solace their beauty must have been to the little white girl captive, in those early days when she arrived after that long six months' journey, 682 miles, partly in canoe, but mostly on foot, from the River Ohio. Perhaps she stood in the exact spot where I was standing, tired, worn and exhausted, with bruised and bleeding feet, and looked at the rush of waters. Perhaps the great beauty of that sight lifted her spirit, as it did mine. What a comfort it must have been to her, not only on that first day, but all through those difficult first years of her life with the Senecas.

She evoked this scene beautifully in the endpapers of *Indian Captive*, with a map that showed Mary's arduous journey from her family's homestead in western Pennsylvania to "The Great Falling Waters of the Genesee" where she stands with one of her Seneca mentors, Shagbark.[49] In the description of her own rapture with the majestic falls, Lois expressed empathy for Mary Jemison and her inner turmoil in a way distinct from, and more intimate than, her feeling for the earlier protagonists she had created.

Visiting the reservation and Letchworth Park gave Lois fresh insights that she applied to writing *Indian Captive*. She did not minimize the cruelty and challenges that life with the Senecas presented to Mary, which Lois bluntly portrayed in crafting her story. Yet Lois realized that "When we look at Indian life from an inside, sympathetic point of view, when we contrast it with the barrenness of the frontier life of the white settlers, we can readily see why Mary Jemison and other captives chose never to come back." That "Indians lived close to nature, in harmony with the universe," impressed Lois deeply, as she began to understand and respect the spirituality of Native people. "The fact that every plant and animals [were] inhabited by a spirit was a solace in itself," she reflected. Lois had learned that Indians "considered it their sacred duty to create objects of beauty," and "all these things made their life extraordinarily rich; and must have made strong appeal to sensitive, artistic persons who chanced to come in contact with them, especially children."[50]

It is remarkable, given the general attitudes toward Native people and others of color during the time period in which Lois wrote, her own religious orientation, and her strict Lutheran upbringing, that she was so open to an alternate perspective of Anglo-American Manifest Destiny. She depicted Native culture with acceptance and complete respect. Acknowledgment of the positive attributes of Native culture in *Indian Captive* became the first step in her creation of books dealing with social justice, fully augmented in her groundbreaking regional series. Madge Klais, who teaches about multiculturalism and the history of children's literature at the University of Wisconsin–Madison, commented that so many of Lois's books "have gone out of print because the writing is undistinguished or the audience for them has vanished, but they are not out of print because their world lacks cultural authenticity or cultural sensitivity." Klais feels that Lois, "perhaps more than any other author of children's books from the 1930s through the 1950s, tried to be respectful of all the people that she portrayed, even those who were not the main characters."[51]

As Lois recalled, the Rochester research—including the day trip to Letchworth State Park—"made my whole story come alive." She returned to her studio "fired with enthusiasm and determination to put as much of this richness as I could into my book." When she began to illustrate the manuscript, she approached the drawings in *Indian Captive* with a similar sensitivity. Dr. Parker felt that these "caught the spirit of ancient days," with "characteristic and most pleasing . . . attitudes of the individual figures and the facial expressions."[52] But Lois became ill in the midst of working on them. She had finished all the drawings in pencil but felt too weak to complete inking them in, as she had done for all her previous illustrations. In order to maintain the production schedule for the publication, she submitted the pencil sketches. These unfinished sketches, reproduced by the printer's skillful use of offset lithography, convey Lois's sympathy for her subject in a way that inked drawings could never have achieved. She felt that the printer, whom she described as "a godsend," made *Indian Captive* her "most beautiful book."[53] And Lois's regionals also benefitted from the experience, because in this series as well, the sensitive rendering of superb pencil sketches reproduced by lithography also complement the empathetic texts perfectly.

Praise for Lois's achievement began soon after publication. The review in the *Library Journal* noted that "this most fascinating book . . . would be invaluable if considered only for its authentic picture of Indian life, customs, and ideas; the addition of the charming yet realistic illustrations and the thrilling story make this a book which all libraries can well afford to

In *Indian Captive* (1941), Molly Jemison observes Beaver Girl expertly making a cooking pot, original illustration for page 137. Original copyright by Lois Lenski. Used by permission of HarperCollins Publishers and courtesy of the Lois Lenski Papers, Special Collections, Butler Library, Buffalo State College.

purchase." Writing for the *New York Herald Tribune Books* supplement, May Lamberton Becker claimed that *Indian Captive* marked not only Lois's "best work . . . a story more than one generation can read," with "Miss Lenski's most successful" illustrations. In her appraisal in the *New York Times Book Review,* Anne T. Eaton commented that *Indian Captive* would appeal to middle-level readers "because the author shows us, with imaginative sympathy, something of the inner conflict of a young person who succeeded in adjusting herself to a new and different way of life, though she did not forget her past or cease to feel herself a white girl." Indeed, Eaton gave Lois her highest praise, for she created a Mary Jemison who emerged "as a real and appealing personality."[54] At last the author had created a universally beloved character who remained center-stage for the entire compelling drama, a crowning achievement for Lois.

Clark Wissler, curator at the American Museum of Natural History and one of Lois's advisors, wrote that "Miss Lenski has succeeded in reflecting the spirit of Indian life in both the drawings and the text to such a degree of completeness that her work can be fully recommended for educational use," the first time that one of her books won such an accolade. Undoubtedly, Lippincott, a publisher of textbooks as well as books of general interest, must have been pleased with this kind of acclaim. The December following publication, the Rochester Public Library had the manuscript material on exhibit, where it "was much studied and admired." Just a month later, Helen Dean Fish learned that the Ohio Reading Circle had selected *Indian Captive* as "one of its 1942 adoptions," which meant the sale of "700 to 1,000 copies." With children "taking a genuine and spontaneous interest in the book everywhere," Fish thought that *Indian Captive* might gain sufficient support to win the coveted Newbery Award. But in May 1942, she told Lois that she had given up hope.

> Now I know the libraries have devised otherwise and I am very much disappointed, even though I know you have not great interest in it or wish for this particular kind of recognition. I know that many librarians will be disappointed for so many have told me that they voted for INDIAN CAPTIVE that I really believed it might be the winner. . . .
>
> You will be pleased to hear that the book is quite active— nearly three thousand copies sold since the first of the year.

One disappointed children's librarian, Natalie Mayo from the San Francisco Public Library, told Fish that although she was "not particularly fond of Indian stories," *Indian Captive* was "one of the finest books I have ever read." Sharing it "in every school assembly and class talk" that she gave, Mayo found that all children responded positively. Not only did she like the fine, dramatic story, she appreciated "the feeling of tolerance in it" and had cast her vote for the Newbery in its favor.[55] Ironically, the winner of the Newbery Award that year was *The Matchlock Gun*, by Walter Edmonds, a narrative also based on a real event, an Indian raid that occurred in 1756 in what eventually became New York. While the father of the family was away from their cabin, the son had to defend the household with the ancient gun. Paul Lentz's beautifully drawn but culturally insensitive depiction of Indians as threatening lacked any nuance.[56]

Although Lois would have enjoyed accepting the Newbery Award for a book in which she had invested so much loving care, she must have been pleased with the book's outstanding sales and its use in schools. She told Mabel that she considered the *Indian Captive* drawings her "finest achievement," and that they were "much in demand for exhibition purposes." Lois eventually planned to "dispose of them" by giving them to libraries in the state of New York, "as it is a N.Y. state story," and she wanted "all regional drawings . . . to go to the region of the story's setting as far as possible."[57] In other words, she did not need to receive a Newbery Award to have a sense that her work's worth as a commodity could add value to a collection in a particular location, a feeling that her book and the artifacts—illustrations, correspondence, drafts—associated with it might establish an enduring presence.

Indian Captive remained in print and remains relevant. A letter that Lois received from an admiring teacher nearly twenty years later bears testimony to her foresight. Lillian Riess from Creighton School in Philadelphia told Lois that "after many years of reading . . . 'Indian Captive' to each new class," she wanted the author to know that it stayed "the most popular book of the fifth grades . . . the one book that I see children fighting to be first to 'read it alone.' . . . I think it has a beauty akin to poetry and a beautiful lesson in courage. It has also encouraged the love of reading and the seeking of your other books, from the library shelves."[58]

In the summer of 1963, Gerhard Lenski's granddaughter, Kathy Lenski, moved with her family from Ann Arbor to Chapel Hill, when her father accepted a position in the sociology department at the University of North Carolina. At ten, Kathy faced "the whole, long, dreary summer" without being able to meet schoolmates. The public library became her refuge, and among the books she found there was a copy of her great-aunt's *Indian Captive*. She recalled that after taking the book home to read, she felt like

> a whole new world had just opened up wide for me! I LOVED Mary's courage; I felt for her during the years that she was not only an orphan, but also an outcast with the tribe; and I cheered her on when she chose to stay with the tribe as an adult, instead of returning to the whites. I felt like I was right there with her, living outdoors, learning new skills. The fact that this was a TRUE story, and had taken place right here in the U.S., caused a blaze of curiosity within me. This is "history"?! Not just the endless names of Generals and Presidents, and dates of elections that I had to study in school? If this was "history," I was all for it!

Although Kathy had never met her great-aunt, she wrote to tell her "how passionate I was about 'Indian Captive.' . . . I was thrilled to receive a wonderful letter from her within the week . . . and thus began a correspondence which lasted until her death 11 years later."[59]

Indian Captive is still popular with upper elementary students. In 2011, fourth-grade students in Mary Ann Sander's class at Lakeview Elementary School in Wind Lake, Wisconsin, conveyed the same message to their teacher. They voted the book their favorite because they admired Mary's bravery and courage and enjoyed exploring the themes of family and inner struggle. In January 2014 Sander decided to read Louise Erdrich's *The Birchbark House* to students, and commented, "As I finish our read aloud . . . with my class this year, I have not seen the same levels of engagement or deep critical thinking in response and discussion as were evident when we read *Indian Captive* . . . it just does not seem to have the same emotional tension and adventurous drama that Lenski provides so well."[60]

Lois had gained valuable experience in becoming an author-illustrator through creating her historical books. In 1952 she told a graduate student in education who was writing her dissertation on Lois's work: "I would be happy to lend you my copies of those of my earlier books which you have not read, if I felt it worth your time to read them. But seriously, I doubt it!

After all, a writer has 'to learn by writing' & these are the books I learned on, and I'm afraid they leave much to be desired. I'm glad most of them have gone out of print."[61] She had begun writing *Phebe Fairchild* without a sure sense of her audience and remained unable to take sufficient control of the story to wrest it from the wealth of material she had amassed. Too many minor characters detract from the protagonist, and the charming illustrations remain more decorative than integral to the storytelling. The book's originality in presenting a realistic snapshot of New England in the early nineteenth century with erudition and grace, however, earned her a Newbery Honor Award, which *Indian Captive* also won just five years later. Yet the difference between the two similar achievements is profound. Within that short time period of intensive effort in only one of the many directions in which she was working simultaneously, Lois gleaned a formula that she needed to reach middle-level readers. She had learned how to create an appealing protagonist whose inner drama matched in interest the external outlines of the narrative—a central character who becomes real to those reading about her. Lois also limited and more fully developed the number of supporting characters and became skillful at providing illuminating illustrations that functioned to enhance both plot and personalities. As the 1940s progressed, these gifts carried Lois to worlds far beyond those with which she had become acquainted through her archival research. She was about to encounter and have her life transformed by "stories from life."

CHAPTER 6

STORIES
FROM LIFE

espite the limited economic opportunities of the 1930s, Lois won significant success introducing her own picture books for the very young and historical novels for older children as well as through her unstinting work as an illustrator for magazines and fellow authors. The Great Depression and the subsequent cultural awakening that recognized the value of everyday Americans transformed Lois's writing in the decade that followed. She fit right into a pattern that children's literature professor Gary Schmidt identifies in mid-twentieth-century American children's literature, when many books

> were clear and unsubtle expressions about the meaning of America and the role of the child as a citizen. These books . . . wanted to inculcate a complex vision of culture . . . they would show an America that was to be extolled and an America that was deeply flawed, and in so doing, the artists and "minders" created a literature that showed a concern about society's problems . . . that argued that artists and those who supported and disseminated their work to children had a responsibility to young citizens to depict America as it was and to challenge their young readers to engage in their country's progress. . . .

> [That literature] was more John Steinbeck than Horatio Alger
> and more Dorothea Lange than Pollyanna.[1]

Visiting South Louisiana with Arthur and Stephen during the winter of 1941, Lois was so captivated by the bayou-dwelling folk that she swiftly converted from the written sources of the past to the oral testimony of the present. In so doing, she became a pioneer in the genre of regional children's literature as she increased her mastery at storytelling and illustrating.

In the first years of the 1940s, Lois began to write books specifically designed for middle-level readers—just as the most successful of her historical books, *Indian Captive*, had been. Her new series emphasized the dignity of working people, a sensibility that permeated the cultural landscape of the entire country during the New Deal years. The tremendous disruption of World War II and its reshaping of rural and urban lifeways also contributed to Lenski's new emphasis of writing for her targeted audience. Most of these regional books from the 1940s through the 1960s reflect the struggle of everyday American families to adjust to successive challenges and crises. What accounted for her work's new thrust and energy? Lois does not tell us. Although her autobiography and lectures for teachers and librarians mention her admiration for the realism and regional specificity that writers such as Erskine Caldwell and Willa Cather and artists such as John Steuart Curry and Thomas Hart Benton brought to their work, she never cites these sources as direct inspirations. Nor does she reference the progressive educators and their critics who debated the very nature of democratic education and sought to provide the nation with an informed—and loyal—citizenry. Lois also fails to acknowledge the works in a similar vein of other contemporary children's authors such as Doris Gates's *Blue Willow* (1940) or Eleanor Estes's *The Hundred Dresses* (1944), both of whom received Newbery Honor Book awards for their efforts to deal squarely and sensitively with topics of social justice. Lois's painstaking, methodical research in the field and her remarkable series of regionals set her apart from these two well-respected authors.

Nevertheless, the strong sense of documentary expression that historian William Stott described as suffusing the artistic imagination of all varieties of American cultural production during the Great Depression revolutionized Lois's choices of subject matter.[2] The ethos of a decade in which American writers and artists celebrated working-class lives inevitably permeated Lois's imaginative endeavors, even though she may not have been completely aware of its immense effects on her curiosity and productivity. Stott argues that the artists and intellectuals of the 1930s tried to probe the essence of their country, to "touch its substance, find and lay hands on whatever would give them, and help give them" a feel for what was genuine. Similarly, Schmidt finds this trend in children's literature as more fully depicting the meaning of democracy "as a fair and just social condition in which every participant has a voice and a stake" in expanding inclusiveness.[3]

Lois's own journey to regionalism began in the same way that her interest in historical fiction had been launched. Whenever she inhabited a new setting, she became so stimulated by what she encountered that she felt compelled to study and come to terms with it. In turn, she created her fictional narratives and illustrations to share a synthesis of these regional reckonings with her readers. Lois's strengths as an author-illustrator aligned perfectly with the regionalism that became one of her enduring hallmarks. In spite of the "intense shyness"[4] she experienced as a child, she never withdrew from her social environment. Instead, she became expert at mentally recording details about the surroundings and events in which she and her family participated. This early tendency to witness rather than put herself into the center of activity suited her new role as a cultural interpreter. Unassuming and modest as she sought out authentic experiences of everyday living, Lois had little problem in gaining the confidence of those she encountered. As the quiet and inconspicuous outsider sitting on her camp stool and drawing in her sketchbook, Lois could easily capture the telling details of an environment without disturbing anyone, taking copious notes to augment her sketches. Just as she mastered the ability to record a scene in her sketchbook, she used her keen ear for dialect to pick up the unique nuances in expression in every region and turn them into dialogue. Lois capably transformed her sketches into illustrations and indicated just where these should be inserted to animate the narrative vividly, and in sufficient detail, so a child reader could revisit the page mentally, visualizing and emotionally empathizing with the protagonists.

Lois accommodated to life's changes by turning her observations and experiences into opportunities that increased her agility as author and illustrator. Just as watching Stephen at play had inspired her ever-more-popular "Mr. Small" series, the Coveys' move to rural Connecticut had whetted Lois's curiosity to learn more about the history of her New England environment through meeting with neighbors and other locals. When the region's winters became too great a burden on Lois's health, her doctor recommended in 1941 that she spend those months somewhere warmer. Lois welcomed this prescription for seasonal change. With children no longer underfoot—Margaret married, Laird a college graduate, and Stephen attending a preparatory boarding school—"it was possible to make new plans and to change the pattern of our lives. The doctor's edict meant enforced trips to the south for three months or more each winter, which served to initiate me into a better love and understanding of our country."[5]

That first winter, Lois, Arthur, and Stephen—on winter break—headed for New Orleans. When they arrived, Lois was not yet seeking a new direction. She already had projects in mind that would keep her busy. Although her deteriorating health first took the Coveys south, necessity soon turned into advantage, allowing the initial trip to Louisiana to catapult her into her most ambitious and most professionally successful arena as the self-proclaimed author of the children "beyond the rim" of normative American midcentury middle-class lives.[6]

Unlike contemporary children's authors such as Marguerite de Angeli and Laura Ingalls Wilder,[7] who wrote about the regions where they grew up, Lois correctly considered herself an outsider in whatever region she was currently researching. She felt that she had some advantage in that role, bringing "a greater receptivity because of the newness of the scene."[8] And as the "other," she intently studied, observed, and listened—literally bringing all her senses to bear on the story she hoped to catch, the work she could already see unfolding. Three decades later in the introduction to an unpublished manuscript, "Stories Behind My Regionals," Lois mentions that while a few other children's authors used the regions in which they lived as the bases for their narratives—as she herself had done in her historical books on New England—"my idea of visiting specific regions in our country to write of present-day life there, was new at the time."[9]

Precedents actually abounded for what Lois was doing, but she may have been unique as both children's author and illustrator in adopting the documentary methods that other artists and writers had been experimenting with throughout the previous decade. In generalizing about the totality of the art of the Works Progress Administration (WPA), for example, Stott notes that the participating artists recorded and clarified "for the American people aspects of their experience, past or present, main-current or side-stream. . . . The WPA artists were free to do what they wanted, but all they wanted to do was document America."[10] Because the documentary imagination revealed the multifaceted nature of the American experience, grassroots regionalism reigned triumphant. In literature, music, theater, and in all kinds of visual arts, examining the seemingly infinite variety of everyday living in America gained new and appreciative audiences. As public cultural works, the output of the WPA artists validated the experiences of everyday Americans, who were scraping by during this economically challenging decade. In fact, Stott claims—with ample evidence—that "documentary is a radically democratic genre,"[11] with "social documentary" designed to encourage "social improvement."[12]

These definitions aptly apply to Lois's regionals. She discussed and revisited her concept of realism in many places—in articles as well as in talks to teachers and librarians—insistent on defending her stories of real lives. She wholeheartedly believed that such stories gave readers "a deeper satisfaction than the mere enjoyment of a made-up story." Her characters helped children completely engage "the life of the book-child" so that the protagonist and the situation depicted became "as vivid a life-experience as their own." Through her gifts in injecting both emotionally evocative and explicitly detailed images and words, Lois convincingly portrayed the hard-working lives of her protagonists. Her readers absorbed detailed descriptions of all sorts of daily tasks accomplished by the book-children—whether setting out strawberries, grubbing "yarbs" (herbs), or cooking for younger siblings. Moreover, young readers might be able to use their empathy with the book-children to help them find solutions to their own problems in meeting "whatever life brings." Lois felt that children instinctively sense the "ring of truth" and try constantly to understand what life is about and how to work through its vicissitudes. Gary Schmidt described her sensing "an America that saw its regionalism as a central aspect of its democratic nature. . . . The result of her desire to express this vision is a line of characters embedded in a series of novels designed to explore aspects of the country's regions by vividly depicting that culture and its regional setting and by creating a strong, empathetic link between the reader and the experience of the Other. What John Steinbeck was doing with *In Dubious Battle*, *Of Mice and Men*, and *The Grapes of Wrath*, Lois wished to do for young readers."[13]

She believed that her books could and should be helpful guideposts to emerging maturation. Engendering growth in empathy trumped other more literary goals. Although adults sometimes bristle at this kind of subliminal or more obvious didacticism, Lois, preacher's daughter that she was, considered it primary for children to work through social dilemmas in order to "acquire a peaceful and Christian approach to living."[14] She used the term "Christian" to encompass a moral and ethical approach to human relations, far beyond the more doctrinally circumscribed definition with which she had been raised. Lois never lost or abandoned her faith in ideals that she found in the tenets of Christianity. While she did not preach or suggest salvation, she offered a constructive and imaginative way to confront and deal with otherness.

Lois imbued her regional characters with personality flaws that had to be overcome in order to succeed at solving the difficulties in their own lives. As she visited different parts of the country, sketching and listening to old and young family members who told her about their lives, she created characters who, in turn, embodied these stories, some almost verbatim. Although all her books' endings had positive aspects that affirmed the directions her characters ultimately chose to follow, the outcomes did not magically improve the material circumstances of their lives. She often included incidents that saddened her characters: a beloved dog gets run over, the pet crow is shot, Pappy throws Billy's handmade dulcimer into the fire.[15] In her 1953 address, "Are Your Books True?", which she delivered to the Association for Childhood Education in Springfield, Ohio, Lois remarked about the positive nature of these conclusions. She always needed, heeded, and appreciated the perspective of her young readers. Once she had asked a group of children if she had put too much unhappiness in a story:

> They replied with an emphatic, "NO! Life is not all happy." We discussed whether or not a book should always have a happy ending. They said, "No, because in real life things do not always end happily." Then one little girl added wistfully, "But I think it should be hopeful. It should end on a note of hope."[16]

Lois saw wisdom in that child's belief and followed it. "In 1964, May Hill Arbuthnot referred to Lenski's regional novels as 'grimmer realism than anything since *Tom Sawyer*,'" but Schmidt feels that what Lois was writing was "much grimmer than *Tom Sawyer.* While the realism of Lenski's novels seems mild and even tame in comparison to twenty-first-century works, what was remarkable was her willingness to speak to the underside of the American Dream."[17]

Lois had not *intended* to write a regional series. Initially, she planned to use the time in New Orleans to complete illustrations for *The Little Farm* and to research and plan a new historical book on early New Orleans. While Lois divided her time between the two tasks, thirteen-year-old Stephen attended a public school in New Orleans for the winter term, and Arthur sketched French Quarter scenes. On Sundays the family drove out to the surrounding countryside. Lois explains how she stumbled out of the reclusiveness of research libraries, archives, and antique bookshops into the daylight of anthropological and *plein air* sketching in Bayou Barataria. "I first discovered Regional America where I first found the little village of Lafitte on a bayou twenty miles south of Gretna [a community on the west bank of the Mississippi adjacent to New Orleans]. I found Lafitte and its people, who so fascinated and inspired me and kept me coming again and again, with sketchbook and notebook, to put down a tangible record of their lives, in what became my first Regional, *Bayou Suzette*."[18]

In late March, Arthur and Stephen returned to Connecticut so that Stephen would be ready for the spring term at boarding school. Lois stayed in New Orleans on her own to complete her research. Three mornings a week, she took the ferry across the Mississippi, where she hired a taxi driver in Gretna to drive her to Lafitte and return for her at five o'clock each evening. On alternate days she rested to conserve her strength.[19] In addition to her sketching and conversations with local families, Lois also took many photographs of the places and people she later fictionalized.[20] She wrote to her longtime friend, Mabel Pugh, the following Christmas: "We spent a wonderful 3 mos. in New Orleans last year—a fascinating place, & I gathered enough material for about 4 books!" In that same letter, however, she mentioned the difficulties of living in rural Connecticut with "war restrictions on transportation, fuel, & food—when you live 6 mi. from nearest store—but we are happy to do all we can to help in the war effort." In addition to rationed travel, Lois confessed that she had been without household help since April, and that she and Arthur had been "obliged to carry on in much simplified style, to save my energy for my book-work, as Mr. C. has had no work for 2 yrs., & no hope of any for the duration."[21] She relied on her relentless pursuit of substantive "book-work" to meet both her own creative and her family's financial needs.

Lois sent the manuscript of *Bayou Suzette* to Helen Dean Fish, her editor at Frederick A. Stokes, publisher of Lois's historical books. Fish was pleased with the story, even though she commented, "The Indian girl [Marteel] gives Zuzu [Suzette] a good run for the title role, and I am not sure that she doesn't deserve it. However, that doesn't matter enough to shift it now and the children won't think about it." Fish asked Lois to consider making the book shorter. "You have frequently yielded to the very natural temptation to put in things that appeal to you in this background, but which will not particularly interest children and which sometimes do not help the story. . . . I really believe that you can go through it with this in mind and make it a more absorbing and attractive story from the children's point of view." Fish reminded Lois that *Bayou Suzette* wasn't truly historical in the same way as *Indian Captive*, and therefore didn't merit "bringing in so much informational detail." The following week, Fish passed the manuscript to another editor at Stokes, who agreed. "Children will be interested in this background and people through character and action," she reminded Lois, and details that "do not actively contribute to this interest will be more or less lost on younger readers." A month later, Lois complied with Fish's suggestions, and her editor now remarked that Lois "had done just the right things" to make it a "stronger book."[22]

As Fish commented, *Bayou Suzette* presents a double set of protagonists: Suzette and Marteel. Which is the real heroine, since each reinforces the strengths and compensates for the weaknesses of the other? Both struggle to comprehend where they fit in as individual, maturing young girls trying to understand the rules and rituals of the societies into which they were born. Ironically, while Marteel may be outwardly rejecting her Indian identity (probably Houmas, since they lived in the area) in order to win over Suzette's family, it's her Native-learned abilities to survive in bayou country that actually win her a place within the Durand household. Marteel rejects the culturally feminine responsibilities of a Creole household, such as housecleaning or keeping confined to her bed/shed/shelter instead of experiencing the freedom of her Indian habits. Still, she hungers for love. Suzette tries to be the upholder of family values and responsibilities, yet she won't accept her mother's verdict that Marteel will have to leave. Through Marteel, Suzette learns more about the bayou backwaters and alligator haunts, develops an appreciation for Indian culture, experiences more of life and adventure, and gains some real perspective when she begins to understand that Marteel has more claim to Bayou Barataria country than anyone in her Creole community.

Bayou Suzette introduces the characteristics that define most of Lois's regionals and bind the series visually and thematically, even though, at the time of its publication, she had not yet conceived the book as the first in a projected series. In fact, in 1944, the year following the publication of *Bayou Suzette*, Lois published *Puritan Adventure*, the last of her historical novels. Only in retrospect, then, did Lois realize that *Bayou Suzette* became the ideal model for turning her curiosity into an evolving methodology to document the lives of children that were essentially missing in mainstream children's literature. It was "New Orleans and fascinating Louisiana . . . literally packed with unwritten stories" that "opened my eyes to the great diversity of pattern in the ways of America."[23]

Here was a niche that Lois was uniquely able to fill, and one that could prove lucrative as well. Her strengths as an observer, listener, and artist were giving her access to new sources—stories from plain folks who had never been asked about their experiences. Gathering fresh material helped Lois envision and cultivate a new purpose to her writing for the nine- to twelve-year-old set. She anticipated, probably correctly, that young readers would encounter many of her regionals for the first time in a setting mediated by a librarian or teacher. As in most of her earlier historical chapter books, Lois provided a foreword to each regional, always in italics, in which she introduced the subject, its significance, and her important resources, both primary and secondary. Once again, she intended these pages for the adult reader. After she completed the series, she looked back on each regional as a "record of a way of life" that described "real people in real situations in a particular setting with a minimum of fictionalizing." Lois wanted to show how both occupation and environment affect families in any given part of the country. "The thoughts, ambitions and struggles of any one family in any environment provide rich material for story-telling. Not only their struggle to meet their daily needs, but their relations with each other and with friends, neighbors and strangers provide a sound basis for drama."[24] All her protagonists faced challenges of daily living, "the wear and tear of human relations,"[25] and her quest was to turn these experiences into fiction dramatic enough to teach as well as to entertain the reader.

Original illustration for cover of *Bayou Suzette*, 1943. Reprinted by permission of the Lois Lenski Covey Foundation and Burrell Covey, copyright by Lois Lenski. Courtesy of the Lois Lenski Papers, 1893–1974, MSS 015, Martha Blakeney Hodges Special Collections and University Archives, University Libraries, University of North Carolina at Greensboro.

Lois's characters in *Bayou Suzette* speak the patois of French Louisiana, which is more challenging for young readers to follow than standard English. She had injected the idiomatic speech she encountered in her research into her historical series in order to project her readers back into the time period portrayed by the narrative. Similarly, in her regionals, while she simplified the spelling for her young audience, she instinctively felt that the dialect and local idioms "give the flavor of a region . . . suggest the moods of the people, the atmosphere of a place." Lois, for example, admired the way the Louisiana bayou folk "transfer our English words into their native French rhythm," and she appreciated the "poetry in the common speech of man."[26] George P. Wilson, linguist of American dialects, commended the author for her innovative rendering of local speech patterns in a simplified style, since doing so "was something of an innovation in children's literature. . . . Had she turned the speech of these people into standard English, she would not have been true to facts—important facts—that reveal people. A child who reads one of her regional books gets the impression that he has visited the inhabitants of the region portrayed."[27] Charlotte Huck and Doris A. Young, authors of *Children's Literature in the Elementary School* (1961), suggested that passages in Lenski's regionals be read aloud "to motivate children's interest and to explain the author's purpose in writing as the people actually speak."[28] Over sixty years later, author Sandra Dutton wrote an article for *Horn Book Magazine* in which she reminisced about her first encounter with *Strawberry Girl* when she was in fifth grade: "I had the feeling that the characters . . . were real. Lenski had listened to the people of central Florida, and I was hearing their speech."[29]

Lois well understood the significance of illustrations in her picture books for the very young. The positive reception to the beautiful and more lavishly illustrated *Indian Captive* no doubt convinced her that an enhanced visual program worked in tandem with the text to amplify the effectiveness of the narrative. Her lovingly rendered pencil illustrations and her protagonists' more fully realized facial expressions and body language play at least as important a role as the dramatic episodes acted out in dialogue by the characters in her text. The endpapers in *Bayou Suzette* function as identical miniature sepia-toned murals, with Marteel and Suzette walking down the narrow path between the Creole cottages and the bayou. The reader is immediately taken into the scene. Facing the table of contents, the compellingly illustrated map of "Barataria Country" contains details from the narrative that the reader can keep consulting as the story unfolds. Often her illustrations reveal the protagonists' personalities as much as (or in some instances, more than) the dialogue and action, such as Grandmère standing on a plank and poling it with her broom through the flooded waters to fetch a doctor for a very sick Suzette. The maps and abundant illustrations, some dominating full double-page spreads, function as reading aids for her young audience. Because Lois "felt that the setting should be adequately shown in pictures,"[30] she was pleased that the publisher was willing to change the format from her historical series. *Bayou Suzette* featured larger pages that made them ideal for illustrations. Lois also was both delighted and relieved that she could submit pencil drawings, which she claimed "my best medium." For publication, they were reproduced in offset, as in *Indian Captive*. Evidently, the publisher also thought that these soft-lead sketches contributed to the making of "a distinguished book,"[31] and one that displayed her mature and inimitable "Lenskiesque" style. J. B. Lippincott and Company acquired Stokes before the publication of *Bayou Suzette*, and Lois told the managing editor at Lippincott that she hoped the paper would be "a warm tinge" of white that "attracts" rather than a "bluish cold white" that "repels," and of a high enough quality and "sufficiently opaque." All these details, she understood, made a book more appealing to readers, even if they were unaware of anything beyond the overall effect.

Given the fact that Lois was married to muralist Arthur Covey, one might wonder whether, or in what way, his work in the 1930s may have affected Lois's move toward regionalism in the decade that followed. During the 1920s, Arthur had designed and executed large murals of skilled workers for the Norton Company of Worcester, Massachusetts, and the Kohler Company of Kohler, Wisconsin.[32] In the post office in Bridgeport, Connecticut, he was able to return to thematic material that echoed the works he did for these industries, all of which emphasized the contributions of blue-collar laborers. The agricultural workers in the Anderson, South Carolina, murals also demonstrated the celebration of those who toiled, in both cases completely within the documentary zeitgeist of the era. The murals for the Torrington, Connecticut, Post Office from the life of abolitionist John Brown, on the other hand, reflected and promoted the social-justice spirit that permeated the cultural works of the decade. Lois had already shown an interest in the everyday life of the past. How could she have failed to be inspired by the sense of dignity that Arthur invested in his portrayals of workers and in his African Americans fleeing the oppression of slavery or bringing in the cotton crop in the Deep South?[33] Lois also garnered much technical ability from Arthur's tutelage. Inevitably, she capably borrowed both the narrative richness and the same sympathy that figures in Arthur's WPA project murals and the works of many of the regional masters, such as Thomas Hart Benton and John Steuart Curry. One can see these influences most evident in the mural-like expanses that grace the double-page spreads and endpapers. Lois expressed her admiration for the endeavors of Benton, Curry, and Grant Wood because they found "America worth painting," not simply in subject matter, but because they "developed also a more forthright technique, painting with directness, simplicity, and vividness."[34] She did not mention how their work might have shaped her own, although she strived for the same attributes in illustrations for middle-level readers from *Indian Captive* forward.

Lois nevertheless needed to distance herself from her indebtedness to Arthur. She never acknowledged the influence Arthur may have wielded over her creative choices once she was no longer his protégée. She also realized that she needed to be the main wage-earner, even if it was socially unacceptable at the time to acknowledge that role. Looking back in her autobiography, Lois wrote candidly about this aspect of her marital partnership, explaining that Arthur

> took little or no interest in my successive books, although he was generous enough to admire my work when it was brought to his attention. He was proud of my books and the reputation I was making in the writing field, and when talking to friends, took a great deal of credit, and rightly, for my training and the help he had given me as a student. But in the books themselves he had little or no interest . . . for a new book, always a red-letter day for me, meant nothing to him. . . . So my books developed independently, somewhat "under cover." [35]

And in the mid-1950s, sharing her enthusiasm for Anne Lindbergh's *A Gift from the Sea* with teacher-friend Emma Celeste Thibodaux, Lois delighted in finding this truly

> a woman's book & says a lot of things that most women (married) think but don't dare to say. But most of all, I think she resents the *emptiness of the modern, wealthy woman's life* in the social class in which she moves in the suburbs near New York. . . . No one with whom she can ever share an honest thought (the way you & I share our *honest thoughts;* why I can't talk to my husband the way I talk to you in letters—He has no idea what I am thinking most of the time.) And I bet Charles Lindbergh was mighty surprised to

read Anne's book—& what's more, I bet *he hasn't even read it!!!* My husband never reads *mine*!!![36]

Lois's own struggles to maintain self-esteem while feeling underappreciated probably helped her explore so movingly the pain and loss that her protagonists often experienced and that she subtly injected into her most expressive illustrations.[37]

Regardless of any resentment toward Arthur for his lack of interest, Lois needed to restrain any overt demonstration of pride in her own significant successes, which helped the family survive financially during the Great Depression. Yet she certainly absorbed the feeling for plain folk and working-class culture poignantly portrayed by Arthur and the regionalists she so admired. The first visit to rural French Louisiana fired Lois's imagination, but the kindling for that conflagration had long been smoldering.

Lois, at forty-eight, had gained a considerable degree of freedom from maternal and spousal obligations and asserted a new sense of self in embarking on her adventures in regionalism. She had never been a bohemian, but she had chosen to flee to New York to become an artist instead of accepting a stable position as the Midwestern teacher she had trained to become. She was also the woman who returned from Europe to marry her mentor and enter into his ready-made household full of responsibilities, and she was now earning enough money to achieve some independence within the tightly bound cultural imperatives of being a traditional wife and mother. Physically and emotionally, Lois needed to create and maintain balance between actively pursuing art, segmenting time for rest because of her health issues, and being available to her husband, children, and grandchildren, just as in her regionals, she balanced text and illustration to achieve a harmonious whole.

Lois's adult readers were thrilled with the publication of *Bayou Suzette* in 1943. The following year, that title won her the Ohioana Library Award for juvenile fiction by a native Ohio author. Louisianans, too, valued Lois's faithful portrayal of the bayou folk. Lois had thanked Jeanne B. Peyregne of Des Allemandes in the foreword. Peyregne felt "honored in having you name me as being of assistance to you" and congratulated Lois for the beautiful illustrations that helped "put across such a lovely story of our bayou folks." An unidentified and undated newspaper review of *Bayou Suzette* (signed "A. D. T." but probably from New Orleans) mentions Lois's dedicating the book to Alex Melançon, "whose bayou stories in *The Times-Picayune* (New Orleans) have endeared him to readers far and wide. . . . There is much of Alex in the story of Suzette and Marteel, much that makes the book a treasure indeed to those who know and love South Louisiana." The librarian for the Orleans Parish school board told Lois that Harnett Kane, a well-regarded author of local lore who had written *Bayous of Louisiana,* "was impressed particularly by the delightful drawings which he felt had caught the true spirit of the people."[38]

Most significantly, Lois gained a new fan and dear friend in Emma Celeste Thibodaux, an early elementary teacher of "backwoods children" in Covington, Louisiana. As Lois later noted, "I met her *after Bayou Suzette* had been published, through her correspondence and her appreciation of that book. Her father was a French bayou-Cajun (tho her mother was not) and she felt that the book was completely true to the life of the French-speaking southern portion of Louisiana." Emma Celeste played several important roles in Lois's development of the Regional and the Roundabout series. Lois credited her as "my general advisor on all my books with a southern locale. She follows the progress of each with as great interest as if she were writing the book herself. She testifies to the authenticity of the background of each, being uncannily able to decipher any false notes that may creep in."[39] Lois had originally intended to make *Bayou Suzette* double in size but then deleted Suzette's adventures in the second half because Helen Dean Fish believed that Lois had "good material left for another story with this same background and possibly the same people."[40]

But Lois never wrote the sequel. The following winter in Florida she became enamored of *that* region, which, she remarked, "called to me in no uncertain terms."[41] Her interest in "Cracker" culture had already been aroused by Marjorie Kinnan Rawlings's books about Florida.[42] Although "Cracker" is often used in a derogatory fashion, the term most commonly referred to poor white herders in south Georgia and north Florida and probably originally applied to piney woods folk who were "whip crackers" driving their livestock.[43] Taking a break from the work on *Bayou Suzette,* Lois and a group of friends took a drive from Lakeland to Tampa, where they passed fields of strawberries. At a roadside stand, they saw a little girl "with flaxen hair and a pert, inquisitive face" waiting for prospective customers. The friend who was driving turned to Lois and joked, "Why don't you write a book about raising strawberries? You could call it *Strawberry Girl.*" The idea struck home.

Lois Lenski photograph of the young girl who inspired her depiction of Birdie, protagonist of *Strawberry Girl*, 1945. Courtesy of the Lois Lenski Collection, Blackmore Library, Capital University.

Although no convenient Bayou Barataria–like setting presented itself, Lois used her wiles to find contacts among Crackers wherever she could that winter and the one following in Lakeland, "milling through the crowds of country people who had come to town to do their trading." She was as intrigued with the local dialect as she had been with the patois of French

Original Pencil Illustration for STRAWBERRY GIRL

Louisiana. Although Crackers looked like ordinary country people, "their speech had a special tang to it. It was colorful and flavorsome, rich in fine old English idiom."[44] As in *Bayou Suzette*, Lois set *Strawberry Girl* earlier in the twentieth century. In the former, one of her informants along Bayou Barataria had regaled Lois with stories of living through three major floods, which helped Lois realize that "no bayou story would be complete without a flood."[45] For *Strawberry Girl*, she wanted to demonstrate the tension between the traditional cattle culture of the Crackers in its conflict with the agricultural industry of citrus and strawberries as it began to take root in Florida. At a livestock auction west of Lakeland where she and Arthur often went to sketch, she found "a little girl whose hair-do intrigued me and which I later used for my heroine." Lois situated Birdie, the "strawberry girl" of a farming family, opposite Stringbean, the son of the neighboring family whose "hogses" ran loose in the piney woods. Lois also saw the model for the original Stringbean, "a skinny Cracker boy who 'couldn't git no fat to his bones!'" And in the corner of a church in the community of Gumbee, near the strawberry fields, she spotted the little girl who became Birdie. Was it the same child she'd seen earlier? Lois only tells us, "That same day

Pages 98 and 99   —LOIS LENSKI   1945

Original illustration of Birdie Boyer, *Strawberry Girl* protagonist, and her mother spreading flour on their strawberry plants to fool String Bean and his father into believing that the two were using poison to keep their cattle out of the fertile field. Original copyright by Lois Lenski. Used by permission of HarperCollins Publishers and courtesy of the Lois Lenski Collection, Western History Collections, University of Oklahoma Libraries, Norman.

I saw Birdie herself plowing the sandy field with an old white mule. That little girl traveled all over the country in my book and came back to me, three years later, bearing the Newbery medal in her hand."[46]

Indeed, the research and writing of *Strawberry Girl* convinced Lois that a *series* of regional explorations was in order. Even before the publication of *Strawberry Girl* and its subsequent success as the Newbery Medal winner of 1946, Helen Dean Fish wrote in July 1945, recommending that Lois grant permission to the Junior League of America to reproduce and record *Bayou Suzette* as one of its selections of regional stories for the Junior League's radio programs. In the very next paragraph, Fish moves on to talk about publicity for *Strawberry Girl*, mentioning that she was "sending an advance copy to Marjorie Rawlings because if she says something very nice about it, it would make a nice advertising line."[47] By the following October, Lois had also granted permission for the audio recording of the book.[48] Dissemination via radio broadcasts meant that Lois's books could reach classrooms and homes in rural America that were far from libraries, a process that proved critical to the way Lois's choice of regional settings broadened as well.

On June 18, 1946, Lois delivered her Newbery Medal acceptance address, "Seeing Others as Ourselves," in Buffalo for the American Library Association. She opened by saying that she was "loath to consider this book worthy of this attention. Rather do I prefer to believe that you have chosen to honor the series of books on which I have embarked, of which *Strawberry Girl* is only one unit, and that you wish to give your wholehearted backing and support to my purpose behind that series." Lois insisted that her approach to the regionals was not "that of a propagandist or even the humanitarian. It is that of an artist . . . seeking a deeper meaning in the commonplace."[49] The "series" at that point consisted only of *Bayou Suzette* and *Strawberry Girl*, so Lois's enthusiastic presumption of support seems premature, even as she announced that *Blue Ridge Billy* would be coming out the following autumn. As she added, "You must forgive me if I find it impossible to talk about *Strawberry Girl* independently. I can think of these books only as parts of a larger whole. In my mind they are indissolubly bound together." Since *Phebe Fairchild: Her Book* and *Indian Captive* had each been designated Newbery Honor Books, Lois probably felt justified in accepting the honor on behalf of a series that was mostly yet to come.

Lois was taken by surprise when she learned that she'd won, for she had "never thought of S*trawberry Girl* in connection with the Newbery Medal or considered it important enough to be considered." Lois was so excited about being named the recipient that she typed up the entire experience as "The Inside Story of Getting a Medal," sixteen densely packed pages "written for certain special friends of mine who could not be there," even though she claimed that "it was a little like being dead and attending my own funeral to hear so many people say so many nice things about me to my face." Although Lois knew a month earlier that she had won the award, she had to keep it a secret. During that time she wrote her remarks, fortunate that the previous fall she had "jotted down some paragraphs" to discuss the purpose behind her regionals, and Helen Dean Fish had mentioned this to the editor of *Horn Book*. These initial thoughts had already become the

Stephen, Lois, and Arthur seated on a bench in the garden with their pet goat, just after *Strawberry Girl* was awarded the 1946 Newbery Medal. Courtesy of Jeanine Covey Gutowski, Vivian Covey, and Michael Covey.

essence of "Seeing Others as Ourselves," which Lois developed into both the acceptance speech and an article for *Horn Book*.

When Lois spoke during the rehearsal for the awards ceremony (recorded for broadcast on NBC radio), she calmed her nerves by imagining herself "talking to my distant friends, to Em' Celeste and Alex in La . . . my family in Torrington . . . 'the girls' (my school teacher friends in Toledo) . . . all of whom I had asked to listen. It was so easy to talk to them . . . it buoyed me up and inspired me." Lois learned from someone on the selection committee that *Strawberry Girl* had been chosen on the first ballot, another boost to her self-confidence. After the presentations, librarians approached her and told her how much children have loved her books, and "how much I had given them in my acceptance speech." During the many celebrations after the banquet, Lois was delighted that "wherever we went, we ate strawberries in honor of Birdie!" Returning exhausted to Greenacres, Lois declared, "I had to repeat it [the detailed story of her Newbery Medal experiences] to all my family before they would let me go to bed." No family members, however, had accompanied her for her most celebrated public moment. Lois had learned with whom she could share her triumphs. The success of *Strawberry Girl* opened all kinds of doors, reinforcing Lois's career move to author-illustrator and, beyond that, buttressing her emerging independence. As she told Mabel, "No! There's no cash, and a medal is about the most useless thing in the world, but this one brings an aura of glory and prestige! Really it does—I've been surprised how impressed everybody is, and what an amount of publicity it means, and how it *booms* the sale of one's books! Everybody just loves the bright gold medal sticker on the red jacket, and cannot resist buying a copy."[50]

Lois's regionals reflected both the larger democratic cultural zeitgeist and the focus on American regions in the emerging field of social studies advocated by one of the giants of Progressive education, Harold Rugg. He specialized in curriculum reform and believed that social studies should be taught as an integrated course to replace the discrete areas of history, geography, civics, and economics. In the first volume of his series, *Introduction to American Civilization: A Study of Economic Life in the United States* (1929), he stated that his goal was "to help young people to understand American civilization, by considering carefully the chief modes of living of our people." Rugg felt that "current conditions in America throw into sharp relief the critical need of teaching our youth to understand American life and its relation to the modern world." Like other Progressives, he responded to the massive changes in the United States brought on by industrialization and urbanization, insisting "that schools bend every effort to introduce our young people to the chief conditions and problems which will confront them as American citizens." He contended that his "new unified course in the social studies" could help students achieve "active and intelligent participation in American civilization."[51]

By 1936, in their introduction to *The Building of America*, the fifth volume in the Rugg Social Science Series, he and the volume's co-author, Louise Krueger, argued that the best way to understand the United States is through getting to know it as it was built, "region by region," woven together "into one story the history of the way our country was settled and the geography of climate and natural resources that made it possible."[52] In "Seeing Others as Ourselves," Lois reinforced the significance of regions and their effect on human behavior: "It is easy to see why a certain environment makes people live as they do, and affects every phase of their lives. . . . When we understand their environment and see how their lives have been conditioned thereby, then we can understand their behavior. We can imagine ourselves in the same situation, and we wonder if we would be different."[53] Leland B. Jacobs, a professor of education at Columbia's Teachers College with an interest in children's literature, wrote of Lois: "Here is a writer who is explicit about her faith that literature for children must come to grips with philosophical and sociological matters that touch the hearts and minds of boys and girls intimately."[54]

We have no evidence of Lois's familiarity with Rugg's work, but *The Building of America*, with its emphasis on regions, was aimed at the same grade and reading level as her regionals. Other textbook companies picked up on the social studies theme and generally emphasized regions in upper elementary grades.[55] Teachers around the country appreciated the regionals, and several sent Lois the units of study they created to demonstrate how math, art, science, geography, and other lessons could make a thematically integrated course built around her books. A Houston, Texas, teacher developed a unit and shared it with her colleagues, one of whom commented, "Children find reading Lois Lenski's books an interesting social studies experience because they lack the traditional dryness of a textbook. . . . [T]hey are geographical too in an interesting way." Another educator in a Methodist orphanage school in Raleigh, North Carolina, evaluated the outcome of the unit: "Children's attitudes and relationships toward home, community and country were inspired and improved. In this study of real people they felt and saw unity, love, and appreciation through toil, understanding, sharing, fortitude, humor, family devotions, security, resourcefulness and sympathy. Here too, they saw many people whose lot was much worse than their own, yet they grew and prospered."[56]

The authors of the teacher's guide to the 1965 fourth-grade social studies textbook, *In All Our States*, ascribed several characteristics to nine- and ten-year-old students, including "wanting to do the right thing." For this attribute, the teacher is reminded: "As part of 'doing right,' the youngster at nine and ten has a higher regard for the truth than he has had at any previous time. . . . This sense of justice and this regard for telling the truth are the germinal stages of a developing system of ethical values." Lois's regionals and her later Roundabout series for younger readers perfectly met such essential developmental tasks. Two of her books are included in the bibliography for the chapter on the South: *Judy's Journey* and *Boom Town Boy*.[57]

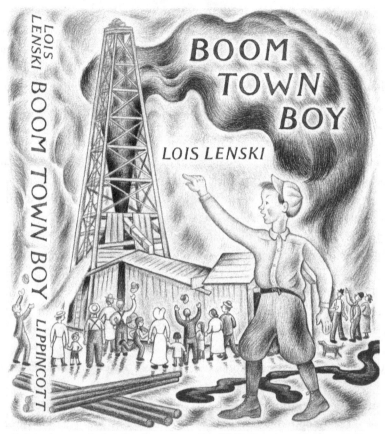

Original cover design for *Boom Town Boy*, 1948. Reprinted by permission of the Lois Lenski Covey Foundation and Burrell Covey, copyright by Lois Lenski. Courtesy of the Lois Lenski Papers, Special Collections, Butler Library, Buffalo State College.

Boom Town Boy (1948) dramatizes the changes that the Oklahoma oil boom brings to the farm family of protagonist Orvie Robinson in the north central part of the state, the area settled by Arthur Covey's relatives during the Oklahoma land run of 1889. While visiting the Covey clan on a family trip to the state, Lois heard so many stories from people who had lived through the turbulent peak of the 1920s oil boom that she set the narrative in that era. The illustrations are among her best, with two different sets of endpapers—those at the beginning of the book showing a bird's-eye view of the Robinson farm and surrounding bucolic land outside of Perry, and

those at the end depicting the same scene spoiled by oil derricks, temporary housing, and cheap "boom town" buildings. The double-page spreads
of an oil town and a gusher coming in on the Robinson farm function
both to respond to the narrative and propel the action forward, just as they
should. But Lois did not control her tendency toward didacticism, which
almost spoils an otherwise dramatic historical narrative. She simply could
not resist contrasting the family's life before and after they got wealthy.
Grandpa Robinson is the voice of sanity, and Orvie is his confederate.
When the family has moved to town and bought more possessions than
they need or even desired, they find they are dissatisfied with their lives.

> "We can't go backwards," Grandpa continued. "Oil has come
> and it hasn't spoiled *my* happiness none. Happiness just don't
> depend on a lot of money. Happiness is within yourself."
> "What do you mean, Pa?" asked Mama.
> "Just what I said," the old man repeated. "*Happiness don't depend
> on a lot of money.* Everyone one of you, except Orvie, thought it did,
> but you've learned by your own experience that it don't."[58]

She doesn't leave much to the reader's imagination or allow the reader to
draw conclusions. *Boom Town Boy* is one of the worst transgressions of this
sort, because the story and the illustrations are otherwise so strong.

Despite the didacticism surfacing at some points in the series, the
regionals made ideal choices for school libraries and "read-alouds" in classrooms as well as popular selections for individual students. Probably not
coincidentally, Lippincott, publisher of the Regionals and Roundabouts,
was also a leading publisher of textbooks.

While curricular applicability may have been peripheral to Lois as she
initiated her series, Wendell Willkie's *One World* was close to the core of
her concerns. Willkie, the liberal Republican who lost to Franklin Delano
Roosevelt in the presidential election of 1940, embarked on a world tour
in the midst of World War II and wrote this slim and highly popular book
in which he pleaded, "Our thinking in the future must be worldwide."
He praised the United States for its diverse grouping of peoples "linked
together by their confidence in our democratic institutions as expressed
in the Declaration of Independence and guaranteed by the Constitution."
Our greatest contribution to civilization, he claimed, was "the ability of

peoples of varying background and of different racial extractions to live side by side here in the United States with common understanding, respect, and helpfulness."[59]

When Lois talked about "Regional Children's Literature," at the New York State Library Association meeting in Saratoga, New York, in 1946, she expressed her gratitude for Willkie's phrase and what it implied: "He meant, as we all know, that we must learn to live as brothers to make the world 'One.'" Yet how can people begin to develop such a perspective if all they can see is their own world? Lois believed that "we must understand our own country and the different kinds of people who live in it" before we can hope to understand the world "beyond our own fence." And to understand "our country as a whole becomes an understanding of its component parts." She believed, and sought to create, illustrated regional literature that could help fulfill Willkie's vision by presenting a locally specific but completely integrated *"way of life."* The reader comes to understand "why the people speak, think and act as they do. And so we come to understand a basic concept behind all experience—the universality of human behavior. The most important lesson that any child—or adult—has to learn is the ability to put himself in the other person's place." Gary Schmidt points out that Lois's regionals were written when the melting-pot metaphor was dominant as a descriptor of American society. But "Lenski wrote to deny both the aptness and desirability of that metaphor, calling instead for larger understandings of the fascinating diversity of American traditions . . . [all of which] could contribute to the American saga in noble and honorable ways."[60]

As World War II was drawing to an end, Bank Street educator Flora Straus wrote an article, "Let Them Face It: Today's World in Books for Boys and Girls," for *Horn Book* that opens with the following:

Our young people, the citizens of tomorrow, face the stupendous challenge of a world in transition. . . . We want to give our children tools for their new tasks. Books are such tools. They can even be weapons for democracy provided they are good enough—real enough—inspiring enough. Through the medium of stories young people can gain a better understanding of the pressing economic and social problems of today. . . . There is need of . . . real inspiration on which to build sound concepts of the world they will want to live in.[61]

In *A Critical History of Children's Literature*, Cornelia Meigs, a Newbery Award–winning children's author and English professor at Bryn Mawr College who was roughly Lois's contemporary, places her series within the realm of American children's literature of the times.[62] While the 1930s had witnessed many books published about children in other countries, some children's authors in the decade of the 1940s "found within the United States of this period situations and problems quite challenging enough for exciting, often moving, stories, and writers of realistic and family stories tuned naturally to American settings. The movement to know-your-own-land had an enlivening effect on American children's literature in those ten years. . . . This same movement emphasized the regional story of the forties, which owed its actual classification to its chief exponent, Lois Lenski."[63]

A lifelong Lenski fan (who wishes to remain anonymous) grew up the daughter of immigrant Sicilian parents who made great sacrifices to enroll her in the most outstanding parochial school in Madison, Wisconsin. As a child, she identified with the protagonists in the regionals, who helped her cope:

> I try to remember what it was about her books that drew me to them. Maybe it is the outsider in all of us. I certainly felt that way as an immigrant child and Birdie Boyer was every blond Irish affluent girl I wished I could be. . . . [The] school was full of Birdies with moms who were active in churches and clubs and did everything so well. My parents were very hard workers but I was a have not. The biggest have not was the fact that my parents had no education like the Slaters and Suzette's family. Maybe, for me, these books were how-to books as in what to aspire to and how to act. There is always a resolution and a happy one. I don't think there is anything wrong with this. Children all need hope and Lois Lenski offered that.[64]

Once she began her regionals in earnest, Lois turned out a new title almost every year, with her sixteenth, *Deer Valley Girl*, published in 1968. Within that tight publication schedule, some are better written, contain more drama, are more beautifully illustrated than others, and better stand the test of time. As a whole, the achievement is unmatched by any other regional writer for young readers. While most of Lois's regionals feature heroines, rather than heroes, as the chief protagonists, gender does not appear to be a controlling factor in the series' universal appeal. *Blue Ridge Billy*, a North Carolina Appalachian story, followed *Strawberry Girl*, with protagonists Billy and Sarey Sue nearly equal in importance. Mabel had told Lois about this part of North Carolina, and Lois thanked her for the advice: "I am glad you sent me to Ashe County . . . for I feel it suited my purpose better than other parts of the mountains where I might have gone.[65] So I'm very grateful."[66] *Strawberry Girl* had strawberry endpapers, no mural-like spreads, but comparing those in *Bayou Suzette* with those in *Blue Ridge Billy*, the reader instantly perceives how distinctly the two environments differ. In the former, the lazy bayou with the pirogues docked at the piers across from the shotgun cottages built closely together form a community. In the latter, Billy's family cabin and outbuildings are nestled at the bottom of a steep hill, separated from other families by the rugged landscape. Lois's belief in the way topography and cultural background shape her protagonists' response to the world is as vividly evident as it is inviting to the reader.

Lois dedicated *Judy's Journey*, fourth in the series, to Emma Celeste.[67] This book is the most poignant and powerful of all, because it deals with the most impoverished of the regional families. The Drummonds are a migrant family who travel along the Eastern seaboard states from Florida to New Jersey, and the endpapers present a stunning visual composite of the experiences that Judy and her family face as they move from place to place. In the foreword, Lois describes the link between this story and her overriding theme of social justice:

> Everything in their [migrant children's] life is against them. As one migrant-teacher told me: "They have never had a break. And yet they are brave, courageous, full of spirit, and anxious to learn. They respond so quickly to all you do for them. They have had so little—every thing you do for them means so much." In this teacher's class, the migrant children are making democracy work. Here mountain white and Northern white, Southern Negro, Japanese-American and American children of foreign descent are living and learning together, peacefully and happily.[68]

When Lois had sent Hugh Johnson at Lippincott the draft of *Judy's Journey*, he wrote that he had originally feared that "in dealing with social conditions that cry out for correction," she would "sacrifice story for the promulgation of propaganda." He was relieved and enthusiastic to find that she had "achieved a nice balance, providing an intrinsically lively story without dulling the edge of the 'message.'"[69]

One of the most vivid scenes takes place when the family is picking beans in southern Florida, their tent set up among other migrants' shacks along a canal bank. Judy knows that Gloria Rathbone, "the prettiest girl" in her third-grade classroom, is having a birthday party the next week, and she decides to make a flour-sack jumper-style dress for the occasion. She is so proud of her dress, and so excited, because she has never been to a party. On Gloria's birthday, when school has been dismissed, Judy sees the other girls in the class walking with linked arms on the way to the party. Judy calls out, "Wait for me, Gloria! I'm coming to your party, too." The girls ignore her, and Judy runs after them.

> Then Gloria switched around and said haughtily, "What do *you* want? Why are *you* coming with us, I'd like to know?"
>
> "I made . . . my new dress . . . to wear to your birthday p-p-par-ty, Gloria," stammered Judy. "I've never been to a party in all my life—"
>
> "You're not invited!" Gloria stamped her foot on the sidewalk. She wore new patent-leather slippers today. "I don't want you—in your old feed-sack dress! And your dirty bare feet—I suppose you don't even own a pair of shoes. Who'd want a big, overgrown bean-picker at their party? I don't, so there!" . . .
>
> They went skipping off down the street.
>
> Judy stood there. She had to believe it now—Gloria had said it plainly enough. She wasn't invited. You had to be invited, to go to a birthday party. Judy didn't know that before.[70]

The pain of that rejection is palpable. With a minimum of dialogue and scene-setting, Lois effectively delivered a powerful example of social inequality, one that even a grade school child could easily recognize and empathetically sense.

Anne Altshuler, a lifelong student of children's literature, moved several times during her childhood. These challenging transitions may have made her particularly attracted to *Judy's Journey*, her favorite of all of Lois's books. She recalled that she discovered Lois's work at the public library in South Orange, New Jersey, which "had shelves of Lois Lenski books. . . .

Perhaps I liked the fact that the Lenski books were fairly predictable. After reading some, I knew what I was getting. I read only the ones about girls. I remember completely connecting with Judy's sadness at being excluded from the birthday party in *Judy's Journey*."[71]

Not only did Lois precisely shape stories such as this one, but her soft pencil sketches also match the artistry of the narrative. Lippincott's managing editor, Dan Walden, told Lois that he believed "the illustrations, particularly some of the full pages, are among the most charming that you have done." The endpapers, in particular, *are* one of her crowning artistic achievements, although they are nearly equaled in several subsequent regionals, including *Boom Town Boy*, *Cotton in My Sack*, and *Mama Hattie's Girl*.

After *Judy's Journey* was published, the School-Library Department at Lippincott wrote to tell Lois that the Catholic Children's Book Club planned to use it as their October 1947 selection, with an initial order of "between 750 and 800 copies."[72] The following year, Mrs. Hugh Grant Straus, chair of the Children's Book Committee of the Child Study Association of America (CSA), wrote to tell Lois that *Judy's Journey* had been selected for the CSA award as

a book for young people which faces with honesty and courage some of the real problems in today's world. Certainly *Judy's Journey* meets this description exactly and I know you will be as gratified as I am that it was our Committee's unanimous choice. We feel that you have handled with great skill this whole area of the submerged children in our population who are badly in need of such a spokeswoman as you. Here you have done not only a "regional" story but one which has universal implications for all America and all children. You have handled it so well that at no time is it a special pleading but rather a picture with profound and inescapable meaning.[73]

Alice Ring, a young fan from Los Angeles, told Lois something similar: "When I read *Judy's Journey* I had no idea there was such a thing as migrants. I've never read a book with such warmth, truth and experience. Tho I am only ten years old I realize how important it is that these migrants have adequate housing, food and clothes. Thank you for giving such a truthful book to the public. I think books should be truthful because it is lots of fun reading about things that you never even heard of. In this way books give sort of a message." Mildred Powell, a librarian from White Plains, New York, was even more succinct in her appraisal: "I think *Judy's Journey* is my favorite of all your books. I admire it especially for presenting the dignity of the underprivileged in a story that children will love for its own sake."[74]

In a letter for a February 1966 newsletter targeting bookshops, libraries, and schools, Lois responded to the most frequently asked questions from her young readers, "Where do you get all the ideas for your books?" and "Are your books true?"

> There is one answer to both questions. I go to the people in the region, and they give me the story. . . . I don't need to imagine characters—I use the real people I meet. I even make sketches of them, so they will look real, I draw the clothes they wear, the houses they live in, the landscape or the city street, or whatever the background is. I listen to their colorful speech and take it down in my notebook, for in my story I want them to speak as they do in real life. I try as hard as I can to make these people come to life on the printed page, as in the story I tell and the pictures I draw. All the things that happen in my stories have happened to some living real person in the region. So my books are *true*. . . .
>
> These children are flesh and blood. I could not make them up. I have learned to love the people in each region as if they belonged to my own family. In fact, the first thing I have to do in any region is to "establish kinship with strangers." I forget myself as I become one of them. I live their life with them, feel with them the dryness of the drouth, or the wetness of the swamp, endure their hardships and share their joys. I have enjoyed many meals at the kitchen table, the very heart of the family. I have listened to heart-rending confidences. Then and only then am I ready to write their story, to speak for them as they would if they could speak for themselves.
>
> Because I love the people in my regions so much, I hope my readers will learn to love them too, and in knowing them, never forget to offer kindness and understanding to those who are different from themselves.[75]

After Lois received the Newbery Award and gained even wider circulation and fame as an author, she enjoyed being called upon as a keynote speaker to address national conferences of reading teachers or librarians. She used such occasions to reiterate her approach to realism by telling anecdotes about the stories from life that she had chosen or describing some of her more vivid experiences traveling around the country on her story-catching ventures. What she appreciated best of all, however, might be termed "invitational writing," that is, responding to the requests of a particular teacher and classroom of students who contacted her to write about *them* and *their* region.

CHAPTER 7

⅃ENSKI AS
STORYCATCHER

After the success of *Strawberry Girl*, the demands on Lois's time for speaking engagements and a busy publications calendar undoubtedly created additional stress that worsened her persistent health problems. Yet with the evolution of ever more roles for Mr. Small, the recently minted Davy series, and the nearly annual regionals, she could now work more exclusively on her own projects rather than illustrating for others. She was driven as much by a desire to engage her enlarged audience as by her need to produce income. Long before the Internet and Facebook created virtual communities, Lois became a networker extraordinaire. The relationships that she initiated (or accepted) and nurtured with teachers and librarians across the country proved to be advantageous to her future enterprises and even more meaningful to her personally. Lois maintained an astonishingly extensive correspondence with an ever-expanding and mutually supportive group of librarians, teachers, and students. Through them, she developed her own blend of mentoring/promoting/obtaining materials, first for her highly regarded regionals, and later for the Roundabout America series for younger (second- and third-grade) readers. These relationships sometimes led to intensive on-site residencies and pre- and post-visit correspondence, which allowed all those involved in her carefully orchestrated engagements to be transformed by the experiences. The result of such collaborations generated a number of outstanding works—almost more anthropological than fictional, actually— that reflected the author's keen recognition that young readers needed, almost as a sustaining nutritional supplement, stories from real life.

Ultimately, the teachers with whom she collaborated became accomplices and assistants in Lois's storycatching adventures. Their shared work turned into abiding friendships with the author and one another. Lois was probably unfamiliar with sociologist Robert Park at the University of Chicago, who pioneered the concept of "participant observation" in the 1920s and 1930s. He advised his students "to live among the people they were studying" in order to get firsthand experience. Her research for the Regionals and Roundabouts mirrored Park's advice. The on-the-street approach that he advocated presented the researcher with information that would have been otherwise difficult to obtain. His methodology delivered a sense of "vicariously . . . participating, as it were, in their experiences [i.e., the lives of those studied], and getting some appreciation of their outlook and philosophy of life."[1]

Lois's research embraced and embodied both the assumptions and the methodology of Park. She acknowledged that she used WPA guidebooks and other secondary references for background reading before embarking on a new regional exploration.[2] But like Park's students, Lois obtained all her stories from life by corresponding with teachers, librarians, and children throughout the country and ultimately residing for an extended period of time in each region she studied. By investing what Lenski termed "the truth in everyday living"[3] in her own fiction as well as in her illustrations, she extended the concept of inclusivity. In so doing, she simultaneously met teachers' desires to make social studies come alive for their students. She validated the lives and cultures of the many students with whom she worked by depicting the environments of rural and urban working-class youngsters in communities not otherwise explored in contemporary children's literature. Lois's evocative drawings and stories also introduced more privileged children to the difficult circumstances under which many of their peers lived. The courage and fortitude her protagonists displayed in dealing with their many familial responsibilities became real to her readers. And upper-elementary students were particularly receptive to what the regionals offered. Anita Fellman points out that "children's literature specialists, drawing on the work of developmental psychologists, identify the ages between eight and ten as those in which children commonly acquire the ability to put themselves in another's place."[4]

Emma Celeste Thibodaux (or Em' Celeste, as Lois often addressed her) from Covington, Louisiana, was the first of the teacher-collaborators in what became Lois's inner circle. Em' Celeste, whose father was Cajun, initiated the relationship, writing to Lois soon after the publication of *Bayou Suzette*. The two women established a long-distance friendship, with over three decades of correspondence documenting their alliance. Not only did Em' Celeste reveal details of her rural Covington students' threadbare home lives, she shared the children's artwork, writing, and their learning difficulties in the classroom setting. When a package of drawings arrived, Lois responded generously with very specific critiques of, and advice about, ways Em' Celeste could encourage her students' work:

> The pictures are really outstanding! You have some real artists this year, & the stories are excellent for so early in the year—I can hardly believe these new ones are only 3rd graders—what experts they will be after their 2 years with you, with such a good start! I have written the children a letter telling what I think of their work. The *funeral* pictures are superb!!! I am going to mount them & some of Steve's & some of the small ones on my studio walls here— for they are a *real inspiration* to me.[5]

Lois also recognized the difficulties of teaching in a poor school that never compensated its educators adequately for their hard work. Dedicated teachers like Emma Celeste often doubled as social workers. Lois sympathized with the plight of one of her students: "The whole story of little Virginia is such a sad one—it is hard to read. What horrible parents! They talk about parents having *problem children*. I think the reverse is true: So many children have *problem parents*." She added, "I'll never forget what Caroline Zachary [a contemporary authority on children and adolescents] said: 'The unlovely child is the one most in need of love.'" Lois was distressed to learn about the depths of these students' struggles, where "there is so much that needs to be done to help them. I wish more of our smug teachers up here (& church workers) could teach for a year in a school like yours. . . . They'd have their eyes opened to conditions they never dreamed of."[6]

Moved by the drawings and stories of Em' Celeste's young students,

Lois wrote an article, "Out of a Paper Sack," that appeared in *Horn Book* magazine in July 1949. She began by telling about a paper sack parcel "tied loosely with red and white string" that arrived about every six weeks: "I have to open it at once. . . . The paper sack takes me to a different world . . . into the lives of a group of children halfway across the continent—children I have never seen." At this point, Lois had never seen Em' Celeste either, but she commented, "I know her as well as I know them." Em' Celeste had shared Lois's books with the students, and their first letters were simple fan letters, telling the author how much they enjoyed them. The correspondence continued, with Lois and Em' Celeste encouraging the students to write and draw what they "*do.*" Whenever students had something to tell Lois, "they were given the chance to express it—right then while the idea was pressing. They did not have to wait until it was time for the language lesson. . . . They did it . . . while enthusiasm was high, before the idea faded and was forgotten. . . . They wrote freely, spontaneously and naturally, because they loved to write. They had ideas to share with a friend and nothing could stop them." Lois noted that since "art is always a re-creation of vivid moments of living," she cherished the children's forthright willingness to share their important memories and ideas expressed in their drawings. In the article, she also mentioned, "I cannot write of my piney woods children without showing my affection for them and their teacher. They have given me great happiness." She kept the walls of her Greenacres studio filled with "a constant but ever-changing display of their drawings. . . . There is something about the simplicity and directness, the lack of uncertainty and fumbling, the clearness of the idea expressed in children's drawings, that not only satisfies but inspires me anew."[7]

Even before Lois met Emma Celeste in person, she supported all her friend's efforts and struggles. As frugal as she was, Lois more than once offered her the means for a respite, explaining, "I happen to have a good deal of money—more than I need or know what to do with—It's all my own—because I've earned it—I call it 'happy money' because it has come from my books which have made so many children happy. . . . Will you let me say 'Here's Your Road to the Sea' and send you 450 a month for the summer, to make it possible? . . . Do make me happy by saying you'll let me!"[8] Unfortunately, no record exists of Emma Celeste's response. Later in their relationship, Lois visited her in Louisiana, met her students, and visited with them and their families in their humble homes. When Lois began her Roundabout America series for second- and third-grade students, she transformed these experiences into the stories, "Piney Woods Girl" in *We Live in the South* and "Janey Lives over the Locks" in *We Live by the River.*[9]

Em' Celeste reciprocated by introducing Lois to a gifted young man from rural northwestern Missouri, Clyde Robert Bulla. Clyde was a self-taught journalist whom Em' Celeste knew only from their correspondence as would-be authors. After reading one of his articles, she encouraged him to try his hand at writing children's books. She was enthusiastic about his efforts, and she suggested that he send Lois his first story for youngsters. She, too, found the story immediately appealing and forwarded it to an editing friend at Crowell, Elizabeth Riley. Riley accepted the manuscript, published as *The Donkey Cart* (1946) and dedicated to Emma Celeste. Incidentally, the following year Lois dedicated *Judy's Journey* to Emma Celeste as well. Lois provided the drawings for *The Donkey Cart*, one of the last books she illustrated for another author. Clyde had written a very short song, "The Donkey Cart," that appeared facing the first page of text, both of which were adorned with her drawings. Perhaps when Lois was working on the illustration for the song, she realized that she and Clyde might collaborate on *her* future publications by adding songs in which she would be the lyricist and he the composer.

Not long after the publication of *The Donkey Cart*, a whole new set of possibilities opened for the regionals when Lois received letters from thirteen upper-elementary students in the classroom of Minnie Foster, who taught in a three-room rural school in Yarbro, Arkansas, outside of Blytheville. The students had listened to a dramatization of *Strawberry Girl* in a *Books Bring Adventure* radio broadcast from a station in Memphis.[10] Now these youngsters wanted to be part of the regionals series. "'Come and write about us,' they begged. 'We pick cotton, we are part of America, too.'" The students let Lois know how much they loved *Strawberry Girl*. Some had written, "It's the only book we ever read that was about real children." When Lois asked what made them feel that the children were real, they replied without hesitation, "Because they say *hogses*! We say *hogses*. Of course our teacher keeps telling us it should be *hogs*, but when we heard Birdie and Shoestring saying hogses we knew they were real children and not made up."[11]

Lois thanked the students for their letter: "You have told many things about cotton that I want to know, and each of you told me something different from the others, so every letter was worth reading." When she learned from their letters that some of the students were planning to use the money they made to purchase her books, she said, "That is the nicest thing I have heard in a long time. Jo Alice tells about the dresses made from feed sacks. You will read about a girl who got one of these when you read the book I am working on now [*Judy's Journey*]—but oh dear, you will have to wait till the fall of 1947 for that." Then Lois peppered them with more questions to elicit still more descriptive responses:

> How does it feel to pick cotton all day long? What do you think about when you are doing it? How long does cotton picking last— from Sept. to Dec.? I was surprised to hear that the same field had to be picked over three times. . . . Do your fathers own your farms or are they tenants who "share the crops" with the owner? I would like to learn more about both kinds of farmers. Do any Negroes and Negro children pick on your farms? Or do they have farms of their own, and cotton of their own to pick? Do they own their farms, or are they croppers? . . . Most of all, I want to know of any exciting things that might happen to anybody in the cotton field, or in any of the work with the cotton. You know a book has to have a lot of things happen in it, and I want my cotton book to be as exciting as STRAWBERRY GIRL and BAYOU SUZETTE.[12]

Lois had every reason to be exhilarated by these letters, because for the first time, she had what she wanted—"a lead and a contact," a cooperating teacher and her enthusiastic students in Mississippi County, Arkansas, the county that produced more cotton than any other county in the United States. Once she learned that it was "predominantly a white sharecropping community," she knew she "could not go wrong." Lois felt that she was not ready "to write a Negro story." She had not yet had enough contact with African Americans to feel comfortable or competent enough to handle such material, even though she had taken copious notes on "Negro Migrants" when she researched *Judy's Journey*.[13] After a few months of Lois's corresponding with the students, Minnie Foster sent a recording of the students' voices to her at Christmas. By March 1947, Lois traveled to the Arkansas Delta, a region she had never previously visited, to embark on her first residency.[14]

Lois was essentially what might be called a landscape determinist, one who believes that human agency is affected by environment. When she arrived in the delta, she was not emotionally prepared for the unrelenting flatness of the "vast seas of fields vanishing at the horizon," where cotton, not yet planted, would dominate, with "not an inch being spared for blades of grass." This was truly a scene of economic deprivation, with "rows of shabby sharecropper houses . . . dirty children dressed in rags . . . a disheveled woman taking gray-looking clothes off the dragging clothes-line—this was the cotton country. . . . Pain and pity engulfed me altogether. . . . Then I panicked. Why had I come? How could I write a book about this?" The devastation seemed unrelenting, and Lois depicted this initial impression on the endpapers: a lonely sharecropper's small house with trash in the yard, clothes on the line, children pumping water, and the unhitched cotton wagon on the other side of the house. But once she met the students at Yarbro School, her spirits revived. "Children are the best cure for disillusionment and discouragement. Just being with them and getting to know them gave me courage."[15] Lois went to school every day, where she was provided with an unused room to conduct "voluntary and private" interviews with the students. She ate lunch with the youngsters, using every opportunity to listen. Not surprisingly, "the more aggressive children volunteered first." One girl bragged, "I got to tell Miss Lenski a lot of stuff, so she can write that book!" That boast opened the floodgates, and other students could hardly wait to contribute tales of their experiences. "They *all* had to *tell me stuff.*" The interviews revealed much about their hardscrabble lives and made Lois even more determined to tell their stories. "I knew that no home, no matter how poor or wretched it might be, no home where children lived was too terrible for me to enter." The cotton children had won her heart. Instead of concentrating on the overwhelming poverty that had appalled her when she arrived in the delta, she focused on the children's "courage in meeting conditions imposed upon them by forces outside their control." Lois visited with families, ate in their kitchens, and loved being adored by the children. "I felt close to them because I thought they needed me."[16]

Lois realized she could not write about the cotton country without experiencing the height of picking season. She spent the following October there, boarding at the home of cotton farmers. "Cotton schools" closed down during the harvest so that all able-bodied family members, including young children, could pick, and Lois even donned a sunbonnet, was given a sack, and spent one day picking alongside the children. They teased her about her lack of skill. She spent more time sketching. "As an artist, I was thrilled with

Original frontispiece for *Cotton in My Sack*, 1949. Reprinted by permission of the Lois Lenski Covey Foundation and Burrell Covey, copyright by Lois Lenski. Courtesy of the Lois Lenski Papers, Special Collections, Butler Library, Buffalo State College.

the majesty and dignity of the figures at work," the figures bent and turning, "the hands darting swiftly from one boll to another, and always the long line of the sack dragging behind in a rhythmical pattern. . . . Day after day I studied these actions and rhythms, trying to feel and comprehend them, trying to put them down in lines on paper." She found her heroine in a field, "sunburned and dirty, hiding her face under a slat sunbonnet . . . but her face lights up when she smiles. When in repose, it reflects all the sadness of the cotton story." Lois did not even change her name, Joanda.[17]

Lois's notebooks from her Arkansas research include snatches of conversations; notes on cotton yields and technical information about cotton planting and harvesting; brief observations of delta towns; a diagram of a cotton planter; descriptions or recipes for "Arkansas Food" with items such as "navy bean pie," "chitlin dinner," and "poke-sallet"; examples of colorful "Arkansas speech" such as "He was a rich man but he *spent himself pore!*" or "as sorry a crop as ever I saw in my life"; and girls' and boys' names.[18] She drew upon this extraordinary collection of source material to make her book ring as true with the audience from Mississippi County as with those meeting her cotton children for the first time. After her visits, Lois also corresponded frequently with the two teachers at Yarbro to be reassured that everything she wrote felt authentic. As she told Minnie Foster, "The main thing I want to know is whether or not you think the story reflects your region & is honest & sympathetic to it?"[19] Teacher Alice Marie Ross recounted the experience of working with the author in a speech made over two decades later. Ross recalled that Lois wanted to plant some ideas that might be new to her readers, such as "the value of hot lunches . . . the enjoyment of library books . . . the value of saving money," and she wanted to make sure that they would resonate with these students.[20]

While Ross felt that Lois's overall portrayal was both "accurate" and "sympathetic," fifty years later, historian Gail Schmunk Murray viewed the ideas Lois was implanting as impositions of her "middle-class educator's voice." But while didactic elements exist, they are well integrated into the narrative and do not detract from the scars of economic deprivation that Lois introduced to children's literature. More recently, Gary Schmidt agrees that Lois dwelt on the "underside of the American dream"[21] in her illustrated narratives that intersected with the interests and imaginations of her readers.

Lois felt so attached to her cotton children that she could not bear to bid them goodbye on the last day of her sojourn in Mississippi County. She knew that her train north would pass near the school, however, and she "went out on the back outside platform to get one last look. . . . [T]here beside the tracks, I saw them all, the children and their teachers and even the grumpy old janitor—all my cotton children waving good-bye." When she could no longer see them, Lois returned to her seat "and had a good cry,"[22] dedicating *Cotton in My Sack* (1949) to "my beloved Arkansas cotton children." By living among them, she had gained a new and extraordinary sense of affinity for the folks she had studied. Many years later, Lois told an audience, "The highest compliment I was ever paid was in the cotton country, when they said of me, 'Miss Lenski is as common as she can be!'" She explained that the appellation was not used in a derogatory sense; the old Elizabethan meaning of the term "common" meant "'earthy,' 'wholesome' or 'good.' When you share people's joys and sorrows, sympathize with them in their trials and difficulties, love and admire them for their courage and fortitude in the face of adversity, it is a rich experience indeed."[23]

Lois worked to balance both her own sensibilities and those of her publisher as she tried to give an accurate and sensitive portrait of her cotton children and their families. While Lippincott editor Helen Dean Fish was "delighted" with *Cotton in My Sack*, she worried over Lois's "use of the word 'colored people'" on several pages. "Of course, you and I know there is absolutely nothing wrong with your motive or the common sense of using this phrase, but in view of the organized campaign of the 'tolerance' people do you think it would be better to use the word 'Negro' with a capital N?"[24] Lois replied immediately. "I purposely used the expression 'colored people' as the least offensive and most apt to please the 'tolerance' people. In actual experience, in real life out in Arkansas, Negroes are always referred to as 'n——s,' by everybody . . . more often, respectfully and lovingly. However I know that this word cannot be used in print." Lois insisted on keeping the word "colored" as the preferred expression in dialogue, since "no Arkansas white person would ever be so formal as to say 'Negro.'" She was willing, however, to use "Negroes" when she as narrator was speaking, for example, "of a group working in the field."

In the book itself, Lois made her stance on racial issues perfectly clear in a conversation between two women that took place in town on a Saturday at the Goodwill, a store "crowded with many people, Mexicans, Negroes and whites." A sudden rainstorm caused all the lights to go out.

Aunt Lessie looked around on all sides, her round face beautiful in the semi-darkness. "We're all the same color when the lights are out," she said softly.

"Ain't it the truth!" said Maggie Sutton.

"Reckon it don't matter a mite to the Lord what color our skin is," said Mama.[25]

Lois also told Fish about Clyde, "a young musician friend of mine" who "composed a simple tune for my song, 'Cotton in My Sack,' and I wonder if you would consider an innovation—printing this song with its music on one page of the front matter?"[26] *Cotton in My Sack* was the first regional to contain a song, placed opposite the second half-title page. Lois did the hand-lettering of the lyrics; Clyde provided the music. Lois was thrilled that her publisher agreed, telling Clyde, "I was really quite surprised that I got their consent."[27] Because she hoped that, by acting and role-playing, students could experience the characters' lives even more vividly, Lois was also able to get the publisher to include a statement that the song could be "freely used or reprinted by any schools or teachers interested, for the use of their children" in hopes that it "will be an incentive to the making of dramatizations of the story."[28] Lois must have been delighted to receive a copy of "THE COTTON PLAY as acted at a rural school in Arkansas" sometime after the publication of *Cotton in My Sack* as well as photographs of parade floats with *Cotton in My Sack* themes in Osceola and Manila, Arkansas, the following year.[29] The greater community of the rural Arkansas Delta obviously had fully embraced Lois's story of the proud-if-poverty-stricken lives of some of its young inhabitants.

Lois's sensitively wrought story and lovingly rendered pencil drawings made *Cotton in My Sack* immediately appealing. As Hugh Johnson, sales manager at Lippincott, wrote to her in the spring of 1949, "Unless I am completely mistaken, I think that this title will set a new high in sales (with the exception, of course, of STRAWBERRY GIRL)."[30] He was right. The following December, Hugh told Lois, "Incidentally, sales of COTTON IN MY SACK up to 12/8/49 . . . [are already] over 11,000 as compared with total 1948 sales of 9,098 for BOOM TOWN BOY."[31]

But more significantly, the methodology that she created in crafting *Cotton in My Sack* set a new standard for its author, affirming that her innovative approach in working with a specific group of children in a classroom

could yield positive benefits to all involved. Of course, *Cotton in My Sack* remained unique simply because it was the *first* invitational regional "to which children and teacher[s] contributed. Working through this larger group made the book, I felt, so much richer, that the practice has been continued since then to improve the caliber of the books; and also because other worthwhile invitations have come from teachers in other regions."[32]

Cotton in My Sack is also the first of an enduringly successful trio of Lois's regionals. Although the second of these, *Texas Tomboy*, was not an "invitational," she utilized her networking know-how to strategize the initiation of a book about a protagonist who grew up on a ranch, the same ranch near

Original illustration of stampede in *Texas Tomboy* (1950), pages 90 and 91. Reprinted by permission of the Lois Lenski Covey Foundation and Burrell Covey, copyright by Lois Lenski. Courtesy of the Lois Lenski Collection, Western History Collections, University of Oklahoma Libraries, Norman.

Eldorado, Texas, where Lois had double-dipped, doing research for *Cowboy Small* and for *Texas Tomboy* in the spring of 1948. *Texas Tomboy's* Charlie Boy is largely the story of Mary's younger sister, Lelah Belle, whose real-life episodes fit Lois's purposes to a T.

During the month of April Lois soaked up all she could from Mary Coupe; her ranch foreman, Bob Whitley; and the West Texas environment.

Moisture was not one of the elements, however, since her visit occurred during the fourth year of one of the many periodic extreme droughts that affected the entire region. The simple ranch house sat "seven gates from the main road," isolated yet "homey," with the "smell of fried chicken or bacon, percolating coffee, a noisy dog barking, turkeys gobbling at the door, and the sound of wind whistling around the corners, a wind that never died down or stopped to give the mind a moment's peace." The lovely endpapers of *Texas Tomboy* depict the ranch house and the outbuildings in their windswept setting. After Lois learned about the Coupe sisters' childhood during the 1920s, she decided to set *Texas Tomboy* in that decade, explaining, "It was so much richer than life lived by children on Texas ranches today, as most of them live in town by the week to go to school and thus become only week-end visitors to the ranch. They do not participate as fully in every detail of ranch life as children of the previous decade did."[33]

One can sense Lois's confidence and pride in the letter that accompanied the draft sent to Helen Dean Fish in August 1948: "TEXAS TOMBOY has been read in manuscript and candidly criticized by a group of 6th, 7th and 8th graders, who have given it the seal of their approval. It has also been carefully checked by several ranch authorities in Texas, people who furnished most of the material. So I feel that from both of these viewpoints, as well as my own, it is pretty good news."[34] Charlie Boy is the most irascible of Lois's heroines, and consequently, her character growth is the most pronounced. As Hugh Johnson wrote her after the book was in production, "I don't think you have ever created such a convincing one-ness of character and environment as you have done here in the case of Charlie and the Texas ranch country. She is an irritating, spiteful, often unpleasant creature, but all of this springs from her deep feeling for the ranch—and the reader accepts her and loves her for it." Hugh was also pleased with the illustrations, which he claimed were "superb . . . particularly, those for the jacket and title page are absolutely the best you have ever done for the jacket and title page of any of your regional books. That jacket, per se, should attract an army of readers!"[35]

Texas Tomboy contains one of the most thrilling of Lois's double-page spreads. Charlie and her younger brother, Bones, have accompanied their father on a roundup. The scene depicts the harrowing night the children spent in the wagon under a wagon-sheet during a storm when thunder and lightning cause the cattle to stampede. As Lippincott's Daniel Walden commented when he received the pre-publication illustrations, "Even though there is only one double spread, that one is very dramatic, and the great amount of detail in the endpaper and the jacket, and the different and quite charming title page will all compensate for the lack of any other double spreads."[36] The thrilling portrayal in many ways is a mirror image of "The Run," a lithograph Arthur created depicting the opening of the Cherokee Strip in Oklahoma in 1893—an incident that he had witnessed when he was sixteen and made the run with his family. Lois loved this work of Arthur's and may well have used it, perhaps unconsciously, as a model for one of her most outstanding illustrations.[37]

After the book's publication, Lois sent an autographed copy to the "grown-up" Charlie Boy, who signed her name "Mrs. Gordon Bird." Now a ranchwoman herself, she wrote, "We are all reading it including the three cowboys and the foreman's family." She found "The *realism* of the book . . . wonderful." She enjoyed reliving many of the episodes but found the "stampede . . . most vivid to my mind. Every word of it is true, and how little Bones . . . cried, cried, and cried. I got him home safely. . . . I remember how 'big' I felt in being able to meet the critical situation so well."[38] Yes, even Charlie Boy herself recognized that change of heart. Mary and Lelah Belle's mother also wrote Lois, complimenting her illustrations, which their mother thought "so correct that I marvel at so nearly attained perfection . . . in the short period of time in which you were here." And as for the story, "Well, it is just so personal and so true that it is hard to believe. Little did I think while living those strenuous days in West Texas that our story would pass on to the children of the world."[39] Nearly eighteen years later, when Texan Lyndon Johnson was president, his daughter, Lynda Johnson Robb, wrote Lois that, as a collector of children's books, she owned a copy of *Texas Tomboy* and was requesting an autograph. "I enjoyed reading it when I was young, and after taking a college course in Children's Literature, I can appreciate it even more." In a handwritten postscript, Lynda added, "I loved your book so much because I was a tomboy."[40] But one did not need to be a tomboy to feel the same way.

Lois's experiences in acquiring the material for *Prairie School*, the third book in this trio of outstanding regionals, were almost as dramatic as the story itself. As with *Cotton in My Sack*, *Prairie School* was an invitational project. Ruth Carter taught in a one-room school and lived in the attached "teacherage," nine miles from McLaughlin, South Dakota. When she read *Strawberry Girl* to her students, they wanted Lois to feature them in a book that reflected their lives on the Great Plains. In May 1948 their first letters reached Lois, inviting her to visit their school just west of the Missouri River, near the North Dakota state line. Ruth also wrote, and Lois remarked, "from one of her letters, a photograph fell out. It showed a half-dozen sturdy, red-cheeked children bundled up in winter wraps, sitting on the rickety porch steps of Maple Leaf School." Lois was intrigued, never having seen the prairie. While she basked in the Florida sunshine the following February, she began to visualize what it might be like in South Dakota, as Ruth told of the children "having a tough time, but they never complain." With the temperature hovering around twenty-five below, "We are having school in the kitchen of the teacherage, and it is crowded, but they are cheerful about it. We are finding out what an old-fashioned winter was like." Lois was hooked. She felt that she had found a "true American epic."[41]

Ruth and her students kept up their correspondence during the following year, and Lois finally arranged a visit in early May 1950. The survival tales of winter rang all too true because after she arrived in McLaughlin, a late blizzard blew in, and Lois, snowbound in town, was unable to get to Maple Leaf School for another week. She spent her time in her room at the house where she was boarding, using the students' correspondence to begin drafting the first five chapters—the first time that she had actually begun *writing* a book in the region she was researching. Finally able to get out, Lois found that she made the trip "appropriately enough, in a skidding jeep during a blinding snowstorm!" Ruth Carter's students were all descendants of hard-working Russian-German families who had immigrated to the area in the early 1900s. Lois saw Ruth as a pioneer herself, having to spend too much of her time devoted to maintenance of the primitive building. "But her most difficult task was keeping the children over-night in storms when it was too dangerous to let them go home."[42] The majority of *Prairie School* is devoted to documenting the courage and coping skills of the children, teacher, and their families as they deal with the terrifying vicissitudes of winter. As Lois told Helen Dean Fish when she sent the manuscript the following September, "I like the idea of breaking away from the family-pattern, set by the other regionals. . . . While the Wagner family is strongly portrayed as a unit, I feel that this is not so much a family story, as the story of a group of families. It becomes a school story. . . . Hence . . . the title."[43]

Prairie School earned positive reviews,[44] and a well-pleased Lois told Emma Celeste,

> I was thrilled to get your last two letters, and to hear that you have enjoyed "Prairie School" so much. I never would have thought of reading it to First Graders . . . so I'm surprised they could get as much pleasure out of it as you report!!! It all just goes to show that the important thing is *how* a book is used—to make it understandable to them! *You* have the knack of making it meaningful by relating it to their own every day life. . . . I hope you liked the Prairie song in the book: 'Born of the Wind'—I think it is one of Clyde's loveliest tunes & portrays all the spirit of real prairie life.[45]

Em' Celeste evidently had marveled at Lois's ability to create dialogue, because she responded by asking rhetorically,

> How did I make them "talk such real talk"? I stayed around & listened to them & took down *their actual words* in *my notebook*, as I do *wherever I go.* This talk is no more real than in *all my other books*—Joanda in "Cotton in My Sack" has pages & pages of "real talk" that I heard in home & cotton field, & so have all the others from other regions. In this book (P.S.) I had the help of this very fine teacher. Some of the incidents, especially the argument between bro. & sister as to whether to go home on that stormy day or stay at school—[were] reported to me in detail by the teacher—who gave me in her letter *the children's actual words.* She was remarkable—few teachers could give an author that kind of help—in sensing what I would want.[46]

Like Emma Celeste, Ruth had become a real friend.

Lois knew that Helen Dean Fish wanted a "Negro story" in the regional series, but Lois still hesitated, explaining that she "did not know Negro life well enough to try to write of it from the inside." Fish understood and encouraged her, "Take plenty of time for your preparation." And that preparation, Lois confessed, "overlapped the writing of several other books." Several children's fictional titles dealing with African American life appeared before Lois tackled the topic. She never directly addressed the issue of racial justice earlier. But in *Judy's Journey*, Lois demonstrated that her concern for children growing up in poverty certainly included those who happened to be African American, Latino, or Asian American.[47]

As Lois contemplated the challenge of writing about children from a different cultural background, she "suddenly realized" that her winter home in Tarpon Springs could truly become a "working laboratory." She already had some contacts with the black neighbors in her winter community, and she "set about to make more." As in the village of Lafitte where she situated *Bayou Suzette*, Lois began by getting to know the children. She visited the then-segregated Negro school and "made friends with certain teachers who made me welcome in their classrooms." She shared books with the students, read stories to them, and helped them "write about themselves and their own experiences."[48]

One winter in Tarpon Springs, she invited children from ages six to fourteen to attend Saturday painting classes in an empty store building in town that Arthur was using as a studio during the week. The best painter in the class was a granddaughter of her Florida housekeeper, whose name we know only as "Mama Hattie." And Lois claimed, "Mama Hattie was a dear friend from the start, even though she was already ill at fifty." Lois became acquainted with Mama Hattie's daughters, who filled in for their mother when she was not well enough to work, "and in that way I came to know the entire family." When Lois walked Mama Hattie home, she would stay and visit, listening to Mama Hattie's "tales of her own childhood . . . and of things that had happened to her children and grandchildren. While we were talking on her front porch, a living drama was taking place before my eyes. It was like a stage and I had a grandstand seat." In *Mama Hattie's Girl*, Lois described and illustrated the scene from the porch on Hibiscus Street, complete with all of its "living drama. . . . There were quarrels and tempers raging, followed soon by smiles and laughter, contentment and peace. . . . [T]here was always something to laugh about no matter how depressed or discouraged a person might feel. Life was worth living and it was certainly lived with vitality and gusto."[49] In the endpapers, Lois portrayed Hibiscus Street pulsing with life, taking advantage of yet another opportunity to set the stage for her readers.

Lois learned that everyone she met on Hibiscus Street had some family member living "up north." Their stories of success resembled those that generations of Europeans had heard from relatives in the United States.

Original illustration of Lulu Belle washing Mama Hattie's feet in *Mama Hattie's Girl*
(1953), page 164. Reprinted by permission of the Lois Lenski Covey Foundation
and Burrell Covey, copyright by Lois Lenski. Courtesy of the Lois Lenski Collection,
Blackmore Library, Capital University.

The children who had the most difficulties getting along, she discovered,
were those "from rough homes that gave them nothing" or "children with
problems caused by a too-frequent change of environment. Children who
shifted from south to north and back again suffered from insecurity and
all its attendant ills." As with European immigrants who arrived to find
that the streets in America were *not* paved with gold, African Americans
who formed part of the Great Migration also confronted disillusioning
problems up north. Although Mama Hattie never went north, daughter
"Imogene" and granddaughter "Lula Bell" did and wrote to Lois during
their stay in the north and after their return. Lula Bell, heroine of *Mama
Hattie's Girl*, was buffeted about, her life "largely controlled by the economic conditions" of her "unsettled parents." Lois compared her to Judy in
Judy's Journey, a child who "had become 'a part of all that she had met.'" Yet
through Lula Bell's love of and concern for her grandmother, her better
self emerged in the end. Writing *Mama Hattie's Girl* was an important event
in Lois's life, as she recounted years later: "I never enjoyed the preparation
of any book—getting the material, choosing the characters from real life,

making sketches, visiting the locale—more than this one . . . never lost the sense of participating in exciting drama, and I was grateful for the experience."[50]

In a letter to Marie Ram, the Buffalo teacher with whom she developed probably her strongest personal and professional ties, Lois reported that she had obtained her southern material "in my little Florida town; & the 'northern' end of it from my niece who formerly taught in an E. Chicago school with ¾ Negro children." Her other "up north" source was a group of African American children she first met in their Saginaw, Michigan, classroom when she visited "by invitation" while in the city on a speaking trip.[51]

Unlike her other regionals, where Lois tries to make the story as locally specific as possible, with maps to reinforce the location, *Mama Hattie's Girl* never references Tarpon Springs. From the prominence of fishing as both pleasant pastime and supplement to meals and the train journey to New Jersey that takes Imogene and Lula Bell through the Carolinas and Virginia, the reader surmises that this is a southeastern story taking place along a coast. Lois never clarifies her decision *not* to pinpoint the location—unless it might have been to protect her own privacy. In the brief foreword, she simply declared, "In the writing of this book I have had the enthusiastic help of children in three schools, two in the North and one in the South. But no attempt has been made to keep the settings or incidents exactly true to either location. My descriptions of both Northern and Southern life are composites, drawn from many sources, and from the experiences of many people."[52] Also unique for the series are the quotations that preface the book, immediately before the illustrated second half-title page. These directly address the common humanity of the characters about whom she is writing, rather than simply their racial identity:

"As my Angel Mother used to say, some of us are Christian folks and some are vagabonds, but all of us are people."—Roland Hayes— from *Angel Mo and Her Son*, by McKinley Helm.

"There are thieves and murderers and wife-beaters among my people. There are also geniuses and saints and many Negroes who walk down God's pathway. In other words, Negroes are human beings with exactly the same faults and virtues as members of the other races."—from *His Eye Is on the Sparrow*, by Ethel Waters.[53]

Although the circumstances and characters in *Mama Hattie's Girl* are African American and pertain to the experiences of the Great Migration, Lois felt that the theme had universal overtones. The move from less-populated countryside or town to an urban center applied to the many Americans who had migrated for better opportunities since the burgeoning of industrial jobs that resulted from the United States' entry into World War II. "Farewell Song: Song of the Negro Children," filled with a mixture of hope and regret, is particularly poignant:

> Lit-tle girl dressed up so gay, so gay,
> Looks like some-one's goin' a-way, a-way.
> Little girl with suitcase new,
> pretty hat and shin-y shoe.
> Don't you leave us all to-day,
> Turn a-round, come back and stay.

> Why you bid your friends good-by? good-by?
> Why you make your grand-ma cry? ma-cry?
> Pretty sights for you to see,
> But how homesick you will be!
> Don't forget your loving friends,
> They will love you till life ends.

> Jour-ney's hard a-long that road, that road,
> Sor-row's heav-y, grief's a load, a load;
> Nev-er been so far *be*-fore,
> Nev-er left your own front door—
> What will hap-pen none can tell—
> God go with you, fare you well![54]

Clyde Robert Bulla thanked Lois for sending him an inscribed copy. "I took it to bed with me and read it in two evenings. It's a fine story, and I know it will do a lot of good. I think my favorite illustration is the double-page spread of the fish-fry. Maybe I've never mentioned it before, but there's something I've noticed about all your books, and especially in this one. It's your characters' names. They always seem so right that you couldn't imagine them being anything else."[55]

The three double-page spreads—the fish fry, the scene of Lula Bell's confusion on Mechanic Street in New Jersey, and Mama Hattie's house on fire—are among Lois's best, in addition to the endpaper scenes of Hibiscus Street.[56] With superb illustrations, outstanding plot development, character growth, and true-to-life dialogue, Lois anticipated a better reception than *Mama Hattie's Girl* garnered. Writing just a year before the landmark *Brown v. Board of Education* decision that declared separate-but-equal education unconstitutional, Lois's sensitivity to African American southern children, in retrospect, seems simultaneously both prescient and cautious. Were libraries and schools ready to buy a book that featured the difficulties, traumas, and joys that *Mama Hattie's Girl* explores? Did they worry that perhaps the subject would only attract African American readers, and only a few of them?

After the book's publication, Lois dreaded the forthcoming reviews, as she confessed to Marie, "for fear I haven't 'toed the line' to please everybody. All I could do was learn to love the people & try to tell their true story in my own way, which I did." One affirmative reviewer pointed out, "There are the fun and the good times. But mostly . . . days bring one serious problem after another—each one of which is followed through with the author's unerring feeling for these people and the kind of realism so often kept out of juvenile writing. . . . The book has its depressing moments, but is a positive affirmation of a people's tenacity, gaiety, and above all, humanity." Augusta Baker, the most influential African American children's librarian of the era, reviewed *Mama Hattie's Girl* in *Library Journal* in 1953. She concluded: "The book has a place as part of a large regional picture and has been done with sympathy and integrity, without caricature or stereotype." Baker hoped that a library collection would also contain books on other aspects of African American life that were not so grim.[57] Few, however, wrote reviews. Was the subject too "risky" to tackle? A disappointed Lois complained, "There are TOO MANY children's books glorifying our past. How we like to escape into the glamour & nostalgia of the past!! The N.Y. Times Book Review for Book Week didn't have half a dozen books listed on *present every-day life*, and the life & problems that children must face every day. Their whole emphasis is on fairy tales, the dream world (now taking form of space control) and our glorious nostalgic heroic *Past*. In these things we can find *safe refuge* from the present—like ostriches, hide our heads in the sand!!! Needless to say *M H's Girl* was conspicuous by its absence—not even listed!!!"[58]

In 1954, the year of the *Brown* decision, Marie Ram likely had shared her frustrations with trying to help her African American students with reading when every basal reading book (reader) depicted only white children. Lois replied, "Negro children in the south (& in the north & east & west) read the same Readers as white children—about *white* Dick & Jane or *white* Alice & Jerry, book characters not only white but *privileged*! My niece who taught Negro children in E. Chicago used to long for books about 'brown children.' Nobody (as far as I know) has ever even thought of such as thing as a Negro edition (except *you*! This proves the originality of your thinking!) The 'White' Readers do *not touch the Negro children's lives*, hence their slowness to learn to read. If they could have Readers about brown children, I'm sure they'd read quicker and better." Sixty years later in March 2014, renowned African American children's author Walter Dean Myers found that conditions had not markedly improved. In an essay written for the *New York Times*, he quoted the statistic gathered by the Cooperative Children's Book Center at the University of Wisconsin that "of 3,200 children's books published in 2013, just 93 were about black people." The gist of his message, long after the publication of *Mama Hattie's Girl*, deals with the same problem facing young readers of color—and their parents, teachers, and school librarians—that Marie Ram had expressed to Lois, and to which Lois responded:

> Books transmit values. They explore our common humanity. What is the message when some children are not represented in those books? Where are the future white personnel managers going to get their ideas of people of color? Where are the future white loan officers and future white politicians going to get their knowledge of people of color? Where are black children going to get a sense of who they are and what they can be? . . .
>
> Black history is usually depicted as folklore about slavery, and then a fast forward to the civil rights movement. Then I'm told that black children, and boys in particular, don't read. Small wonder.
>
> There is work to be done.[59]

Lois suffered another more personal disappointment: Mama Hattie, whom she "loved very deeply," never lived to see the book published.[60] Although regretting that she missed the opportunity of honoring Mama

Hattie with her own autographed copy, Lois paid tribute to her in 1956. In a talk entitled "Otherness," delivered at a social studies conference at State Teachers College in Indiana, Pennsylvania, she addressed the need to recognize and learn to deal with people from different social and/or economic backgrounds and to look for shared commonalities. She was no intellectual snob and cited Mama Hattie to make her argument:

> For three years until she died, I had a fine relationship with Mama Hattie, a character in one of my Regional books. Although I had a college education and she went only to the third grade, although I am white and she is black, although I have much and she had little . . . we found that we had much in common, as we compared our respective ways of life and the problems of living. She used to say: "I never went to school, but I've got mother-wit to bring up my children." She had an instinctive wisdom that I held in high regard, and her passing left an emptiness in my life.[61]

Lois's no-nonsense appearance and demeanor also made her easily accessible, as these positive attributes and real-life stories created audiences across the country. She may have been surprised to find how quickly a dedicated teacher and a classroom of children, eager to embark on a literary adventure helping an author, could persuade her to return to the Midwest for another regional so soon after *Prairie School.* In 1951 a Cedar Rapids, Iowa, classroom contacted her about developing a corn story, but these urban students knew little about growing corn. Still, word quickly "got around" that she needed youngsters with firsthand experience, and she received letters from all over the state. She excitedly wrote Emma Celeste, "Did I tell you that the rural CORN teacher who started this idea of wanting me to do a CORN story wrote to a women's radio commentator, who has a program called Kitchen Klatter & told her about it, & the radio woman in Iowa is talking about it on her program & I'm getting letters from housewives who live as corn farmers?"[62]

Most of those who wrote, however, sent her secondary literature. They failed to understand that she really was looking for compelling evidence that the "child's every-day life in his own family, *as lived today* . . . was important enough to become the contents of a book."[63] On the other hand, those who wrote offered insights that Lois might not have gleaned elsewhere,

Ruth Carter, Lois Lenski, and Marie Ram relaxing during research for *Corn-Farm Boy*, 1954. Courtesy of Illinois State University's Special Collections, Milner Library.

since they were "interpreting the woman's point of view."[64] Enter Celeste Frank, who taught children from seven to fourteen in a one-room school in the northwest Iowa community of Remsen. She knew exactly what Lois wanted and felt confident that her students could provide it. As in Lois's other experiences with classroom informants, Celeste and her students carried on a lively correspondence before Lois's residency there during the summer of 1953 "at the height of corn-growing season." Lois worked out all the details of her itinerary well in advance so that one can almost hear her breathing a sigh of relief, as she happily confided to Em' Celeste: "Laird & Marion & Paul will be here to take care of my husband in my absence & cook for him. That's why I am free to really be 'on the loose' again & do what I please. . . . If my health picks up & I don't get too tired, I'll really have quite a jaunt & lots of fun."[65] According to Ruth Wagner, an Iowa educational journalist who documented the summer venture, Lois pointed out that the Iowa book would cover ground quite different from *Prairie School*. After all, "corn is a basic food, the corn belt is spread over seven states, and the growing of it is a dramatic adventure which lends itself to a 'good story.' 'The children are really writing this book for me,' she told the publishers, 'so I want to strike while the iron is hot. In contrast to the South Dakota blizzard, this will be a *hot summer* story.'"[66]

For the first time, Lois was able to connect two of the teachers in her enlarging inner circle. Ruth Carter and Marie Ram arrived in South Dakota to get acquainted with Celeste and participate in the storycatching process. Lois rode on trucks and tractors and reveled in walking "between the dark rows of tall hybrid corn then bursting into tassel" as she "listened to a girl de-tasseler tell of her work." But she found most "invaluable" to the research process the help of two eleven-year-old boys, Noel Leinen from near Remsen and Ronald Dougal who lived at Dunlap. "From them I learned how a corn-farm boy thinks and feels as well as what he does outwardly. They shared their love of machinery and the hazards and dangers of farm life." Ronald also impressed Lois with "his deep love of birds and animals."[67] *Corn-Farm Boy* radiated with the boys' enthusiasm and energy. In the foreword, she underscores the larger purpose and ultimate value of her endeavor: "It is my firm belief that the happenings of daily life, episodic as they may appear, form the only sound basis for plotting an honest story—a story of vital family relationships and the give-and-take of daily life in a chosen setting."[68]

Just as Emma Celeste enticed Lois with tales of her students' adventures as well as with their own stories and artwork, and Ruth Carter provided verbatim testimony from her students, Celeste Frank became a collaborator in the creation of *Corn-Farm Boy*. Lois did not have the opportunity to visit the stockyards in Sioux City while she was in Iowa, and she needed eyewitness details for the chapter "Market Day." Although Sioux City was only thirty-five miles away, Celeste had never gone to the stockyards, so Lois sent her on a mission to be "not only eyes and ears for me but *nose* as well. . . . She wrote afterwards that being my proxy . . . to get all the impressions that an author and illustrator might need, was an exhilarating experience."[69] Back in Harwinton writing the book the following fall, Lois told Marie Ram:

> I'm deep in the heart of Iowa these days. I've planted & cultivated my corn and have been pulling a big crop of cockleburs lately. Looking forward to shelling my last year's corn, a trip to the stockyards to sell my hogs, and then corn-picking before the snow flies! I had accumulated so much material, and over the two winters that the children were writing to me, I was absorbing more than I realized. After going over my materials, sorting & reviewing them,

Original illustration for *Corn-Farm Boy* (1954), page 49. Courtesy of the Cedar Rapids Public Library, Cedar Rapids, Iowa.

I just plunged right in on Chapter I. To my amazement, the story began "writing itself"—my family took charge and things began happening, sometimes so fast that my pen could hardly keep up. I found myself jotting down only key words of sentences without punctuation or capitals or anything—just to get the ideas down quickly. It's really *fun* to write when the story moves like this. Of course, I run up against snags now & then—points I'm not sure about & will have to check later, but I just leave a blank space & gallop merrily on![70]

Lois may not have seen the hogs transported to market in Sioux City, but her joy in writing that story and the other episodes in *Corn-Farm Boy* makes it sound as though she was in "hog heaven." So was Celeste Frank, when she received her own copy of the book after its publication. "As I read, I am with Noel continually. You have surely captured his personality. . . . What a lovable character you have made of Dick [the protagonist, based on Lois's young informants, Noel and Ronald]. We helped in giving you a Noel but you've breathed a soul into him—beautiful character. That is the part that impresses me most."[71]

Publication day created a sensation for Lois's inner circle beyond the Remsen community. Ruth Carter and Marie Ram from Buffalo had visited Iowa to participate in the research process; now Lois was lassoing in Minnie Foster and Alice Ross from Yarbro to make them feel that they were all actively experiencing the warmth of mutuality and support. Celeste Frank received a telegram from "Arkansas Cotton Children," congratulating her and explaining that students in Osceola, Arkansas, would be celebrating publication day with a "corn-boy party" of their own and would send pictures and stories to document their interregional solidarity.[72] Several days earlier, Lois had also mentioned the occasion to Marie Ram: "Tomorrow is the Big Day at Remsen! I asked Celeste to try & get the program recorded on a tape-recorder (So I can have records made.) It's her big day—hope you have sent her a telegram to reach there tomorrow. My 'cotton children' here [in Luxora, Arkansas, where Lois was researching yet another regional] are sending one."[73]

The Iowans clearly loved Lois's attention. The Iowa children had expected the famous author to be "of a different social standing, but the person who stepped from the plane was in their own words, 'a good friend—just like one of us.'"[74] Lois loved feeling that kinship with those she was researching. She was also discovering the intense pleasure of being in her element—an element that she had engineered herself—by responding so fervently and passionately to the invitation to share children's lives in different parts of the United States. She was relishing every aspect of storycatching—observing, listening, eating at farmhouses with hard-working families—becoming in every way the "participant observer" described by Robert Park. But she had moved beyond that model as she began to link her teacher-informants into a network to nourish her research and writing and to encourage them to establish ties with one another. Toward the end of her article on Lois's research, Ruth Wagner mentioned that "Miss Lenski has two pet dreams—for children in the various regions of our country to correspond with each other and to share adventures of their everyday lives; and for regional teachers to be exchanged in much the same manner as we exchange teachers with foreign lands."[75] Lois beams from the photographs taken of her in Iowa; at last, she was achieving at least part of that dream.

Lois had not shied away from presenting the financial difficulties in farm life. At the conclusion of *Corn-Farm Boy*, Dad and Uncle Henry (the brother-in-law who actually owned the farm) "were friends again, and were making big plans for next year's crops. . . . They talked about contouring and decided it had been worthwhile. Dad did not mention moving away and Uncle Henry seemed satisfied. Dick felt relieved that the farm lease would be renewed. After all, the farm was home."[76] The last item glued in the *Corn-Farm Boy* scrapbook tells the rest of the story. It contains Ray Leinen's notice of a public "closing out" sale on January 27, 1955, with a small article from the *Remsen Bell-Enterprise* newspaper dated the same day:

> The Ray Leinens are having their farm public sale south of Remsen today and I hope this small caliber blizzard does not prove costly to them.
>
> The Leinen place was the main setting for Lois Lenski's new book, "Corn-Farm Boy," and all the Leinens, particularly young Noel, were drawn into the story, with illustrations of the farmstead and caricatures of Noel.
>
> But there's one singularity. Mrs. Lenski told repeatedly about certain difficult situations anent the Leinen farm operations and of their "threats" to leave the farm, come next spring. And now they're doing just that.[77]

Nearly sixty years later, Noel Leinen confirmed that his family left the farm to move to Sibley, Iowa, where Ray Leinen worked with implements, instead of continuing to farm in a new location. Noel retains vivid memories of Lois's many visits to the farm near Remsen. She was willing to try everything, getting on the machinery, taking a ride on the tractor, and sharing meals with the Leinens. "She was such a down-home person," he recalled, "so easy to speak with, so easy to be with. She had her meals with us. Of course, she was always wanting more in her letters." When asked how his family members felt about her selecting their farm to be depicted in the endpapers of the book and in other narrative details, he laughingly replied that they felt "pretty special. . . . We thought we were 'hot stuff!'"[78]

CHAPTER 8

CATCHING MORE STORIES

L ois's storycatching benefitted teachers, students, and parents while also honoring the chosen community. The process yielded a unique series of books and engendered warm and evolving relationships, such as the friendship that Lois developed with Marie Ram. Like Emma Celeste, Marie was an early-elementary schoolteacher. Lois's decision to pursue the Roundabout America series for less mature readers (seven to nine years old) very likely grew out of her close association with these two teacher/protégée friends. Lippincott's sales manager, Hugh Johnson, must have discussed the proposed series earlier than his letter of November 21, 1950, when he thanked Lois for giving "us another crack at the 'Roundabout America' series." He also asked her for "a dummy and a manuscript and enough specification suggestions to make it possible for us to thrash out some estimates so that we can report to you, on the basis of those estimates, what kind of books we can give you and at what list price." The following year, he wrote Lois that "all the educational salesmen were *very* enthusiastic" about the new series, clearly conceived for the classroom market. The books were to be developed under the educational department at Lippincott, responsible for the promotion and sale of the textbook edition of the first two books.[1] *Peanuts for Billy Ben* and *We Live in the South* were published the following year. One of Emma Celeste's students became "Piney Woods

Girl" in the collection of four stories that made up *We Live in the South; Peanuts for Billy Ben* was a short chapter book.[2]

Marie Ram also initiated her relationship with Lois through correspondence. Although Marie had been teaching elementary school for many years, she felt unsure of her new position. She had been assigned to teach "primer" to pre-literate youngsters in Buffalo, New York's Annex 61 School, built to serve a temporary housing project for World War II veterans and their families from all over the United States. During the fall of 1949, she was looking for "attractive seasonal literature" for her students. Through the Work with Schools department at the Buffalo–Erie County Library, Marie was introduced to Lois's picture book *Now It's Fall*. After witnessing her students' positive response, Marie was impressed with Lois's "deep understanding of small children"[3] and enthusiastically wrote the author, "They loved your verse."[4] In her initial letter, Marie described her unusual classroom setting. "Our school is a lovely wooden bungalow situated on a temporary housing project where home means a crowded, drab barrack like structure built on a filled in stone quarry, a former city 'dumps,' where children are starved for beauty, space and normal living conditions."[5]

The description of the school and the demographic mixture of her students immediately intrigued Lois, and the two began an active correspondence. The following summer Marie enrolled in a graduate seminar in elementary education, "Minority Groups in American Culture," at the State Teachers College at Buffalo (now Buffalo State College). There her professor, longtime educator Hertha S. Ganey, introduced her to Lois's regionals. Marie immediately saw the parallels with her own pupils' diverse ways of life that she determined were "unique and different," and she decided to write a paper on Lois's regional books "as a human relations factor in interpreting minorities to American youth." In response to her questions, Lois related that the simple tools of her approach—sketchbook, notebook, and pencil—together comprised her entire "technique." Due to her "atrocious memory," Lois felt compelled to jot things down. "I encourage people to tell me stories of their experiences . . . and use them as the basis of incidents" for future books. She advised Marie to do the same with her young students. "If you start young children dictating their experiences to you as stories, they soon become expert at 'story-telling,' & improve as they continue. Plenty of opportunity to do it is all the 'technique' they need."[6] In responding to Lois's suggestion, Marie created what she called "experience charts," using the students' own words. "I wanted each child to identify with the chart and with the reading. . . . After the charts became old, instead of throwing them out . . . I would put a date at the top and a 'Dear Miss Lenski,' and then a signature: 'with love, First Primer.' And then we'd roll them up on broomsticks and send them to Lois."[7]

The two women's interests intersected beautifully. Marie's initial paper grew into her 1952 master's thesis, "The Regional Stories of Lois Lenski." That academic success helped her reach for another, and Marie wrote her 1958 doctoral dissertation in education, "An Analysis of the Lois Lenski Literature from a Sociological Point of View."[8] Meanwhile, in the classroom, Marie's students kept telling their own stories. And Lois prodded Marie for more details of her students and their lives in the project. Lois was thinking of using these stories for her own new venture—stories of real urban children: "If you can gather any first-hand 'housing project' material for me, I may be able to use it later; as I'm hoping to use city life in both a Roundabout & a Regional now in planning stage. I don't need facts so much as 'human interest stories'—Those dictated stories of your project children—if elaborated & continued—would be perfect—giving a child's point of view on it."[9] The collaboration grew exactly as Lois had envisioned.

I'm intrigued by your preliminary suggestions for "focal points of our *project story*." They are all so GOOD—and I long to hear more about each. Doubtless, the children will be able to tell you plenty as soon as school opens—"The Store Truck" is wonderful! "Made from old school bus!" Fine! "4¢ merry-go-round traveling kind"— this sounds so "story-booky," it's just too good to be true & would fit perfectly into a Roundabout book. Also "The dumps & all the treasures there"—what bliss! As for "the clinic"—I suppose that's the place you go to be bandaged when you've fallen down & got a bad cut? Not so pleasant, perhaps, but life in a "project" has its ups & downs. Even Allen & pumpkins sound marvelous enough for a story! So you see—of little human incidents like these, are stories built, stories which will later come alive for young readers. *Get* the children (or I should say: *Let* the children talk of these things), and jot down what they say. They'll make each focal point a human adventure; & each will tell what happened to ME there. And that's just what I want to show.[10]

Project Boy began to emerge when Marie's room-mother, Lou Larson—quite conveniently, also the mother of Allen (mentioned above)—was drawn into the group. Lou became a third partner, taking photographs, writing summaries, diagramming the family's apartment, drawing pictures in pencil and crayon on Big Chief tablet paper of features in sufficient detail, which Lois could use as models for her own illustrations. Lou's participation was exceptional, since she was not an educated professional but one of the "folk" herself. Lois was especially pleased with her drawings: "They are remarkably good, especially the perfection of details. I think I would be able to reconstruct them all right from these drawings."[11] The materials mailed from Buffalo proved so helpful that Lois only spent one intense weekend in the spring of 1953 as Marie's houseguest, visiting all the places provided by Marie, her students, and Lou.[12] When Lois turned in the final version of the manuscript, she complained that she did not get exactly what she wanted in the book. "At the last, I had to do a drastic job of cutting. . . . The manuscript ran to 70 typed pages, where it should have been only about 50 or 55. So I had to leave out 4 or 5 of the between-chapter verses, omit 5 or 6 illustrations & cut some long paragraphs of text. . . . How I hate doing this! It always mutilates a story terribly, but the extra 16 pages would have made an increase in retail price necessary which pubrs. didn't want; they want to keep all books in Roundabout series at same price, 2.00. And it was my fault for making the story too long in the first place."[13] The substance of *Project Boy* (1953) was not diminished when it became the third in the Roundabout America series.[14] After the book's publication, Lou wrote, "The author has captured the feelings one has when living in a project; the frustrations, the hopes of a brighter future and the will to take nothing and make something of it. . . . The drawings make me re-live the old project, and especially our old apartment. . . . 'Project Boy' is a book worth reading and remembering both by children and adults."[15] Both Marie and Lou were probably deeply gratified that, in a note on the brief foreword page, Lois thanked "Mrs. Allen H. Larson, project mother, and Mrs. Marie L. Ram, project teacher at Annex 61 School, Buffalo, N. Y., for their generous help in the writing of this book."

A few years later, Lois began distributing her manuscripts and illustrations to various university libraries interested in children's literature. As a direct result of their association with Lois, Marie and Hertha Ganey encouraged her to consider making the Edward H. Butler Library at Buffalo State

one of the recipients. When Lois visited Buffalo on May 24, 1957 (declared "Lois Lenski Day"), to present her gift to the college, she once again stayed with Marie and her husband. As Marie recalled, "At this same time while she was in Buffalo, she did her research for another Roundabout, *High-Rise Secret*."[16] Coincidentally, Lou Larson once again served as the principal informant, because she and her family were among the many residents who moved from the temporary project for veterans into the Dante Housing Project after its construction.

Project Boy and *High-Rise Secret* are the only two of Lois's Roundabouts that take place in the same urban location. Lou Larson and Marie Ram must have presented a convincingly thorough case, with enough specific incidents and episodes to lure Lois back to Buffalo. Although Allen Larson is not the protagonist of *High-Rise Secret* (1966), Lou's letters and newspaper clippings suggest her enthusiasm for contrasting both the promise and ultimate failure that the newly constructed twelve-story project offered its residents. Like many well-meaning but socially disruptive urban redevelopment housing efforts of the 1950s, the Dante Project was located in

The merry-go-round truck visits the projects in this original illustration for *Project Boy* (1954), pages 16 and 17. Reprinted by permission of the Lois Lenski Covey Foundation and Burrell Covey, copyright by Lois Lenski. Courtesy of the Lois Lenski Papers, Special Collections, Butler Library, Buffalo State College.

an isolated industrial setting lacking sufficient recreational facilities and accessibility. Bound on one side by "a high-level bridge for the New York Thruway, teeming with traffic, on another, railroad tracks with boxcars and coal cars, a dead-end canal, and beyond, Lake Erie with its freighters and river boats," living at Dante proved daunting to those who had to negotiate such challenging circumstances and profound isolation.[17]

Lois began to consider a book about a high-rise project long before she actively engaged in the research for *High-Rise Secret*. Evidently, Marie had written about the construction of the Dante Project (which became the Porter Project in the book), and Lois responded skeptically, having read about a similar project recently dedicated in the New York City area. As urban planners approved the construction of high-rise public housing in the nation's larger cities, she was prescient in her skepticism. "All this new 'public housing' is built on the same plan as Dante, and it worries me. I wonder if we are just exchanging an old form of slums for a new form. There's something wrong with the new ones when mothers don't like to live there with their children, and I can see many disadvantages to skyscraper life. In many ways, the old 3 or 4 flight walk-ups (which I'm describing in *We Live in the City*) were better. But who can hold the old slums up as models?"[18]

Lois's ideas about urban housing projects were also shaped by Harriet Arnow's strong and memorable 1954 novel, *The Dollmaker*. The narrative focuses on an Appalachian family living in hastily and poorly constructed housing for World War II industrial workers in the Detroit area. Lois told Emma Celeste, "Marie Ram has just returned my copy of '*The Dollmaker*,' by Harriet Arnow, so I am re-mailing it on to you. . . . She's doing for adults the same kind of honest realism I am doing for children; only for adults, you can really call 'a spade' 'a spade' & can speak *more plainly* than for children. I'm sure she really *lived* every minute of this book herself."[19] After the publication of *High-Rise Secret* in 1966, one reviewer agreed with Lois's assessment. "Without being brutal, Miss Lenski writes of the problems of the children, parents, and janitors confined in treeless areas where 10 automatic washers serve 600 families, police protection is inadequate, and everyone hears family squabbles through thin walls. Although the children are the most important characters, the adults are well defined, showing a good cross section of the types of people that make up this world of cliff dwellers."[20]

At this point in her evolving regional series, only *Mama Hattie's Girl* dealt with urban life, when Lois contrasted Lula Bell's positive and negative experiences up north with similar polar opposites back south. Lois had not yet written a completely urban regional when the secretary in Dina Gianni's Lois Lenski Book Club at Chinatown's Commodore Stockton Elementary School invited her to come to San Francisco. Lois was so impressed with the letter she received in December 1952 that she quoted from it in the *San Francisco Boy* foreword:

We have been reading the Roundabout America books you have written, which tell how the children live, work and play in other parts of our country. We are Chinese children and live in Chinatown. We eat our rice and other foods with chopsticks. . . . We wear our Chinese costumes on certain days. . . . Some of the children work after school. Some children work in the jeans factory, cutting threads off jeans and folding them. Others wash glasses and dishes in their parents' restaurants. Some children work in the laundry. They deliver, count and fold towels, put paper and cardboard in shirts and wrap bundles. . . . We go to Chinese school after American school and learn how to read, write and spell in Chinese.

Would you like to know more about us? Then come and visit us. . . . We think it would be a good idea for you to write a book about us.[21]

All the book club members signed the letter, which was soon followed by the arrival of individual letters. As Lois recalled, "I decided at once that they were the best letter-writers in any of the schools in the United States. And then came the drawings and paintings, these made mostly by four Chinese boys. They depicted the streets, houses, interiors, as well as people, and were drawn and painted with genuine artistic skill, which quite overwhelmed me, as I had seen nothing like it before . . . and all the loving letters assumed that, of course, I was coming!"[22]

Lois was busily working on *Corn-Farm Boy* at the time but was tantalized by the students' talents and their equally persuasive powers. As she wrote Helen Dean Fish, "At first I thought of the possibility of doing a Roundabout, but more and more I believe the setting and drama are rich enough to be worth a Regional. It would kill several birds with one stone: It would be a corking *city* story (of one of the most colorful and fascinating cities of the U.S.) and also a California story, both of which have been repeatedly asked for." Then Lois confessed, "I had not intended to use any foreign-background people in this series, leaving that to other authors who have been specializing in it."[23] But the students' letters wore down her resistance. "They are begging me to come out there and one Chinese family invites me to come and live with them. It is a unique opportunity to get at the inside of present-day Chinese life in a great city." Who could say no? Lois added, "I feel that my best books come when the region itself is enthusiastic and urges me to do it, rather than when I arbitrarily choose a region and try to stir up an interest which may not be there."[24]

Helen Dean Fish did not live to see the fruits of Lois's San Francisco adventures. She died early in 1953,[25] soon after this correspondence. Lois's letter to Em' Celeste recognized the critical role that her longtime editor played in developing her career as an author. Fish had worked hard to shape her protégée's writing skills, and Lois typically resisted the sound and well-considered advice or only grudgingly accepted it. Perhaps in response to the years of contentious push-and-pull between editor and author, Lois revealed her strong negative feelings about the relationship:

> Another shock—My editor (Lippincott's)—Helen D. Fish (whom I never liked much) died of a heart attack on Feb. 5—had not been ill at all, so it was quite unexpected & a loss to the company— guess she was very capable. She's been my editor since my very first book—she accepted it in 1927—So it's hard to believe she's actually gone. They're in an upset state till they get a new person to replace her. And I've just been told who it will be—Eunice Blake, my Oxford editor! It means re-shuffling of editors for me—Well, it's good that I know her, & she knows me & believes in my work— So I'll have to do my re-adjusting at the Oxford Press, instead of at Lippincott's–[I thot [sic] she had a pretty good thing of it at Oxford & was surprised to hear she would change. But of course one never knows the inside.][26]

Lois and her Chinatown students corresponded throughout that school year and the next. As some students moved up a grade, "new and equally enthusiastic children had taken their place and the Lois Lenski Book Club was still flourishing" when Lois finally made the trip to San Francisco in June 1954. For *Corn-Farm Boy*, she had amassed many stories but spent time searching for an underlying and unifying plot. In contrast, she found the plot for *San Francisco Boy* before she even traveled west. She later acknowledged that it "was given me by one of the boys, James Sue, through his letters in advance of my coming and through later conversation, in which he elaborated and gave more concrete details."[27] Teacher Dina Gianni told Lois, "I have a wonderful story from James and will continue to take down his stories. He comes to me when he is in the mood for writing or painting. The other day while he was painting & everyone was so quiet—he called out—'Mrs. Gianni—you know when I grow up, I'm going to be an author and illustrator.' We all were quite amused and had a good laugh. His remark was so spontaneous."[28]

Before his family moved to Chinatown where his father cooked in one of the restaurants, James had lived across San Francisco Bay in Alameda.

Commodore Perry School student James Sue's original watercolor depiction of his former Alameda home, San Francisco, California (ca. 1953). Courtesy of Illinois State University's Special Collections, Milner Library.

There the large Sue family lived in a house with a yard, garden, fishpond, trees to climb, and kind neighbors, all of which he missed terribly in the crowded three-room apartment and congested streets and neighborhood of Chinatown. As Lois said, "He was bitterly homesick. . . . I know he greatly enjoyed writing and dictating his Alameda experiences, for they came alive in his letters to me. He was a sensitive boy of deep feelings and this was shown in his fine paintings as well. Long before I decided to actually go to San Francisco, I felt that James' homesickness and his gradual adjustment to city life was a worthy theme for this book." It is almost uncanny to see how closely Lois followed the "script" that James had described in words and pictures when she created the main male character, Felix, the "San Francisco Boy" himself. In one of his dictated letters, James wrote:

> I want to tell you all about my life when I lived in Alameda. The picture shows our backyard when we lived in Alameda. We lived

there until I was seven years old. . . . In the picture my brothers Joseph, Jason, Jackie, Leon, and I were taking care of our garden. We had a lot of tomato plants in our garden. We had corn and watermelons growing too. We grew all kinds of vegetables. We had a pear tree, a plum tree and lots of pretty plants and flowers growing in the yard. We had a good sized fish pool with four gold fish and a black fish. Bamboo was growing in our yard too. We used bamboo for fishing poles. In the front of our house we had a cherry tree. In the spring the blossoms looked so pretty. Near our garage there were lots of beautiful bright red roses and golden poppies. I loved our house in the country. I wish I was there now.

My father changed jobs and we moved to San Francisco. We did not want to come. My mother didn't want to come, either. She was going to miss canning her own fruit. She used to can her own pears, cherries, and plums. . . . In Alameda there were many Chinese, Colored, and American people living near us.[29]

Dina's brother drove Lois and Dina to see and photograph James's Alameda home and talked with his former neighbors, an older African American couple "who said kind things about the Sue boys."[30] In *San Francisco Boy*, Lois calls this couple "Grandpa and Grandma Reed," whose grandson, Timmy, often visited and played with Felix and his brothers. She never identified any of them as black, only once mentioning Timmy's "dark face."[31] Lois described the Alameda home very much as James's did: "Felix showed Mei Gwen just where the tomato plants grew, and the corn and the watermelons. He pointed out the cherry and pear trees, and the bamboo stalks for fishing poles. He showed her the fishpool, which was half full of water and still had two gold fish and one black fish in it. He showed her where he had buried his turtle."[32]

Lois also garnered details from other boys' stories in creating her protagonist, Felix. Dina wrote enthusiastically after the book's publication: "I could see parts of James Sue's stories thru out and I'm so happy you could use so much of his dictated letters, the colored folks, the description of Alameda, the trees. . . . How you could possibly think of putting so much of the children's contributions in the story is a miracle and I'll never know how you did it. . . . With our hero Felix, I could see the experiences of James, Marshall, Homer, Sherman, Russell, Frank, Kendall, and Roger."

Although James actually had a baby sister, in *San Francisco Boy* Lois created Felix's slightly younger sister, Mei Gwen, as a composite character based on many of the stories related by the book club's girls. Dina was ecstatic. "With our heroine Mei Gwen I could see all my little girls who had babies [their younger siblings] to take care of and shopping chores to do with the brown shopping bags." Dina listed several of these students with their roles in the book: "Alberta (Jeans Factory) . . . Ellen Lee—noodles & laundry . . . Patricia Lee—Fisherman's Wharf & her Italian friends. . . . All the combined experiences for the heroine and hero made their lives very full and exciting. The composite characters are wonderful! All this made me realize you meant what you said in the forward [*sic*] when you stated without their help it couldn't have been written."[33]

San Francisco Boy is a beautifully illustrated and well-written regional. The endpapers depict a highly stylized schematic of the city, bustling with people of all walks of life, only some of whom are Chinese. The reader immediately grasps the cultural and topographical diversity: a perfect introduction and reference point for the narrative that follows. More importantly, as with so many of the "invitational" books Lois wrote, the project transformed all who worked to make it a reality. Leliah Cain, the librarian at Commodore Stockton Elementary, tape-recorded Lois's meeting with the Lois Lenski Book Club when she first arrived in San Francisco. Lois was overwhelmed by the students' enthusiasm, telling Marie, "The experience proved so novel that everybody had a question to ask, even repeating questions that had been asked before. And I was nearly smothered by juvenile Chinese humanity!"[34] Leliah had written to the author the previous spring to tell her the principal had mentioned that the correspondence between Lois and the book club constituted

"the most worthwhile project ever undertaken in our school," and I certainly agree with her. The real value of the entire project is the enthusiastic interest of the children. . . . These children are anxiously waiting for your new books. The books "belong" to them in a far more personal way than by mere purchased ownership, because—after all, don't they "know" the author?—hasn't she written to them personally and over and above all, hasn't the author personally autographed their books? . . . You and Mrs. Gianni have given these children something that can never be taken away from them. Reading enjoyable books—well written, and attractively illustrated—is always a pleasure, but reading books by someone you "know" has far greater meaning and interest. I am sure that when these children have grown and have children of their own in school one of their outstanding memories of school will be their association with the Lois Lenski Club and the author Lois Lenski![35]

On September 21, 1955, the Children's Reading Room in the main branch of the San Francisco Public Library at the Civic Center displayed the original illustrations from *San Francisco Boy*, while hosting a Publication Day reception in the Commissioner's Room. Lois excitedly told Emma Celeste, "All the Big Shots are to be there—the Supt. of S. F. Schools, the Asst. Supt., Supervisors, Principals, Head of School Libraries, all kinds of librarians, school & public, not to mention the Chinese children members of the Lois Lenski Book Club, who contributed to the book." The Chinese PTA provided the refreshments, and the students were taken to the library on school buses. Lois couldn't be there, but she'd sent telegrams to Dina and the children's librarian at the public library.[36]

The feature covering the event in the city's *Call-Bulletin* newspaper included a photograph of Dina surrounded by students—all of the girls in their traditional dress—with an inset of book club member Homer Ng, the *Call-Bulletin* newsboy whose story became part of the protagonist's narrative. Gilbert Woo, editor of the *Chinese Pacific Weekly*, also ran a review of the event, and the *San Francisco Boy* scrapbook contains a translated typescript. Woo introduced his audience to Lois by describing her as a "well-known writer of children's stories" who "uses simple language with which to express thought-provoking and deep ideas that are welcomed by children." He mentioned that the author "spent considerable time visiting in the homes of these [Chinatown] children and enjoyed many personal contacts with her young friends and their parents." Most significantly, Woo points out, "The main subject discussed as the S. F. Boy is of Chinese descent, although Miss Lenski does not make the distinction and call him Chinese Boy or Chinatown Boy. Perhaps a race purist would not approve of the idea of her selecting an Oriental boy and calling him the S. F. Boy, but this book should be of far-reaching and immeasurable influence. Not only our Chinese children are being introduced to other children throughout the United States but the whole of San Francisco is being honored by Miss Lenski's book."[37]

Nearly a half-century after the party at the library, James Sue still had fond memories of working on the book. He found Dina Gianni a very good and "encouraging" teacher, and remembers Lois as being "very gentle and friendly and like a teacher, very patient, and very encouraging. I remember her collaboration." He actually described her as "very motherly." Aside from his service during the Viet Nam War, James spent most of his life in San Francisco, and much of that time in Chinatown. Although he did not become an artist, living "next to Golden Gate Park now," James retained the same keen appreciation of being out-of-doors and free. "I love nature," he mentioned. "Every chance I get, I am out there."[38]

That love of nature and place that James holds dear also claims the souls of Irene ("Dago") Story Freeman, the central protagonist in *Houseboat Girl*, and her younger sister, Debbie Story Saylors. Neither ever wanted to leave the banks of the Mississippi River where they spent their childhood. Unlike *San Francisco Boy* and the other invitational regionals, the "invitation" for *Houseboat Girl* came "from the river itself," because, Lois claimed, "the river is an invitation . . . to all kinds of people who love it and live on it." Literature and history prompted her "love of the Mississippi River and its tributaries" and initially whetted her curiosity.[39] The *Bayou Suzette* research and Em Celeste's stories about her students' lives by the smaller rivers and bayous in south Louisiana also contributed to Lois's interest in planning the Roundabout called *We Live by the River*. Through successive visits, Lois learned that some families still lived in houseboats *on* the river itself. Reading Harlan Hubbard's *Shantyboat: A River Way of Life* convinced her that she had to find a houseboat family to showcase. In 1944 Harlan Hubbard and his wife, Anna, had built their own houseboat on the Ohio River near Cincinnati, where they lived for two years before floating all the way to New Orleans. They arrived in March 1950, and *Shantyboat* was published three years later. Lois wrote to Hubbard immediately after reading the book,[40] asking for his help in locating the Story family that he had described meeting in 1949 during the Hubbards' meandering down the Mississippi. Hubbard introduced Lou and Henry Story, "both of them river people by birth, ancestry, and inclination . . . the river between Memphis and Paducah was their home."[41]

Hubbard told Lois that "the Storys are one of the best river families we know" and offered to write to them about her interest. Lois and Lou Story began corresponding in the spring of 1954, and Lois found Lou's letters

Lois Lenski sketches Henry Story knitting a fishnet on the porch of the Story family's houseboat with his youngest children, Debbie and Pete, watching her (1954). Courtesy of Illinois State University's Special Collections, Milner Library.

"full of character, information and a spirit of friendly cooperation." Early the following fall, Lois visited with the Storys almost daily for six weeks on their newer houseboat tied up at O'Donald Bend near Luxora, Arkansas. Although Lois stayed in the home of a high school teacher who lived nearby, she spent her days at the school attended by the four Story children or aboard the houseboat visiting. Newspapers in surrounding communities took note that "a book about Arkansas was so successful for the author that she returned here to gather material for another publication." Another noted, "the author who had already traveled to the state to do research for *Cotton in My Sack* has returned to assemble material for a book, 'Boat on the River,' she plans to write soon. She interviewed the children in Mrs. B. B. Wilson's class Friday at Luxora."[42]

Lois immediately identified Irene ("Patsy" in *Houseboat Girl*) as her "ideal" heroine, because she was "happy, lively, talkative," loved to keep pets, was just the right age, and "a delight from the very first day."[43] Henry Story looked like Abraham Lincoln, and though he had never learned to read or write, "knew every twist and turn in that ever-changing body of moving water, the true instinct of a real riverman." In *Houseboat Girl*, Lois described Patsy's dad, Mr. Foster, as looking "so much like young Abraham Lincoln, he went by the nickname of Big Abe."[44] As the houseboat traveled down the Mississippi,

> Patsy studied the map each day. Each new page was tacked to the wall and showed a new stretch of the river. All lights and buoys were clearly marked.
>
> "If I could only teach Daddy to read . . ." said Patsy.
>
> "What's the good of a map?" asked Daddy. "The channel has changed a dozen times since it's been printed."
>
> "Well, it's fun to look at anyhow," said Patsy.[45]

When Lois sent the manuscript of *Houseboat Girl* to Eunice Blake in early 1957, her Lippincott editor thought it one of the "nicest Regionals, and I grew very fond of the family, particularly of the father." But she was troubled that Lois brought up the question of his illiteracy, wondering if it wouldn't seem insensitive to "the feelings of your friends on the river." When Lois asked Lou about this issue, she did not object, because she had already told "everybody."[46] Lois included this information to let her young readers know that she valued all kinds of people and all kinds of knowledge, and that she did so without in any way diminishing Henry's character and intelligence.

Lois's "Picture Map of Houseboat Voyage of Foster Family down Mississippi River" comprises two pages, landscape-style in the book. It is a graphic masterpiece, tracing the Fosters' journey down the Mississippi from where they began near Paducah, Kentucky, to O'Donald Bend, above Luxora, and includes snippets from the narrative. At a glance, readers can grasp both a chronological account and a sense of the geographical dimensions that they will travel with Patsy and her family. The map also functions as a necessary and convenient visual reference to which readers will return time and again as the houseboat and narrative move downriver.[47]

Because Lois needed to understand the Storys' manner of subsistence living in order to write and illustrate accurately, she found Henry a patient teacher, carefully explaining whatever he was doing as she sketched and took notes. Lois was thrilled to be able to spend so much time with the Storys, and her independence during that late summer was guilt-free. She reported that Arthur "was happily traveling in Europe with good friends, and I was free until his return. . . . I soaked up sunshine by the barrel and gained five badly needed pounds from being lazy, with no household responsibilities and no running-my-legs-off."[48]

Of course, Lois's "river education" continued both immediately and long after her Luxora residence, through correspondence with Lou over the next three years during the writing of *Houseboat Girl*. Irene (Dago) also kept in touch, sending Lois a "most interesting account of the Story family's trip down the Mississippi in their houseboat in the summer of 1954," just about the time that Lois met them. Lois marveled that Dago was able to type the letter: "how she ever got a typewriter or who she may have found to type it for her, I have no idea." Dago described in some detail the story of how she had learned to swim, an incident that Lois amplified in *Houseboat Girl*, including a caption in the picture map near the town of Wickliffe, Kentucky: "Two months stay. Sold fish. Here Patsy learned to swim and got a dog."[49]

About the same time, Dago thanked Lois for sending her copies of *Flood Friday* and *We Live by the River* and wondered when she could expect to see a copy of *Houseboat Girl*. "I am so anxious to read the book you are writing about us and the river I can't hardly stand it."[50] She didn't have much longer to wait, since the book's publication was the following fall. Both Lou Story and Harlan Hubbard wrote as soon as they received copies, immediately before the book's release to the public. Lou unreservedly expressed her pleasure:

> Read the book and gee we are all proud of it. Peg & I went to Post office and got it . . . it took us 1 hr to get home for looking at Pictures and laughing. Every nite Peg & I read to Henry he really enjoys it said. You could really write a book. We read and laugh as so much sounds just like us and that Pasty [*sic*] is so much like Irene. We thank you a million for a copy of it. I am going to write the Hubbards and tell them of book and hope they get a copy and read it. It is lots more interesting than one he wrote.

Harlan Hubbard wrote with similar enthusiasm. "We rejoice to see *Houseboat Girl* in a book with appropriate illustrations. It could be done only by one who went to the river and lived with river people, and we congratulate you for having put the Storys into permanent form."[51]

Lou continued to tell Lois about the local response to *Houseboat Girl*. "Honey you have no Idea what a stir up the book has caused." When the Metropolis, Illinois, librarian received a copy, she telephoned the local radio station

> and had it go over the air—as soon as it hit air—her phone begun to ring. Paducah news woman wanted book first so she could read it and put in Paducah paper and she come to my house Tue after noon wanting me to tell Irene our Radio Station here wanted her (Library woman) and Irene on radio Monday morn at 8:30 she called school and made it ok with her teacher. . . . We go by town in stores we hear different one's not know us asking others do you know the Story that they have book about at Library.[52]

Several months later, Irene sent Lois a photo of herself with the following inscription on the back: "To the nicest and sweetest woman I've ever met. Thanks for everything and I hope you'll never forget me I know I'll never forget you. Love always to Miss Covey, Irene Story."[53] Still called Dago by her siblings, Irene and her husband now live far from the Mississippi River in Toccoa, Georgia, north of Atlanta, near the rest of her husband's family. There they've raised their four boys and six girls and live on sixty acres, surrounded by their children and grandchildren. What she misses most about the Mississippi is just being able to see it every day. She fondly remembers Lois, whom she found a "very likable person and wonderful artist. She even rode the school bus home with us . . . she was fun to be around. She wanted us to act natural . . . but we didn't know any other way to act. We were pretty simple people." Debbie Story Saylors ("Bunny" in *Houseboat Girl*)[54] was only five the summer of 1954, but she remembers how Lois "kind of hung out with us" while she was doing research for the book. The Mississippi River still remains central to Debbie's life. Her husband, James—also the son of a fisherman—grew up on the St. Francis and the Mississippi. The two live now in Helena, Arkansas, and Debbie claims, "Given the chance, I would be out there right now. Every day I need to go down to the river . . . to get the mud between my toes." Irene and Debbie's brother, Pete ("Dan" in the book), was a tugboat captain all his adult life— first in Louisiana and on some of the coastal waters, and eventually back in Metropolis, where he piloted on the Mississippi.[55]

During the summer of 2012, Debbie and Irene and their husbands planned a river reunion. Each couple took their pontoon boats to Metropolis to begin a nostalgic journey down the Ohio and Mississippi to Helena. The *Metropolis Planet* ran a feature article, "Houseboat Girl Returns to Ohio River," with a photo of the two couples, a sketch from the book of Patsy looking at the houseboat from the porch of their Metropolis home before the journey downriver, and a third photo of Irene holding her boat's life ring, named "The Houseboat Girl." Although the river was choppy and they ran into three storms that thoroughly soaked them and their belongings, they all enjoyed themselves immensely. Both Debbie and Irene complained about the changes that increased industrialization has brought to the rivers, although they still thought the scenery beautiful.[56]

Houseboat Girl is one of Lois's last completely satisfying regionals. Not only is the ever-changing setting itself intriguing if not exciting, but character, narrative, and illustration complement one another. Lois published sixteen titles in the series, from *Bayou Suzette* (1943) to *Deer Valley Girl* (1968). In between these books and other projects, she wrote eleven Roundabouts, from *Peanuts for Billy Ben* and *We Live in the South* (1952) to *High Rise Secret* (1966). These two series alone represent a staggering achievement, even though the quality of the books in both series varied from title to title. The reputation of the Roundabouts never equaled that of the Regionals. Ambitious in scope, Lois designed them to compete with traditional basal reading books by controlling vocabulary and sentence length while offering the early-elementary students more real-life tales of their mostly working-class counterparts around the country. The books' lesser production values—smaller size, lack of illustrated endpapers and double-page spreads, and simplified inked drawings—indicates that they were designed on a tight budget. The chapter books, like *Project Boy* or *Little Sioux Girl*, in which Lois had the space to develop a single protagonist, had the potential to be more convincing and interesting, although *High Rise Secret* is weaker than the others. But the "We Live in" titles are universally disappointing. Even though some of the story settings contain colorful elements, the brevity and disjointed nature of the books fail to provide much interest. As one reviewer of *We Live in the Country*, no fan of Lois's, declared,

> Lois Lenski is the most purposeful of writers . . . she pursues the entirely admirable aim of showing how other children live. In four

stories she gives glimpses of life on a chicken farm, among share-croppers, on a sheep farm and in the timber forest. The writing has what one must assume to be a conscious lack of distinction, as if the author wants nothing to distract from the authentic ordinariness of her material.

The result is a book which is admirable in intention and much less enjoyable in performance.[57]

While no Roundabouts are still in print today, the Regionals remain remarkable works. In the classic titles, such as *Strawberry Girl*, *Judy's Journey*, *Cotton in My Sack*, *Texas Tomboy*, *Blue Ridge Billy*, *San Francisco Boy*, *Houseboat Girl*, and *Prairie School*, Lois "caught" stories from and about children across the country whose lives, as depicted in both narrative and illustration, easily fascinate readers. Although the level of complexity of research and writing in the series looms far above what it took to create and illustrate her picture books, Lois's illustrations are no less essential in the longer chapter books. They convey much of the cultural and dramatic content and create the memorable images that remain fresh decades after reading one of her books. Many people say, "I remember her illustrations more than I remember her stories," but the two facets of her storytelling are truly interdependent and balance each other admirably. Even allowing for the didacticism—mostly restrained but sometimes, as in *Boom Town Boy*, out of control—Lois's regionals leave us an indelible, invaluable, and intimate portrayal of children's lives across the country in the first six decades of the twentieth century. In *Children and Books* (1957), at the height of Lois's most productive decade, May Hill Arbuthnot summarized the value of the regionals:

There are dangers in such a series of books. They might easily turn into obvious propaganda and stereotypes. The values of this series are to be found in their objective realism and compassion. Young members of under-privileged families meet their own kind. . . . And they take heart, because always the ups and downs of these hard-pressed people yield a ray of hope. Things are, or give promise of becoming, better. As for the well-cared-for children of suburbia, these books give them a picture of family love and loyalty that makes these families worthy of respect.[58]

Bradford Koplowitz sees Lois as an "innovator and pioneer" and values her gift for narrative: "She wrote more plainly and realistically than other children's authors by using material and characters from real-life observation. . . . She took chances by writing about people and places which were little known, and subjects which were considered taboo. . . . Lenski's commitment to writing in a realistic style is what makes her work not just endure but thrive." And Gary D. Schmidt, writing in 2013, concurs when he says that Lois's purpose, like John Steinbeck's, suggested that "the American scene was more complicated than it might appear," because beneath its shining image lay "ugliness, poverty, and injustice that must be faced." It's worth noting that no reviewers ever mention the tremendous role her illustrations play in making her works memorable to middle-level readers. Lois *did* approach her storytelling as an artist, capturing as much realism in her lovingly rendered drawings as in her carefully crafted verbal descriptions, much as artist Thomas Hart Benton approached his *America Today* mural in 1930: "Every detail of every picture is a thing I myself have seen and known. Every head is a real person drawn from life."[59]

In the twenty-first century, Lois's Regionals and Roundabouts have become valuable themselves as source material documenting lifeways that have diminished or vanished, like the shantyboat families along America's major rivers. Lois's own journeys to those stories both transformed her sense of self and created a similar impact on those like James Sue, Noel Leinen, and the Story sisters. Young readers also experienced her books in ways that shaped their sense of being in the world. Lois once explained to an interviewer that as much as children enjoy fantasy,

> there comes a time . . . when make-believe does not satisfy their curiosity about life. About the age of ten or twelve, they begin to be curious about people and the world about them, not only their own small world. And the world of the privileged child is really quite a small one. But that larger world, beyond their horizon, where other people live and move and have their being, they want to know how people behave and why and how to get along with people, even those different from themselves. In all these things, I hope and think that my regionals will help. Certainly, I feel that they satisfy certain yearnings that other books do not meet.[60]

In that interview, Lois was asked about fan letters from children, and she responded that she answered "every one by longhand. Sometimes it gets to be quite a task, but I feel this way. If I skipped some of them, I'd be afraid that I neglected the child who needed an answer most." She read from an "amusing one from Hawaii," which began:

> "Dear Miss Lenski, prepare yourself for a shock. This is no ordinary letter." And it wasn't either. "Your book, *Houseboat Girl*, has inspired me to write a book called 'Down the River.'" This girl outlined her entire plot, quite different from mine, and in some ways better. I wrote and told her that I wished I'd had her letter before mine was published because she'd given me some very good ideas.[61]

As recently as 2012, an acquaintance wrote that she had read *Cotton in My Sack* in elementary school

> so many times that I felt like part of the family. . . . Joanda and her story just felt like it was "mine." My life couldn't have resembled hers less, though . . . I had access to everything Joanda was missing in her life.
>
> I think I was intrigued by the totally different world I encountered in this book. . . . I loved being part of a big family, and I loved experiencing the trials and triumphs of their lives. I admired them for their strength, and I also yearned for them to overcome their failings. The way that family inched away from dependence and poverty was inspiring to me. . . .
>
> I think it was the character of Joanda herself that really touched me. From the very first we learn that she is fascinated by words—the image of her reading the upside-down wallpaper is indelibly etched on my memory. . . . She is eager to grow up and better herself, but also has a great pride in where she comes from.
>
> Finally, what has turned out to be a prophetic side of the book is that I met and married a man who came from a family of Arkansas sharecroppers. I feel that I understand quite a lot about their background, and respect them strongly, from knowing this book so well. I know that it is only a stroke of fortune that provides our place of origin, and I believe that even under those difficult

circumstances people had the same dreams, joys and sorrows as anyone else.[62]

Lois Lenski would have loved that latter-day fan email, because cultivating a sense of the worth of each individual's life lay at the heart of her own impulse to impart narratives that opened children's minds and hearts to a world beyond their comfort zones, just as she had done by storycatching in regions that she had not visited previously. She expressed her own transformation poetically in the essay "Place and People," originally written in 1956 for the *Illinois State University Journal.* She said that in the early days of her regional adventures, she wished that she could disguise herself "in an invisible coat" so that she could "be more truly one of them [those she was researching], to see and not be seen . . . to feel and sense and live with them as they do themselves, as they would if I were nowhere around." Because she could not magically make herself invisible, she claimed that she worked to reach a state "where I—the real ME—no longer exists. . . . I am no longer a person, I am an intermediary . . . a mere link in a chain, I take on the personality of the place, of the person, I sink my soul in his."

> Land that never knew my birthplace,
> Land accepted, chosen, prized;
> Land unlike my native region,
> By adoption realized.
>
> Land unknown but never alien,
> Land so new of me a part;
> Once I gave it understanding,
> There I buried roots and heart.[63]

CHAPTER 9

INNOVATIONS AND COLLABORATIONS

n the 1950s, Lois was writing, illustrating, and publishing picture books, Regionals, and Roundabouts with astonishing frequency. She somehow found the energy to venture into other areas of interest, once again emphasizing her belief in the ultimate value of encouraging children to respect and get along with one another. She had devised her regionals from an inherently simple but hard-to-achieve precept: Know Thy Neighbor, with overtones of the more difficult, religiously universal, Love Thy Neighbor. Now in the immediate post–World War II era, she used her skills as an author, illustrator, and collaborator with Clyde Robert Bulla (1914–1970) to design experiences in which both upper-elementary, middle-school youngsters, and even preschoolers could be ever more fully engaged with the reality-based worlds she had created.

The process began to develop in 1948 with the response to the publication of *Judy's Journey* and the notice given to it by the Child Study Association's award. The prestigious recognition for a book for young people that "faces with honesty and courage some of the real problems in today's world"—as the chair of the committee in charge had explained to Lois—stimulated interest in the possibility of her creating additional stories about migrant workers for use in religious school settings.[1] While *Cotton in My Sack* opened Lois's eyes to families living in poverty such as she had never before encountered, the resiliency of her "cotton children" deepened her sense of social justice. Telling Judy's story only strengthened her resolution to convey the reality—and hopes and dreams—of some of the poorest, hardest-working, and most mobile families in America. In the midst of the postwar economic boom, Lois wanted youngsters to realize that many families across the country remained stuck at the bottom.

In her foreword to *Judy's Journey*, Lois had praised the Home Missions Council of North America (HMC)—under the auspices of the Presbyterian Church of North America—for the work the organization had done, beginning in 1920 along the Atlantic seaboard, "providing health centers, child care centers, religious counseling, and inter-faith church services" to migrant workers and their families. Two decades later, the HMC network had spread to the West Coast and the Midwest. In 1948, the year following the publication of *Judy's Journey*, Edith Lowry, HMC executive secretary, told Lois that several radio stations had requested permission to broadcast radio transcriptions of the book. Lois stipulated that the material used would have to be taken from the first half—"or preferably the first quarter—of the book, so that the child hearer will be led to the book and will read it." According to the author, "Too many broadcasters are telling the entire plot of a good book in a fifteen-minute broadcast, which will keep the child from reading the book." Not surprisingly, Lois only wanted to allow her books to be shared "over the air" to entice young readers into reading the book itself.[2]

Lowry also invited Lois to join the National Migrant Committee, to which Lois replied, "I am not much of a 'joiner,' preferring to work independently for causes I believe in." Still, the author was so impressed with the work of the committee that she consented. Delighted to have her aboard, Lowry expressed her wish that Lois might suggest "ways in which this migrant situation could be interpreted through children's literature."[3] Lowry was in the process of designing a leaflet promoting the use of *Judy's Journey* and was requesting permission to use some of the original artwork to add interest, which Lois graciously granted. By the following month, Lois was telling her about a group of fifty or so Sunday school and vacation Bible school workers from the Connecticut Council of Churches (CCC) who were planning to meet in her studio to "discuss ways of using the book with Sunday School and Bible school children." Lois was "particularly interested in the fact that they themselves have found the book, and are using it,

Vacation Bible school children making a *Cotton in My Sack* mural in Lois Lenski's studio in Harwinton, Connecticut, mid-1950s. Reprinted by permission of the Lois Lenski Covey Foundation and Burrell Covey, copyright by Lois Lenski. Courtesy of the Lois Lenski Collection, Special Collections, Dean B. Ellis Library, Arkansas State University.

and that the request has come from them." Lowry was excited about "the Connecticut project" and hoped to find similar interest elsewhere. After the CCC meeting, organization member Edith Welker asked Lois to plan a course of study to acquaint religious youth groups with the plight of poor working American children from migrant and sharecropping families. Welker hoped Lois would author an issue of the booklet "Thoughts of God" to further explore the way books could lead to human understanding. Lois agreed to do so.[4]

That very year she wrote to Emma Celeste in a similar vein, "I tried to tell my brother (preacher of a rich congregation in Wash. D.C.) about some of my experiences with the 'underprivileged'—It was as you say: 'Like a tourist *on a streamline train* riding past a Negro shack'—I could not help but remember the story of the Good Samaritan, 'They passed by on the other side.' Oh, I wish I could do a story that would really put over this obtuseness of 'nice' people."[5] Lois was just about to have her chance to do so, with two projects focusing on migrants that began to emerge nearly simultaneously: one for the CCC and one for the Home Missions Council.

Emma Celeste had initially put Clyde in touch with Lois, and their first collaboration was the song they wrote for *Cotton in My Sack*. She had recently been thrilled during a return visit to Arkansas when she heard large groups of children singing the song. She learned that it was to be performed by "1500 children in a group" at a music festival the following spring. Lois responded to the news with a special plea to the "cotton children" to remember that

> whenever they sing it, they must remember that thousands of non-cotton-picking children will be singing it, in a vast chorus with them. This was a new idea to them—they just can't get used to the idea that their "very own book" will be read by children in the rest of the country, not only in Arkansas! This leads me to think that songs can be made a real bond of understanding between groups. If Michigan and Wisconsin children learn to sing the cotton song, it should help them to a better understanding of the cotton life.[6]

Lois recounted the incident to Lowry, wondering if a group of children were studying the migrants, "perhaps in vacation Bible school," they might want to participate in dramatizations of the material. She explained that Clyde would be glad to write music for *Song of the Migrant Children*. Lois had already submitted the lyrics.[7] In an undated typescript, "Play-Acting Real," Lois outlined her belief in the value of such dramatizations: "Children should be allowed to 'play-act' daily in school, just as they do in their own yards at home. They need not be taught how—they know instinctively. At first incidents can be taken from their own out-of-school experience. Then they progress to 'the experiences of others.' So they go to books and find there a wealth of material to draw on, incidents from the lives of other people different from themselves."[8]

Ultimately, Lois wrote three plays about migrant children for the National Council of Churches, and she and Clyde collaborated on a number of short songs for each, which were copyrighted in 1952 with the following notation: "The plays are offered for experimental production. No part of plays or songs may be reproduced or quoted." Each play concerns a family of a different ethnicity, and in each the family encounters various forms of prejudice and mistrust on the part of the settled community, even as they seek acceptance—and work.

Strangers in a Strange Land deals with the experiences of an Appalachian coal miner and his family, displaced from their former home when the coal played out and the mine closed down. They travel by wagon across the Mississippi River to Arkansas, where they hope to find work picking cotton. Lacking money for lodging, they look for a safe place to camp and choose a churchyard. The very idea horrifies the upright people of the church—who are afraid the migrants will enter the church and put their dirty feet on the newly upholstered pews. The policeman in the community tells them to move on. Only the grocer and a poor woman seem to take interest in their dilemma. When more hands than were needed showed up to pick cotton, the family heads home, disillusioned and humiliated by the treatment they received. Lois's underlying theme—that, by rejecting them, the church people are, in effect, rejecting the teachings of Jesus—remains unstated. There is nothing didactic in the play, but the words of one of the songs drives home the family's plight, repeating the biblical lines that echo the title, "We're but strangers in a strange land," followed by, "We've not met a helping hand." [9]

Lois had earlier sent the words to Clyde "for a new hymn to be called 'I Was a Stranger.' . . . This is almost exactly as it stands in the Bible—I've changed 'clothed me' to 'gave me a coat.' I hope it will make a good tune." She already had a vision for how it should work and sound. "Somehow I feel it will, & that it can be sung responsively—by high & low voices. The final sentence can omit the words 'Inasmuch' & 'my brethren,' if the rest will make a sort of chorus refrain, which can be repeated, perhaps, more than once." Lois wrote Emma Celeste about the actual event upon which the denouement was based. "This incident took place in Ark., & I heard those school children say those things—had my note book there & took it down verbatim—I was Dora Mae [one of the schoolchildren in the play], & rode after 'the terrible people' in a commandeered truck, caught up with them, where they had stopped for water at a poor sharecropper shack, & talked to them, learning their whole true story." And she confided to Clyde that she was "thrilled to get approval from Home Missions Council" for her manuscript of *Strangers in a Strange Land:* "no censorship, altho it is pretty strong & outspoken, especially regarding the shortcomings of 'the church' & 'church-people.' As these migrant plays are intended to be put on by 'church groups' I thought there might be objections, but none, so far, at least."[10]

The following year, Lois was pleased to be able to tell Clyde that she had heard from the Home Missions Council about a successful production of *Strangers in a Strange Land* in Yonkers, New York, in which "Mr. Bulla would have been gratified to hear his songs sung so hauntingly and sweetly by a 15-year-old girl who stepped completely into the part of the grandmother & really lived it." The Home Missions Council also reported that "this production did achieve something in bringing home to participants & audience the feeling of what it is like *not to belong*."[11] This is certainly the kind of achievement that Lois and Clyde had hoped their work would induce.

The HMC wanted Lois to include a play about Mexican American migrants in the Midwest in the trio she had proposed writing. Lois had to stretch and "find some one to help . . . with Mexican speech," since she knew very little Spanish. She anticipated that one of the lyrics she planned to create would be "a little Mexican girl's song sharing her longing to go to school and learn to read out of a book—very poignant if I can make it so." In *A Change of Heart*, a Mexican American family has settled in a migrant camp in southern Illinois, near a small farming community where they have found seasonal work. But the "good people" in town look down at them:

> MRS. ROGERS (*staring off R*): Oh, look at those ragged, dirty children. What are they doing in here?
>
> MRS. EDWARDS: That's one of those Mexican families. Remember the gypsies that used to come begging at the back door, Peggy, when we were little girls? Now, we have migrants. And I don't know which is worse.
>
> PATTY: Are they bad people, mother?
>
> MRS: ROGERS: Not exactly bad, Patty, but undesirable. They are not in our social class. We just don't want them around.[12]

However, Mrs. Rogers accompanies the Home Missions community worker to the Riverbend Camp, where the migrants live, and experiences an awakening of empathy:

MRS. EDWARDS (*turns to Mrs. Rogers*): But Peggy, I thought you wanted to run the Mexicans out of town. What's come over you?

MRS. ROGERS (*acts embarrassed for a moment, then lifts up her chin, looks from one face to the other in the group and says proudly*): I never realized how the Mexicans themselves feel about these things till I went out and visited their camp. I stepped into their shoes for the first time. I don't quite know what's happened to me . . . but I guess . . . I've had a change of heart. (*Pauses.*) Meeting adjourned.[13]

The African American mother and her two children in *The Bean Pickers*, not unlike Judy's family in *Judy's Journey*, follow the crops up the eastern seaboard from Florida to New Jersey. This play is more complex in structure, as three "neighborhood children" within the script offer a running commentary on the main drama. One of the two migrant children gets hurt working in the field, and the field walker who oversees the workers tells the mother that her children cannot stay in the field if they are not able to pick beans. The injured child needs to see a doctor, but the mother has no way to get to town. As the three try to walk along the road, no one stops to help a poor African American family. The three neighborhood commentators cannot stand that "the play" ends so unhappily, and they decide to rescript the last scene. At last Lois can neatly insert the Good Samaritan reference that she had earlier mentioned to Em' Celeste:

HELEN: But the woman didn't want colored people to ride in her nice car.

BEVERLY: Well, plenty of white people don't like to associate with colored people. They wouldn't ever ask them to come and have dinner with them, for instance.

ROBERT (*indignantly*): Are they afraid the color will rub off?

BEVERLY: I suppose colored people can be nice too. I'm sure I feel sorry for this poor woman and for poor Ralph with his cut knee and for Rose Ann with her sore eyes; but what can *I* do about it?

HELEN (*thoughtfully*): All our life we've known the Golden Rule: Do unto others as ye would that they should do to you. But we all forget it. I'm sure that woman in the last car never even heard of it. If she had a cut knee and was standing by the roadside, begging for a ride, I just wonder how she would feel, when all the cars went whizzing by.

ROBERT: She was full of prejudice. She couldn't see under their skin. She couldn't see the Negro mother's courage and cheerfulness. She couldn't see her trust in God. . . .

HELEN: How could she go on trusting in God, after people treated her like that? She must know that it is God's way to work through people. There must be other people who . . .

ROBERT (*eagerly*): Well, in the story of the Good Samaritan, the third man who came along really helped! He "bound up his wounds, poured in oil and wine, put him on his beast, carried him to an inn and took care of him."

HELEN: Let's plan SCENE IV. Let's make the story of the Good Samaritan come true. We'll be in the next car ourselves. . . .[14]

As Lois explained in the introduction to *The Bean Pickers*, "Here we have more than a mere play. We have a play within a play. We show how the play has the power to touch and even change the attitude of the children who take part in it." She also explicitly tells those who will introduce the play to religious or vacation Bible school students, "No faces should be darkened for playing the Negro parts. If it is felt necessary to say outright that the characters are Negroes, a sentence to that effect may be added to the introductory dialogue. But perhaps a more effective way is simply to present the Negroes as lovable human beings without a race label. The audience will easily deduce the fact from the words of the play, and from the Negro mother's lullaby with its haunting melody." In the closing paragraph of the introduction, Lois notes that all three plays "are the personal contribution of the author and the composer to the migrant cause. May they help to bring about wider understanding and love of 'our brother'!" That Lois and Clyde provided these very tough and masterful little plays pro bono underscores their commitment to awakening young consciences to the plight of migrants and, by extension, to the struggles of undervalued or unrecognized American citizens of all stripes. And this was two years before the Supreme Court's historic 1954 ruling, *Brown v. Board of Education*, that declared segregated education unconstitutional.[15]

In August 1952 Lois asked Marie Ram to read her three migrant plays, "especially the between-scene dialogues, where I'm trying to have the children *themselves* evaluate the play & the social situation involved & realize their own responsibility. . . . Thus the play becomes double-barreled—(1) acquainting them with situation (2) arousing their concern about it by awakening their emotional response to these human adventures."[16]

Lois must have felt emboldened to be more forthright in creating plays that directly address social injustice and inequality, very likely possible because the three were to be performed in a specifically religious setting. An undated typescript, simply entitled "Migrant Plays by Lois Lenski," appears to be a rationale that the author presented to the HMC in response to suggestions that the organization seems to have made or to questions that were raised about the plays. Her well-argued explanation provides further insight into the motivation for undertaking the project:

> The primary purpose of these plays is their effect on the children who take part, rather than their effect on the audience. I am trying to relate the plays to the children's own lives, so that the experience will have real meaning for them. I am trying to give the actors the vicarious experience of not just talking about a migrant, but of being that person. Only when this experience becomes a profound emotional experience for the child-actors will the effect on the audience be deeply felt. The child-actors are not just "taking a part." They are feeling and thinking like that other person: and so they must also speak as that person speaks.
>
> Perhaps we underrate the ability of our Juniors to really *think* and *feel:* to understand and express what we adults call "mature ideas." My wide experience in discussing my Regional books (which present many provocatively mature ideas) with boys and girls of 5th and 6th grades . . . makes me know that children of this age are quite ready to assimilate and understand the ideas presented in these plays. In some instances, some guidance and explanation from a leader may be necessary. All the plays should stimulate earnest discussion of the group using them, no matter what their age . . . because I am trying to stir children of Junior age into greater thoughtfulness of others, and because I believe them capable of it, I have written these plays for this age.[17]

Lois mentioned that the plays had already been tried out, and she believed that "*'real speech'* (dialect) could help . . . as nothing else, not even costume, to put himself more vividly and dramatically into the life of another. . . . It helps the privileged child to realize the reason for the poor speech—lack of a chance to go to school, for instance." In June 1952 she had written Emma Celeste about a performance of *The Bean Pickers* that took place in a Connecticut neighbor's barn, in which she had seen "an 8 yr. old 'bean picker,' Ralph, just such a little backwoodsy boy as you have down there (we have them too on our back roads here, where 'better class' call them 'Raggies')" enter into the part completely. "He learned his lines quickly, never forgot his cue, & said his lines as if they *meant something.*" The following month, another performance of the play made as much of an emotional connection with the author as with the children participating: "I had only 4 half-days . . . to teach them the play & rehearse them . . . But they did it well & it really *went over*. . . . It exhausted me each day, but I just *loved* doing it."[18]

Lois thrived creatively by entering fully into her writing and the subsequent theatrical productions, even when they absorbed and dissipated her energies completely, a pattern repeated throughout her long career. Obviously, the joy of going overboard in fulfilling her passion to inculcate empathy in children of the upper-elementary age group more than compensated for the aftermath of intense fatigue. Lois's experience with the HMC and its work with migrant children was so positive that she later created a trust fund to guarantee a semiannual income to the organization. Lowry thanked her: "To know that this fund is something permanent to help migrant children gives us great reassurance."[19]

The poignant and well-developed migrant plays gave vacation Bible and Sunday school youngsters and those who worked with them excellent vehicles for discussing class and racial prejudice. Lois accepted Edith Welker's offer to write "Living with Others" for an issue of a small periodical, *Thoughts of God for Boys and Girls,* published in 1952 for the Connecticut Council of Churches. Doing so fulfilled Lois's specific aim that she reiterated in "A Story from Strangers," an essay written in 1966—possibly for a talk with teachers: "Children should be consciously taught how to get along with their own parents, with their brothers and sisters, with friends and relatives, with strangers, and with people they have never seen; with people who are like themselves and with people who are different. . . . The wear and tear of human relations comes to us all and we must somehow work our way through it and acquire a peaceful and Christian approach to life."[20]

The strongest lines in the eighty-page booklet appear in the first sentence of Lois's introduction: "Religion is putting into action what we believe." She then asks, "How shall we do this? How can our actions show others what we believe?" As one of the children in a "discussion" says, "We show our worst side to the people we live with. . . . We save our best for company." How can we change this pattern that is so destructive? The stories, questions for discussion, poems, prayers, and songs that follow, she explains, have been written to be provocative, assuring the reader, "You will come to your own conclusions about the behavior of people; about your own behavior in relation to others; about how to live with others."[21]

Lois created an original prayer, "Three Circles," as an opening that succinctly, if rather prosaically, summarizes the thematic content of the booklet. The prayer begins by asking blessings for the family; it then forms ever-widening concentric circles that next encompass friends and community members, and finally embrace "those we do not know" around the world. The prayer asks that "the spirit of Jesus" might radiate from us "like the waves of the sea . . . making God's blessing known to all."[22] Lois had never written prayers before she tackled them in "Living with Others," as she confided to Em' Celeste:

> You see, I was brought up in a church where only the preacher does the outloud praying. In the Lutheran church, even the preacher does not "make them up" as he goes along. They are printed in the book (hymnal or prayer book). . . . No Lutheran preacher ever extemporizes or invents a prayer . . . never knowing what he will say next or where to stop. My father was a Lutheran preacher (& Dean of Theological School teaching young men to be preachers) but I never heard him invent a prayer in his life. As for me, I have NEVER prayed out loud in front of other people IN MY LIFE. The last couple of years, while I've been hobnobbing with these Congregationalists & Presbyterians & Methodists here in Conn, & up at the Northfield Conference where nearly *all* denominations were present, I was *scared pink* for fear some one would suddenly ask me to "offer a prayer." I would have had to stutter and mumble & say "I never prayed out loud in my life, & I don't know what to say."[23]

The challenge of writing "Living with Others" made Lois aware of the need to create prayers "to get our privileged children to sense something of the life of the under-privileged & their needs." Afterward, she felt "half ashamed" of these prayers, even though she realized that it was a completely new direction for her to take. She overcame her hesitancy at self-expression when addressing God, because she felt empowered in what she saw as her mission. She wanted to help children think about their relationships with family, friends, peers, and strangers in order to live more closely with the example set by Jesus. Considering the household in which she grew up, this was a mighty step for Lois to take as she approached her seventh decade.[24]

In presenting her plea to youngsters, Lois's faith appeared to guide her in ways that differed from her upbringing. She wanted to be as inclusive as possible, under the larger banner of Christianity. She told Emma Celeste, "I'm glad I've decided to do MY work for children OUTSIDE the church instead of INSIDE—I was brought up IN the church, a preacher's daughter—but have gradually edged out. I could never do any work for children WITHIN the church (any church)—It's too narrow & confining—the air would choke and stifle me."[25]

She hoped that readers of "Living with Others" could use the examples cited to actively access their own ideals and become more compassionate in their dealings with others. She was thrilled to learn that in "at least ½ doz. towns in Conn . . . the booklet is being used as a 'course of study' for their Bible Vacation Schools; so there are a lot more children there using the booklets—So one can never tell how far the waves extend when you throw a stone in a pond of water," she told Em' Celeste.[26]

In 1952 Lois also worked with Clyde to create a third religious publication, *We Are Thy Children: Hymns for Boys and Girls*, published by Thomas Y. Crowell. She and Clyde had written two of the songs included in "Living with Others" specifically for their hymnal: "Do Unto Others" and "We Are Thy Children." The closing lines of the latter encapsulate the main message of the booklet as well as the overarching theme in the larger body of work that Lois produced for middle-level readers:

> In judging others may we have no part,
> Unless we look into the heart.
> We are Thy children, our love we prove
> When we, like Thee, our brother love.[27]

The content of *We Are Thy Children* corresponds to that of "Living with Others," but it is everything that "Living with Others" is not. First of all, it is a beautiful hymnal, its title and the authors' names flanked by very Lenskiesque floral branches, which have been handsomely embossed in gold on its slate blue cloth cover. The hymnal is slender (just thirty-two pages), graciously sized and horizontal in format (nine inches tall and eleven inches wide) so that it can easily remain open on the piano to the desired page. Each hymn has its own page—or double-page spread—with both lyrics and simple-to-follow but beautifully written melodies. Lois's pen-and-ink drawings, accented with a watermelon-red wash, enrich each page. Although these illustrations are similar in style to those in "Living with Others," the larger, well-formatted pages allow for much more detail and sufficient space to set off the music and add visual depth to the lyrics, important qualities that contribute to the overall aesthetic success of the hymnal. Aside from the migrant plays, which are simple scripts, Lois's best work demonstrates her skillful use of illustrations to amplify the meaning of the passages (lyrics or prose) she has written.

Collaborating with Clyde while creating lyrics and illustrations for *We Are Thy Children* also allowed Lois to work with the Crowell editor, Elizabeth Riley, to whom she had sent Clyde's manuscript for his initial book, *The Donkey Cart*. One immediately picks up the affection between the two women from the tone of a letter that Riley wrote to "My dear Lois" in January 1952, after the manuscript had been submitted and reviewed by a group of churchwomen:

> At long last I received a report from the Methodist ladies (I had received one from the Baptists a while ago but was holding it for the second report) and what a report it is! One would think they were dealing with a Hollywood movie. Their adjectives begin with "good" and go on up the scale. They certainly are most enthusiastic about your work. . . . I think your hymns must have won them over! They thanked me several times for giving them the opportunity of seeing the material in advance. . . . They are so grateful for the concepts that are brought out in "We Are Thy Children" and I am delighted that you are using this as the title of the book. . . . I am more delighted that they think the book will be useful in their Sunday Schools. Of course we knew it all along.[28]

Lois responded just as delightedly: "Hooray for the Methodist ladies! I am thrilled to hear that we will have their enthusiastic support. You realize, don't you, that this group acts in an advisory capacity for the religious education of about fourteen denominations; so their approval really means something. Whenever they approve 'concepts' you may be sure we have hit the ball on the head." Lois then conveyed the good news to Clyde: "They [the Methodist ladies] made a few minor suggestions for changes in wording, nothing drastic, & on the whole, heartily approve 'the concepts' back of the hymns & are grateful (in advance) for getting them in book form!!!!"[29]

Elizabeth Riley concurred with the decision made by the Committee on Religious Education that the hymn "A Child of God" was too adult for the hymnal. Lois's response lacks the defensive tone of her earlier back-and-forth communiqués with Helen Dean Fish. She simply informs Elizabeth about why she feels that the hymn is valuable, even for the younger reader:

About A CHILD OF GOD. I agree with you and "the ladies" that this is my most adult hymn. . . . Clyde . . . did one of his loveliest and most catchy tunes for it. I find now that it is one of the tunes that comes back to me, and keeps running in my head more often than any other. For this reason alone, I would want to keep it. . . .

Now, may I ask you, why should we not have one semi-adult hymn in the book, something to grow to? Yes, it is symbolism—one of the most beautiful in the Bible. . . .

In the Sunday School which I attended all through my childhood, we always read Psalm I responsively every Sunday, with these words in verse 3:

"And he shall be like a tree planted by the rivers of water, that bringeth forth his fruit in his season; his leaf also shall not wither; and whatsoever he doeth shall prosper."

For years and years I was intrigued by these words, because of the vivid word-picture which they built up in my mind. I confess I did not understand them. No adult tried to explain them to me, or even thought they needed explaining. We just read them over and over again every Sunday. Not until I was grown up did I understand their meaning; but I am glad now they were a permanent and secure part of my childhood. They mean so much to me now that I feel they represent the basic theme of this book—the whole meaning of "religious education" lies behind these words.[30]

The hymn remained, and Lois's frontispiece—the finest artwork in the hymnal—illustrates the verse that appears on the title page along with a verse from Psalm 40:3. "And He hath put a new song in my mouth, even praise unto God." Lois's argument to keep the hymn in the book demonstrates her thorough appreciation for the gradual aesthetic and conceptual awakening of a growing child. She insisted that children have rich experiences of religious potency that resonate even without being fully understood and that gain in depth as the child grows to appreciate this heritage.[31] The hymn itself is succinct, lovely, and soothing:

> A child of God shall be
> Planted like a tree
> Beside the river free,
> A wondrous sight to see.
> The tree shall never lean,
> Fed by waters clean;
> His leaf it shall be green,
> Nor fade away unseen.
> The tree shall grow with care,
> Its blossoms shall be fair,
> Good fruit forever bear,
> Rich beyond compare.[32]

Although they were exchanging lyrics and music as they worked closely on *We Are Thy Children*, remarkably, Lois and Clyde had not yet actually met. Their collaboration took place cross-country, since he lived in southern California while she was in Connecticut or Florida. Clyde referred to this unusual work style in the "Composer's Foreword": "I watched the mails for her letters, hoping that in each one there would be the words of a new hymn. Some of the verses suggested music at once. Others I carried in the back of my mind for months before a melody came to me. . . . It has been a happy and absorbing experience, from the first song to the last."[33]

As Lois recovered from yet another hospital stay in the early fall of 1952, she reported to Em' Celeste, "It all boils down to the same old thing— poor blood, not enough red blood cells, due to alkaline stomach, & that in turn causes arthritis." Hospitalization had actually served as a source of inspiration for such a self-disciplined and religious author. She explained, "During some of the prolonged tests, I composed poems & hymns in my mind—just *made* myself think of these things, to keep from thinking of the pain & discomfort. It is hard to do—but one can do it—I made the 5 days a real 'retreat'—of communion with God, asking to be shown more clearly the work He wants me to do. . . . It was a year to thank God for—the kingdom of God is within you if you'll let it come there." In her next letter to Emma Celeste, she apologized "for feeling awfully BLUE. . . . I'm so sorry I wrote you in one of those infrequent moments." Yet that blue period had led Lois to a deeper understanding of herself and had helped her shape that understanding into productive work—her best and most reliable refuge: "I've learned to SHUT DOORS in the mind. When you get to my hymn book, you'll find one hymn called 'I will open wide the door of my heart & let Jesus come in.' This is *opening* the door to constructive thoughts, to thoughts of children & their happiness, to thoughts of God and growing things, to thoughts of Jesus & all that He stood for."[34]

Lois also rejoiced in the rewarding experience she found working on *We Are Thy Children:* "I had *so much mail it took me 3 hours to read it* leisurely and I thanked God for all the good, good friends He had given me, people like *you*, who share their rich experiences & insights so freely with me— Clyde, too, with all his lovely music enabling me to give our lovely hymns to thousands of children—Eliz Riley & the 2 girls in her office who have all worked so hard & lovingly to make the hymnal a thing of beauty to be loved & prized & *used* in many, many homes—How rich one's life can be when it is out going."[35] Louise Seaman Bechtel, influential children's book editor for the *New York Herald Tribune*, wrote a glowing review of the hymnal: "Both text and music have been slowly tested with children over a period of years. Some adapt Bible stories and settings. . . . There are morning, evening, Christmas hymns, and finally a prayer for peace. So little is available in conventional hymn books suitable for small children that this book will be widely welcome. Mr. Bulla's music is easy to sing and to play. The many decorative pictures give the book charm and make it a picture book as well as a song book, for ages five to twelve."[36]

Lois had such satisfying experiences collaborating with Clyde on songs for the regionals, for the migrant plays, and for *We Are Thy Children* that the two embarked on a completely new secular venture for younger children—producing books that encouraged participation. While the songs included in the regionals and the migrant plays facilitated dramatization, the song-based publications that the Lenski-Bulla team produced met the needs of children ages three to nine. *The Songs of Mr. Small;* the Read-and-Sing series; and finally, a recording, *Frank Luther Sings Lois Lenski Songs,* paired with these books to extend their listening and reading skills through self-expression. That Walck hired multitalented recording artist Frank Luther demonstrates the high degree of dedication to excellence the publisher placed in the project. One of Luther's many specialties included recordings for children, including nursery rhymes and popular stories.[37]

Lois claimed that the read-and-sing idea came to her when she was sharing a Mr. Small book, *The Little Farm,* with grandson Davy, then age four. Because Davy had heard the book read to him often, "he knew the text by heart. He just began out of his own sheer joy in the book to sing it, all the way through, to a little tune he made up as he went along." Lois said she "listened in amazement," then universalized the experience. "Why can't children learn to sing their books as well as read them?" she wondered. She thought that if children could "sing" the books they enjoyed, perhaps that would help them, later, learn to read those same books.[38]

The Songs of Mr. Small (1954) was the first publication in this vein. Of course, the Small books already existed, and Lois and Clyde did not attempt to retrofit them with music. Instead, Oxford brought out a completely different edition, larger and vertically oriented (eight by ten inches), enlivened by pen-and-ink drawings with watermelon-red and turquoise accents. The twenty-one songs reference the varying personae portrayed by dapper Mr. Small. The book's personality is much akin to that of *We Are Thy Children*, with about equal proportion of words and music to decorative visual touches. In the foreword, the authors explain that the songs more vividly dramatize Mr. Small's actions. Thus, the child "does not just sing about Mr. Small. He is Mr. Small. . . . The songs will help, even more than the heard or spoken word, to bring Mr. Small alive. The child as Mr. Small makes the auto go . . . trots on the pony. . . . In the songs Mr. Small speaks for himself." In the first song, "Big Mister Small,"

Mr. Small assumes one role per verse for eight verses, as in these sample verses:

> Big Mister Small
> Has an airplane, too,
> He flies up very high.
> He banks and turns,
> He loops a loop
> Way up there in the sky.
>
> Big Mister Small
> Is a cowboy now,
> He rides the range all day.
> He breaks a bronc
> And if he falls,
> Jumps on again to stay.[39]

The authors assume, probably correctly, that children already familiar with, and undoubtedly attached to, Mr. Small through the book series would be those most attracted to *The Songs of Mr. Small.* The recording truly serves as a companion piece.

Lois and Clyde then created a completely new Read-and-Sing series—*I Went for a Walk* (1958), *At Our House* (1959), and *When I Grow Up* (1960)—of little books for little hands, similar in size and feel to the Mr. Small books and dedicated to grandchildren: Paul (Laird's son), and Michael and Vivian (Stephen's two older children). Patricia Cummings, children's book editor for Oxford University Press, immediately applauded the idea when Lois introduced the concept to her in 1956. "We're really very keen about your idea of 'Read-and-Sing' books. This seems to be the ideal solution for making it painless for the child (or the adult buyer) to be exposed to songs. And so far as we can tell the idea is unique, in trade book publishing anyway." Cummings thought that the series should begin with "IN OUR TOWN," evidently the original title for *I Went for a Walk*, and agreed with Lois's decision that the illustrations be pencil sketches with a single accent color, but wanted the size to be distinct from both the Mr. Small and Davy series. The size should be right for a child's hands, but "large enough to include music notes, too, even though the music will be only the simple, easy-to-read melody." All three publications measure six inches high by seven inches wide and share a similar format with the pencil sketches and single-color wash. In the later two books, the design is simplified and uniform throughout: the left side of the page contains a simple verse, with two lines of music and verse repeated within the musical notation, facing one large image on the right. Cummings approved of the change in format, telling Lois, "We like your arrangement of verse and music on the left-hand page and illustrations of the right-hand pages. Having the family larger will certainly make the book completely 'au courant'!" All three publications are equally charming, with the whimsical magic that Lois's drawings universally cast.[40]

Finally, in April 1960, after the first two Read-and Sing books were published and *Songs of Mr. Small* and several other picture books were included in textbook adoptions in Philadelphia and Washington, D.C., Lois wrote Henry Walck (who had recently acquired the children's book list from Oxford University Press to form his own company) to tell him that she felt that a *recording* of the Mr. Small and Read-and-Sing songs would help "a vast number of children to learn the songs" that these publications present. "Many schools have no pianos, and few teachers can play a piano," she argued, "so unless a music supervisor teaches the children a song, there is no opportunity for them to hear or learn it." By making a recording of these songs, "the books would be more widely sold and used, and thousands more children would learn to know and love the songs." Walck jumped on the idea. By the following month, he planned to engage, once again, the highly recommended recording artist Frank Luther who, he told Lois, would "direct as well as do the singing. We will have an orchestra consisting of a piano and two instruments, probably strings. The record will be 12" long play in monaural but we plan to tape it in stereo as well so that we can produce a stereo record later when libraries and schools obtain that equipment." The first side of the record contained "Songs of Mr. Small"; the other side held the songs from all three Read-and-Sing books. For the artwork on the record jacket, Walck added, "We hope to adapt the jackets of the four books for the art work . . . the SONGS OF MR. SMALL on one half and the three Read-and Sing books on the other." The record and the third Read-and-Sing book, *When I Grow Up*, would be issued and promoted simultaneously.[41]

The promotional material for *Frank Luther Sings Lois Lenski Songs* describes him as the "popular 'Father of Children's Records'" and explains the connection between the books and the recording: "an ingenious index on the record jacket enables the listener to locate easily each song on the record and in the book." Included are reviewers' comments. As Spencer Shaw, children's consultant for the Nassau (New York) Library System, notes, "the words sung by Mr. Luther are predominantly monosyllabic, yet colorful, illustrating a vocabulary suitable for the intended age group. The contents are filled with people, happenings, elements usually noticed by the very young in their immediate environment . . . a child's sphere . . . which he may cherish." Spencer Shaw felt that Luther "respects a child's impressionable mind by carefully avoiding pretense or a sugary style." Accompanied by a three-piece orchestra directed by Tony Mottola,[42] Frank Luther's voice is a clear and cheerful tenor, positive and bright, with no hint of condescension—the perfect voice to articulate and accompany the serious pursuits of Mr. Small and the Read-and-Sing children.

Emma Celeste had still other ideas about the kinds of songs and music that the Lenski-Bulla team *should* provide for the youngest audience, the being-read-to children. In letter after letter typed on a broken and difficult to decipher typewriter or an uneven scrawl, Em' Celeste sent Lois her ideas for "picture music." In early June 1953 Lois told her:

> The piano publisher, Mr. Hansen, wants me to do a book to *introduce pre-school children to piano . . . before they start taking lessons*—to get them *interested* in the piano & the sounds it can make. This is really what you have been telling me all these years—this "method" your own—& at last it is beginning to register with me. I'm not sure that I can "put it across," as I feel that I am not enough of a musician. But maybe with Clyde's help, & your help & God's . . . maybe . . . well, there's no harm in trying!!![43]

She still felt unsure of exactly what Emma Celeste had in mind, but it seemed to match what Hansen wanted, and Lois was determined to understand more concretely Em' Celeste's framework and instructions. "You speak of pasting pictures on. What kind of pictures?" Lois needed to know. Laird's son, Paul, "just turned 3," was visiting his grandparents at Greenacres for several weeks. "His parents want me to 'get him interested in music.' So he is the perfect 'guinea-pig' for us. Remember he is barely 3, so still a baby in many ways—much, much younger than the 6 yr. olds in your school or in Abita [Louisiana] on whom you used this method," Lois told her. Lois had tried to show Paul middle C "as a place to start," but he showed no interest. "So far, all he has done at the piano is to bang." Was his truly the age that Emma Celeste was describing? After another explanation from Em' Celeste arrived, Lois triumphantly reported, "I tried *Drum-hammer* & *3 bears* with Paul & he loved them. I drew a drum & hammer on keys with pencil—he liked that. Later, I drew 3 bears, one on high C (little bear) one on middle C (mama bear) & one on low C (Daddy bear)." Lois was beginning to catch on and taking great pleasure in it. "Well—I never dreamed I'd embark on a song career at the age of (nearly 60!!) One never can tell what life will bring! But this new venture is really FUN!"[44]

Lois and Clyde capably turned Emma Celeste's ideas and her revisions of theirs into *Up to Six, Book I: Picture Music for the Pre-School Child*, published by Hansen Music Corporation in 1956. As Lois and Clyde explain in their introduction: "PICTURE MUSIC will not, and is not intended to teach the child to read notes. . . . At six or seven is soon enough. But for three or four years before that he can be enjoying sounds of his own making on the piano. He can learn to listen to these sounds and he can learn how to use not just one, but all his fingers on the keys." Beating the drum, ringing bells, ticking the clock were all sounds—and images and short stories—that Lois and Clyde provided. A boxed note at the bottom of the brief foreword informed the adult reader that the book even contained a "perforated insert of pasted pictures which can be used over and over again, since each illustration is printed on a special self-adhesive paper. Just peel off protective backing and smooth it on. It also removes easily."[45]

Parents or supervising adults could use these simple little illustrations by Lois exactly as she had used the pencil sketches for Laird, all thanks to the ingenious research of Emma Celeste, confirmed by Lois in her interactions with grandson Paul. In fact, the authors' introduction to *Up to Six* recapitulated Lois's experiences with him: "The child's first impulse is to bang on all the keys at once, hitting here, there and anywhere. This makes noise. He likes it but never listens to it, never tries to control it. He just bangs. Banging is a good thing. He is learning sound." But that is not enough for an active and inquisitive youngster. "He wants to play the piano, to make sounds come out with the pressure of a finger. He does not want to read notes. He wants action, and his fingers have to learn to move like feet learning to walk. He can and will read pictures—so the pictures in the book are printed large. He will not read notes, so the notes are printed small, for a guide to the adult." Lois and Clyde mastered Emma Celeste's tutelage so well that they could instruct others. The conclusion of the introduction echoes the sentiments Lois expressed twenty years earlier in her article "Let Your Child Draw; Don't Teach Him," published in *Better Homes and Gardens*, in which she admonished parents: "Let him draw what he will in his own way." In *Up to Six*, she and Clyde write:

> The notes and song-words given in the book are intended merely as suggestions. The child is to look at the picture in the book, be stimulated by it, learn from the pasted-on picture where to start— then go ahead and use his fingers and his voice. . . . He needs no other "teaching." Sometimes he will play with his left hand, sometimes with his right. What difference does it make? He is learning to use his fingers, to listen to sounds and enjoy them and to make up his own little songs.[46]

Incredibly, Emma Celeste and Clyde never actually had a face-to-face meeting, even though their significant friendship initially shaped his career and facilitated the collaboration of these major children's authors. In many ways, Emma Celeste was their absentee partner, providing anecdotes and real-life experiences as a teacher sensitive to her students' intellectual and emotional needs. Emma Celeste's comments and insights became integral to Lois's stories and Clyde's music that enlivened the plays, the songs, and, finally, their introduction of children to the piano keyboard itself. All these interactions kept an often ailing and aging Lois young, vital, and open to new ideas and new opportunities that simultaneously expanded her repertoire while enlightening and enlarging her audiences.

CHAPTER 10

FRIEND
OF CHILDREN

espite Lois's often-debilitating health issues, she experienced her most expansive, creative outpouring during the 1950s. She described this unlikely combination of illness and output in the last chapter of her autobiography, *Journey into Childhood*, calling creative thinking "one of the best cures for pain, illness, and physical discomfort. It fills one with a sense of well-being, and indescribable joy which carries one's thoughts and imagination along, so that one's body can be forgotten."[1] Lois continued to consolidate the friendships and collaborations she cultivated, including the children with whom she worked at home in Connecticut, at her husband's studio one winter in Florida, and in the regions to which she traveled. She recognized and fully appreciated the joy she took in imbuing her life with purpose—a commitment to writing that encouraged children to sense the worth of every human being. Her work therefore fulfilled both a creative and a spiritual quest: to produce books, poetry, plays, and songs that promoted human understanding or helped children face the realities of life with courage, dignity, and integrity. This sense of mission fueled her, even as she faced personal and physical challenges in her final decades. Lois expressed such feelings in "I Sing the Life I Live," a poem dedicated to Stephen's youngest child and her second granddaughter, Jeanine, and which opened *The Life I Live: Collected Poems*, published in 1964:

> I sing the life I live,
> I sing the things I do,
> I sing of all I feel—
> My joy, my sorrows too.
>
> I laugh, I cry, I give
> To others as I go;
> I sense, I feel, I hurt—
> These are the things I know.
>
> I sing of others' lives,
> I sing the things they are;
> By sharing all they feel,
> My life is richer far.[2]

As author and illustrator, Lois needed the presence of children to stimulate and rejuvenate her own creative juices, even though her visits with family required a good deal of preparation on the part of her hosts. Her pernicious anemia required her to follow a very demanding and specific diet and allow adequate time for rest. Such demands only exaggerated Lois's sometimes "prickly" nature, just as she had demonstrated in interactions with her longtime editor, Helen Dean Fish. One of her great-nephews recalls that "It was always a bit of a big deal when she would come. . . . She would always send detailed instructions ahead of time to my mother—precise needs, food preferences/requirements, etc." Although Lois always brought a book for him, he mostly remembers "being quiet and not really being a part of conversations—but just thinking we were with somebody important."[3] Visiting with Stephen's family in the 1960s, Lois had to spend a good part of the day resting. To engage with her grandchildren during this "down" time, she created a post office game. The children were to slip little letters to her under the door, and she would slip letters to them in return. The children loved this game and even now retain some of these notes.[4]

In the years after her children had grown and moved away and when no grandchildren were visiting, Lois covered the linoleum floor of her studio with newspapers, put two huge piles of newsprint on a table, and invited preschool neighborhood children into her Greenacres studio on Saturday afternoons to paint. "They do not miss a single Saturday. They come running in, shouting, 'I have an idea!' 'I have an idea!' They gather around to tell me what they want to paint, their faces lighted up with eagerness and expectancy," Lois wrote in "Let Them Create," an article for the February 1952 issue of *The Horn Book*. Her delight was in being able to "sit on a chair and watch as the miracles begin to happen. For there is no greater miracle in this world than the growth and blossoming of a child's idea."[5]

Marilyn Reynolds Coronado was one of the Harmony Hill neighborhood children who looked forward to those Saturday painting sessions. She remembered that Lois always put out brushes and black tempera paint, instructing the children to outline everything in black first. When the outlines dried, other colors were available, and the children would choose whatever colors they wanted, one at a time, with a brush for each color, to fill in the objects they had rimmed in black. Then Lois would place a long sheet of paper from a roll on the floor, and the children painted grass and sky. For the final "mural," Lois cut out all the outlined objects and attached them to the paper, making an assemblage, which she hung on the wall opposite her desk. Like the regional children with whom Lois worked, Marilyn found her consistently nice, "always smiling," dressed in very plain clothes. Lois also referred to the benefit she derived from taking time away from her writing and illustrating to offer these and similar sessions: "I cannot create my books without the help of children. I go to them to observe, to listen and to learn. Only with their help and inspiration do my stories and pictures grow and develop." Even in writing and illustrating picture books, Lois felt the need to "catch up with the very essence" of a child's "being, so that it shines through and wins his ready yet inarticulate acceptance." She once asked Marilyn to write a story about a chicken hawk for *We Live in the Country*. Marilyn recalled, "She kept after me, and finally I did it," and Lois used Marilyn's brother and sister as models for the drawings of the children in the story.[6]

While Lois was observing her young neighbors and being inspired by them, she was suffering from complications of arthritis and fallen arches, and standing was difficult. She wrote Emma Celeste that at last she had found some corrective shoes that really helped, but conceded, "They look terrible—like big clumsy gun-boats—or men's farm boots—but they *feel* wonderful. No more pain in my foot." More than sixty years later, Marilyn's brother, Robert Reynolds, commented on those shoes: "Memories are funny. Somehow the big chunky shoes she wore made an impression on me." And his cousin Jane Reynolds Pallokat, whose grandparents lived across from the Coveys, added, "He is right about those shoes!"[7]

Joan Kirchner, whose family's property on Harmony Hill bordered the Coveys to the north, has her own memories of visits in the 1950s. Like Marilyn and Robert, she remembered participating in painting murals at the studio, her memory a variant of Marilyn's. "She did have a mural that she had all the neighborhood children work on," Joan reported. "She had a roll of paper that she spread all the way across the floor. It was long, and we each had a spot, and everybody painted houses and trees. . . . I think we were just supposed to do our [own] house, and she put it up on the wall, and it was up on the wall for a long time." (A photograph of children standing in front of the mural is one of the illustrations in "Let Them Create," and a photograph of Lois sitting on a daybed, with the mural behind her, appears in *Journey into Childhood*.) For Joan, however, being a member of a group was not enough. She eagerly awaited the Coveys' return from Florida each spring. "When I would see them, I would appear at the door. When Mrs. Covey—which I always called her, Mrs. Covey—would be ready for company, she would invite me down to her studio, and I would paint, and I can still remember the smells of the turpentine and paint. It just permeated me. She would always say, 'Outline things with black paint first, and then you fill in,'" the methodology that Lois explained in "Let Them Create." While Joan worked on the floor, Lois sat at her desk and wrote. As far as instruction, Lois had simple suggestions. "She always said to do your outlining first, and then color in. She didn't really say anything like 'Do this,' or 'Do that'; it was more of a guidance rather than direct instruction." According to Joan, Lois also took a similar approach in teaching her to write poetry: "She told me about scanning, how to make it work, how to make the lines even, the rhyming. Then she said, 'I'll show you how to make your own little book.' And she got some paper, got a needle and thread and she, in the crease of the book, made some binding, and on the front, that's where she wrote, 'My Poems.'"[8]

Stephen shared a memory associated with poetry from 1943, when he was twelve. Lois wrote a poem, "Forgetful Tommy," which Stephen claimed was "based on the fact that I could never remember where I left my belongings!" About the same time, his parents had given him "a small lino-type

Unknown child's original drawing of Mr. Small, sent to Lois Lenski as part of her fan mail, undated. Courtesy of the Lois Lenski Papers, Special Collections, Butler Library, Buffalo State College.

press, complete with several fonts of type." With his mother's "patient assistance and guidance," Stephen "interpreted her illustrations in linoleum cuts, and hand set the type, printing an edition of the book." *Forgetful Tommy*, published by "Greenacres Press, 1943," is even listed in the Lois Lenski bibliography, "Ohioana Authors." Lois was evidently quite proud of her son's artistic ability. "Forgetful Tommy," dedicated to "S. J. C." also appears in the anthology of Lois's poetry, *The Life I Live*.[9] The Harwinton children's experiences reveal a unique kind of intimacy through creative endeavor in which Lois excelled. More than one of her grandchildren remembered that she was "warm, but distant" or "a very determined personality, never lost in a room with others. . . . Her presence was never unnoticed. She was engaging, attentive, not forceful, but not shy with her opinions."[10] Her mentoring brought the same empathetic understanding and guidance that the students who worked with her experienced while she was researching her regionals.

Lois's interactions with African American children in Tarpon Springs offered insights she otherwise would have missed, and without which she would never have been able to write and illustrate *Mama Hattie's Girl.* She visited "the (then) segregated Negro school" and befriended the principal and those teachers who welcomed her to their classrooms. Having established these relationships, Lois became a frequent visitor. She gave children books and read stories to them, "including some of my own which they helped me write about themselves and their own experiences." The Saturday painting classes gave her additional insights. Held in Arthur's studio (before they built their own home with studios for both of them), the atmosphere was markedly different from the classroom. Lois found the children "free and uninhibited." As she recalled, "Along with the wonderful paintings which they produced, I listened to confidences which allowed me to share their lives."[11]

"Each winter return to Florida gladdened my heart," wrote Lois, who benefitted physically and psychologically from the increase in sunlight and warmth.

The Coveys had initially chosen Tarpon Springs because rentals there were more affordable than real estate in Dunedin or Clearwater. She told Emma Celeste in 1948, their first winter in Tarpon Springs, that it was a "Greek sponge-fishing town . . . the *only* place that fitted our needs . . . as this town is not so 'touristy,' thank goodness." Although Lois always relished their Florida winters, Arthur, at first, resented "feeling cut off there from his professional contacts in New York." Gradually he, too, sensed that the warm weather benefitted his health and realized that Tarpon Springs gave him "more painting subjects . . . than in any of the other Fla. towns." Lois found the apartment they rented a great retreat, with its "good sized screened porch, with two cots for resting—which gets sun all thru main part of day—lovely trees & shrubs all around, & very private & quiet," and "2 big studio rooms, each 24 × 30 . . . at the rear end of a large old rambling house so well off the street, but only 2 min from center of town (5000 pop.)

and about 10 min. walk from the boats." Lois was not nearly so ready to return to Connecticut as Arthur, who looked forward to being closer to his older children and grandchildren.[12]

The Coveys' comfort in their Tarpon Springs surroundings increased greatly in 1951 when they decided to build a one-story home and bought a secondhand car to leave there. They had purchased two adjoining waterfront lots "with a fisherman's storage building on them." As she described in her autobiography,

> We added a large studio at each end . . . and turned the original building into a tiny living room and dining-kitchen area. . . . We each had our own privacy. At his end of the house, Mr. Covey could still stretch large canvases, splash oil paint and spill turpentine. He worked on his major mural commission, the ceiling paintings for Trinity Lutheran Church at Worcester, Massachusetts, during the early 1950s in this room. At my end of the house, with door closed, I could pound on my typewriter for long hours, undisturbed. . . .
>
> There were other allures, the chief one being the beautiful outdoors. . . . Mr. Covey . . . never tired of the scene or lost his skill in portraying it. Many of his finest watercolors were Florida subjects. Across the waterfront of our lots was an eighty-foot dock over a bayou, where fish leaped and sunshine danced on the waters.[13]

Lois wrote excitedly to Emma Celeste: "Here I am in Heaven!—That is, Florida, which is about as near to Heaven as I'll probably ever get. I'm sitting out on our dock in the warm sun . . . writing, as I listen to the pounding of carpenters' hammers inside our new home. . . . There is more built-in furniture to be made, linoleum to be laid, painting of kitchen cabinets, etc. But we hope to get moved in by the end of next week." The new arrangement simplified their seasonal journey by allowing them to travel by train and leave art supplies and all necessary household gear in their winter quarters. To her great pleasure, Lois could also now garden year-round.

Lois once told her great-niece, Kathy Sherpa, that she was like the daughter she never had, a memory Kathy cherishes. When she and a friend decided to drop in on "Aunt Lois" to surprise her during spring break in 1972, they found that the address to which Kathy had been writing since initiating their frequent correspondence nine years earlier "turned out not to exist!!" The two adventurous young women went to the local library, "and sure enough the librarian knew Aunt Lois's real address. She said Aunt Lois had disguised it all these years to avoid sightseers" but divulged it to them. Over forty years later, Kathy described Lois's house and the time spent there in loving detail:

> There was a long kitchen that separated the two sides of the house. It had windows all along it. She had placed hundreds of cobalt blue glass objects in the windows, and they literally glowed! She also had plants EVERYWHERE—inside and outside, including many begonias. She told me that she was planning to write a book called "All About Begonias," because she had learned so much by growing them over the years. As you passed beyond the kitchen, on the right was Uncle Arthur's studio, with murals and many paintings lying all around. As you passed beyond the kitchen on the left was Aunt Lois's studio: she had an upright piano; the cotton picker's sack from her regional "Cotton in My Sack" hung from the ceiling, and every child who had been in that book had signed the sack; she had an easel, and had been sketching; she had a desk with a typewriter, and piles of papers. It was beautiful! Her home was right on the edge of a body of water. We spent the day with her. It was a wonderful day![14]

By the time Kathy visited, Lois was living in Tarpon Springs alone. On February 6, 1960, Lois wrote very simply to Clyde Robert Bulla, with whom she had developed a great deal of trust through their many satisfying collaborations: "I have sad news for you. My dear husband died in his sleep Thursday [the previous] night. My friend, companion and helpmate of nearly forty years has left me, and I must travel the rest of the road alone. The children are coming today." In *Journey into Childhood*, Lois mentioned that Arthur had become very ill during the last two years of his life, but the "Florida sunshine" helped him recover and improve. Then on February 4, the day before his death, he told Lois how well he felt, and she went to his studio "to look at the bold, vigorous drawing on his easel." He told her, "I'll finish it tomorrow!" But he died in his sleep sometime that night or early the next morning at the age of eighty-two.[15]

Lois acted swiftly to ensure his legacy. In late May, just months after Arthur's death, Lois made a significant gift of "paintings, mural sketches,

Lois Lenski at her typewriter, Tarpon Springs, Florida, undated.
Courtesy of Jeanine Covey Gutowski, Vivian Covey, and Michael Covey.

etchings, lithographs, drawings, and watercolors by her late husband" to
Southwestern College in Winfield, Kansas, where Arthur had first studied
art. In the biography in the brochure designed for the occasion—not credited to Lois but undoubtedly her work—she explained, "Arthur Covey's art
was his life." The closing paragraphs of the presentation contain a succinct
overview of her appreciation for her husband's life work:

Out of his affection for this particular region of the United States,
out of his love for Kansas and Oklahoma soil, in which his first

roots were put down, and out of his gratitude to the College where he first began his art study, it was the earnest wish of Arthur Covey that a collection of his paintings find a permanent home here, to honor his life-long friend and first art teacher, Edith Dunlevy.

These paintings are not only the work of his two hands that once held the plow, but they are the reflection of his great soul and spirit. In them, although he has left us in the flesh, he will go on living, so that future generations may know him as well as we.

The following year Lois endowed the Arthur Covey Memorial Art Scholarship at Southwestern College in honor and memory of her late husband, to be awarded to "the student-artist who demonstrates the finest ability and desire to continue in further preparation for a professional art career in Drawing and Painting." At the same time, she gave the college library Arthur's collection of art books, establishing "the art section of the library as one of the finest collections of its kind in this area, especially in the field of the history of costume."[16] Arthur had consulted these books in executing his many historically based murals.

In August 1960 Lois told Clyde about the "beautiful & inspiring memorial service for Mr. Covey" held at Trinity Lutheran Church in Worcester, Massachusetts, where Arthur's final and most difficult series of murals decorated the ceiling. Although she was recovering from having a collapsed lobe of her right lung removed (a repeat of the operation performed the previous fall on her left lung), Lois felt that she could not miss the ceremony. "The triumphant recognition of his life's work was my reward. (A beautiful stone tablet was installed in the nave & dedicated to his memory)."[17]

Between 1961 and 1965, Lois donated Arthur's biographical material, correspondence, business records, notes and writings, artwork, project files, a scrapbook, printed materials, and photographs to the Archives of American Art of the Smithsonian Institution, again to honor and preserve the legacy of his long and productive career.[18] Widowhood, the sorting and organizing of her husband's effects, and her own advancing age and deteriorating health very likely motivated Lois to think about the projects on which she might want to focus, the destinations for her own work, and the processes needed to make accessible the artifacts of her career as an artist, author, and illustrator.

After Arthur's death, Lois at first retained the Coveys' annual living arrangement of Connecticut summers and Florida winters, but she now spent only three months in Harwinton instead of six. After two summers trying to maintain two houses, she realized that the effort took more energy than she cared to devote. Distributing the effects of Arthur's career very likely made her aware that she would soon do the same for herself and that she needed to simplify her life by giving up Greenacres. "I spent two summers clearing out the contents of his [Arthur's] studio and finding a depository for a record of his life's work," she wrote. "Then I began on my own."[19] In a letter written to Clyde in June 1962, Lois laid out what most concerned her at this critical juncture of her life and invited him to join her in the process of coming to terms with her materials and the legacy she wanted to leave:

> I wonder if you would consent to be my Literary Executor, after my death? I have to re-write my will this summer & must select some one. Since Mr. Covey's death, there is no one in the family who is equipped to do it. . . . There will have to be various questions decided, as to reprints, mostly, after I am not here to do it myself. You would be "in the know" because you are in a similar situation.
>
> If there is a possibility that you could undertake it, how would you like the idea of a trip to Conn. this summer? Marie Ram will be there with me part of the time, & we will be working on contents of my studio, getting more things ready for distribution to Libraries. It would be a good time to acquaint you with details you would need to know. I don't think it would be a burdensome task for you, but it should be some one in the book field to make the necessary decisions as they come up. You are so much younger than I, you should outlive me for many years.
>
> Think it over, no need to decide right now. But if you like the idea of a trip to Conn., maybe you could find some story material in New England. . . .
>
> Write me how you feel about it.[20]

Lois was thrilled with Clyde's acceptance, reassuring him, "No one could do it better than you." She then made the offer of time spent at Greenacres more specific. Marie Ram would be there, acting as a summer personal assistant to Lois, and the author was looking forward to their

Lois Lenski reading from *Flood Friday* to a group of children in Unionville, Connecticut, 1956. Courtesy of the *Hartford Courant* and located in Illinois State University's Special Collections, Milner Library.

meeting, because she wanted them both to "become acquainted with my various literary materials" so that the two of them could "perhaps be of service to Laird in deciding about their disposal." Lois described the need to assemble the "manuscripts and the other multitudinous materials connected with my work, and to distribute them to a number of libraries, most of them in universities, who had begun collecting my work."[21]

She had actually begun distributing her illustrations much earlier, well before Arthur's decline and death. In September 1956 she sent a mimeographed letter addressed to "My dear Library friends" around the United States, explaining that having spent her career illustrating and writing books for children, she had faced a dilemma: "What about all those accumulated illustrations?" When they overflowed her filing cabinets, Lois "decided to do something—to give them back to the children who inspired them, who have loved them in printed books." Earlier that summer, she (with Marie Ram, at least some of the time) had begun "preparing the illustrations for their future and permanent homes." They had cleaned; cut mats for them, "(over 200) myself," Lois claimed; "mounted, labeled, signed, sorted, selected, covered, and at last bundled and packed these drawings and shipped them to you . . . a labor of love." Lois explained that she had tried to make assortments of illustrations that typified her work—those from her picture books, from the series for middle-level readers, and those created for other authors—so those viewing them would get a sense of her "development as an illustrator." She concluded with a statement of the purpose and deep personal meaning of the materials she bequeathed so generously: "Dear librarians, when you give these drawings a home in your Library, when you use them, display them, share them with groups of children and adults, service, repair and preserve them, I shall be there at your side. For each drawing is a part of me, a bond between me and my beloved readers everywhere."[22]

Even as she busily organized and distributed materials over summers in Harwinton, often with Marie's help, Lois was still writing and illustrating new manuscripts. Marilyn Doesken Perry, Lois's great-niece (one of Esther Ferne's daughters), spent the summer of 1960 visiting Lois and assisting with typing. Marilyn recalled fifty-five years later that her great-aunt "made me feel competent and appreciated, the whole experience . . . incredibly wonderful and made me feel like visiting royalty . . . one of the high points of my high school years."[23] Lois was also still accruing honors and artifacts, even as she began sending her materials to libraries and collections. On May 8, 1959, she received her first honorary doctorate of letters from Wartburg College, a liberal arts college affiliated with the Evangelical Lutheran Church of America, in Waverly, Iowa; followed by an honorary doctorate of humane letters from the University of North Carolina at Greensboro, awarded June 4, 1962. Four years later, Capital University in Columbus, Ohio, presented her with an honorary doctorate of literature, as did Southwestern College in Winfield, Kansas, in 1966.

In 1969 two prestigious awards provided Lois significant recognition, reminding children's librarians and other adults in the world of children's literature that her books, in particular, could be sources of strength for young readers. First, the de Grummond Collection of Children's Literature at the library of the University of Southern Mississippi, Hattiesburg, presented her its first medallion. The silver "coin" bears Lois's image on the front and the inscription "Out of her great riches she gives gifts to the children of all time," and on the reverse side, the central image selected by Lois came from the cover of *Judy's Journey*, with "Awarded by the University of Southern Mississippi" (USM) above and "Lois Lenski" inscribed below. The same spirit prevailed later that year at a conference of the Catholic Library Association in New Orleans where Lois was honored with the association's Regina Medal. In her opening remarks, presenter Sister M. Julianne, O.P., stated, "Today, as we award the Regina Medal to you, we, who know you through your books, consider you a 'friend worth knowing.'" She then elaborated on the theme:

> In giving succeeding generations sincere and authentic portraits of life, Miss Lenski has introduced them to many friends, while she herself has gained many admirers.
>
> A "friend" is someone who is attached to another by esteem, respect, and affection. Esteem for Lois Lenski's writing comes from the authenticity with which she writes. Reality is the substance of our lives, and Miss Lenski makes it a practice to be true to life while she inspires a child with splendid ideals. . . .
>
> Numerous events in our country today are examples of the hate that kills, the fear that paralyzes, the prejudice that shrivels, the suspicion that stifles and the ignorance that stunts. Understanding, openness, trust, and love, positive qualities evident in Miss Lenski's writings, help to counteract these tragedies. Her descriptions of life in many regions of our land enrich our lives. They lead the reader to be open, to appreciate and to love the persons encountered in her books.[24]

In mentioning "the hate that kills" and "the fear that paralyzes," Sister Julianne was very likely referring to the events of the previous year that shocked and horrified the American public—especially the assassinations of Reverend Martin Luther King, Jr., and Senator Robert Kennedy. The concluding remarks of Lois's acceptance speech gave her the opportunity to reiterate her major thesis: social justice through mutual understanding. "My books have served two purposes, I believe, in revealing certain less well-known ways of life. They have taken the blinders off the eyes of many of our advantaged children. . . . My books have also given new prestige to the children I have written about—cotton children, mountain children, city children, river children and others, previously neglected." She was proud that an eighth-grade African American child reading *Judy's Journey* in Chicago could say, "We never knew that white children had a hard time of it too," and that another child felt "as if I was right there living with the people in the story."[25]

Lois was still working on her picture book series and Regional and Roundabout series during the 1960s, but aware of her own advancing years, she also embarked on new projects closer to her heart: an anthology of her poetry, a collection of Christmas stories, and her autobiography. All three may be considered efforts to complete the circle in the limited number of years she felt remained. Each fulfilled a separate but interrelated need, and all three looped back to her childhood. In the foreword to her collected poems, *The Life I Live* (1965), Lois calls this "the happiest of all my books" because it contains "a lifetime of love and devotion to children." She wrote no poetry during the 1930s and 1940s and only returned to it as she began to write lyrics for the songs she decided to include in her regionals—after her introduction to Clyde Robert Bulla as the illustrator for his first book. She explained that she had included American folk songs in her first regionals but, in her research for *Cotton in My Sack*, found that the only cotton-picking songs were "Negro in origin," and she wanted to create some for "the white cotton-picker," too, who had been underrepresented in folk song collections. Lois explained her motivation for getting back to poetry, which she saw as "the basic fabric behind all my work for children," since poems included themes that were her "life's blood." Although her poetry dates to the 1920s, most of the verses—some never published previously—composed for *The Life I Live* date from the 1950s and 1960s. This was a time period fraught with illness and restrictions on her physical activities. Lois found poetry restful, the one creative activity that could be managed in bed. She took pleasure in collecting and categorizing a lifetime's worth of verses, and as she put it, "To note what a strong thread of 'understanding others' runs through them all."[26]

Some of the poems are truly specific to their original context, with a useful index of titles that includes information about when the poem was written and in which publication it originally appeared.[27] Not surprisingly, some of the most successful poems were not previously published and work beautifully here, such as "House or Home" (1952):

A house is a building
With walls and a door;
A home is a house,
But also much more.
A house is a place
To eat and to sleep;
A home is a place
To laugh and to weep.
A house is a shelter
From wind and from rain;
A home is a haven
From sorrow and pain.
A house has four walls,
A roof o'er your head;
A home is a center
Where kind words are said.
A house may protect
From storms above;
A home is a haven
Of kindness and love.[28]

Another poem that appears here for the first time, "A Book Can Take Me" (1960), addresses the purpose behind Lois's entire body of work in a few short lines:

A book can take me
out and away,
To another world,
to another day;
To another life
I have never known,
To another life
unlike my own.

A book can open
for me a door
To another life

unknown before;
A book can give me
understanding new,
Of people and places
my whole life through.[29]

Finally, several later poems reveal something of the pleasure that Lois derived from her gardening, which soothed her spirit both in Connecticut and in Florida, best expressed in "My Garden" (1963):

A carpet of green,
cool depths of shade;
A burst of color
That paint never made.
Gray pattern of vine
Or stem or leaf,
Tender new growth
Stands out in relief.

A sea of loveliness,
A world of its own,
Inside the gate
I wander alone.
Here peace and joy
And deep content,
Here tranquility
To me is sent.[30]

Lois provided charming line drawings that enliven, rather than illustrate, most pages. Some are cartoon-like yet expressive stick figures, while others resemble those from the Roundabout series or *We Are Thy Children*. The overall effect of these lovingly decorated pages reveal the happiness Lois invested in amassing the verses. Her publisher, Henry Z. Walck, probably realized that another Lenski publication practically guaranteed good sales and would highlight the other books in their catalog from which she drew material.

Lippincott issued its own Lenski anthology in 1968, *Lois Lenski's*

Christmas Stories. The holiday delighted Lois as a child and remained important throughout her life as a combination of ideals: a remembrance of family
love and a striving to emulate Jesus as the lamb of God, both coupled with
aesthetic beauty. As she states in the foreword to the collection, "Despite
the cheapness and commercialism which has changed it [the holiday] in
modern times from an essentially religious festival, it still retains its vital
and universal appeal. . . . For in this rapidly changing world, its message of
goodwill is still, as it has been since the birth in Bethlehem, the one thing
the world most needs." As she wrote to her nonobservant son and daughter-
in-law in December 1960: "I hope that you will remember and perpetuate
some of the Lenski and Covey family Christmas traditions, which Dad and
I established during all those years at Greenacres. I hope you can take the
children to at least one beautiful Christmas service at church . . . perhaps
a children's program, which they would be able to understand. Without
church, the whole meaning of Christmas is lost."[31]

As in *The Life I Live,* most of the contents have been repurposed from
earlier publications, since Lois featured the holiday in many of her books
in her historical series as well as the Regionals and Roundabouts. She also
included a version of the Anna, Ohio, Christmases of her youth, which she
fictionalized as "The Pink China Bonbon Dish," originally appearing in
The Christmas Annual of 1939. Lois commented that the story was "sparked"
by a memory Miriam had shared. She had seen a beautiful bonbon dish
in the window of the dry goods store, the perfect gift for her mother,
although she had no money for it. In the fictional version, Lois's younger
sister "borrowed" the dish, intending to pay for it later. Guilt overwhelmed
her, she confessed, and the story has a happily resolved ending. Actually,
Lois told the story more autobiographically many years before in *A Little
Girl of Nineteen Hundred,* in which she, not Miriam, had taken something
from the store without paying for it—an English walnut. She repeated
this version in *Journey into Childhood* when she wrote about being a child
with "an exaggerated moral sense." She, like her fictional counterparts,
was plagued by guilt before owning up to her parents, who never "said
one word about it, so perhaps they understood." This exact phrase appears
in both *A Girl of Nineteen Hundred* and in *Journey into Childhood.* That she
fictionalized the memory twice—and felt it significant enough to include
in her autobiography, published two years before she died—reveals a great
deal about Lois's hyperactive conscience. And that "exaggerated moral

sense" penetrated all the books she created for middle-level readers, as she worked to move from moralizing to imbuing "meaning," best expressed in her essay "Beyond the Rim of Our Own World": "Direct moral teaching of earlier days has gone out of storybooks for children, and a new kind of moralizing has come in. Perhaps it would be wise to discard the word moral entirely. So let us say that our modern books for children do not have a *moral*, that they do have a *meaning*. The *moral* is not stated in so many words, the *meaning* is implied—it has to be dug out."[32] Lois also wrote new poems and a short play for *Christmas Stories*, but the bulk of the offerings that she lovingly revisited, selected, and revised demonstrate the way Lois reshaped her own narrative as well as those she created in fiction.

Shortly after Lois completed these projects, she learned that Stephen's marriage was ending. During the summer of 1970, the grandchildren— Michael (age fourteen), Vivian (celebrating her thirteenth birthday while there), and Jeanine (age six)—spent five weeks with Lois. Michael considers her "very supportive" to be willing "to take in two adolescents and a young child." Because her energy was no match for theirs, Lois "arranged to have an older teenage girl" act as a companion during some of the day, so that she could work and rest while they enjoyed places around Tarpon Springs such as the beach or a "nearby swimming hole." Michael has vivid memories of specific events: "fishing several times in the bayou with bamboo rods off of the dock/patio in back of Lois's house, walking into the town of Tarpon Springs with Lois, visiting Lois's next-door neighbors, the Leonards (he was a deep-sea fisherman by trade and later took me out on the Gulf for a week of fishing)." Lois "had a map on the wall of her kitchen/eating room" and had the grandchildren "plot the positions of the summer's hurricanes." She also shared her work with them, showing them "illustrations she was inking in for what must have been one of her last books." She also spent a lot of time with correspondence and business letters. Looking back, "Vivian empathizes with Lois's predicament of having to take care of an adolescent preteen/teen girl who was upset about the breakup of her parents' marriage." And in retrospect, Michael remembers that the three "were behaving as children of the early 70's behaved, while Lois had brought up children many years before, when children behaved less rebelliously. We were all fish out of water. There was no 'listen and respond.' . . . I don't think we offered much discussion, and Lois was probably a bit conflicted over her son's divorce."[33] But she was there for them as a base of support, as only a grandmother could be.

In preparation for writing her autobiography, Lois asked her long-term correspondents—Mabel Pugh, Emma Celeste Thibodaux, and Marie Ram, among others—to return any extant letters they had saved so that she could use them to reconstruct and flesh out the chronology of her long career. Lois used the letters directly in drafting the first handwritten version of *Journey into Childhood,* then incorporated them in her own words in subsequent revisions. As discussed in earlier chapters, the results of this practical methodology are not altogether successful, although the fault may lie less in the methodology than in the impression that the storyteller wanted to conceal perhaps more than she was willing to reveal. Stephen Covey and Kathy Sherpa both mentioned that Lois was not pleased with what she felt to be excessive editing and was ultimately disappointed and dissatisfied with the publication.

In March 1972 Lois asked Kathy if she would be willing to be the "Lenski Photo Archivist" because of Kathy's expressed interest in old family photographs. When her father died, Lois had managed to rescue his negatives dating from the time she was a child. She decided that these ought to be kept by someone "with the name Lenski (which in these modern Women's Lib days, you will probably keep, even after you marry)." Lois enclosed in the letter a clipping from "a recent issue of Sat. Review" regarding "some Women's Lib publications" that she thought would interest Kathy, especially "the mention of Emma Goldman on the 2nd page." Lois may have already told Kathy of her fascination with Goldman during her Art League student days. This discussion prefaced Lois's sharing her high degree of frustration with her autobiography. The passages below reveal her feeling that the emergence of the women's movement—between the time she wrote *Journey into Childhood* and its publication—had so altered women's perceptions of their own history that the book might seem irrelevant. In fact, *Journey into Childhood* was even somewhat anachronistic by the time it reached the public:

> Four years ago (five rather) when I was writing JOURNEY, there was not so much publicity on "Women's Lib." In fact I don't think I had even heard this new movement mentioned, so I did not put in my account of career-vs-family to fit into that cause, at all, as "now" readers may be apt to think. I simply told the facts of my

experiences, and I still don't think a woman can do BOTH, without making many compromises. The only way I did it was by earning the money to pay for household help to do the house chores I (theoretically) should have been doing myself. Of course, I had the added burden (or difficulty) of poor health. Maybe women who are stronger physically than I ever was, could have done BOTH more easily than I did. . . .

While I greatly appreciate your admiration of my book, I realize there are many lacks in it. I had a change of editors midstream, even the first one who had suggested I write the book, became unsympathetic to the idea, must have been having editorial troubles, so she up & left. The new one, who took her place, did not relish taking over a book from her predecessor & so was equally unsympathetic. Four years went by with delay after delay, meantime costs went soaring, so it became more & more difficult to get it published at all. Also the mood of the reading public has changed. I think it would have been better understood & appreciated 4 years ago than now. . . . One of the compromises was drastic cutting of many portions of the book. As I wrote my first editor (who slashed it unmercifully) "all the enrichment has been removed, & it is nothing now but its bare bones."[34]

Lois was also frustrated that the edited version of her autobiography did not adequately convey a sense of the way she created books. She bemoaned the fact that "the section of the Regionals was entirely removed, with a vague promise they might use it in a second & separate volume, which now, the second editor says she does not want." And Lois complained that other deletions shredded the heart and soul of her story. She admitted that she probably had to be "thankful that any of it got into print."[35] But before she died, Lois wanted to make sure that her work created its own financial legacy to benefit less privileged youngsters' access to good children's literature.

She established the Lois Lenski Covey Foundation, Inc., in 1967 "to advance literacy and foster a love of reading among underserved and at-risk children and youth." After considering the possibility of establishing scholarships for those interested in bettering the lives of at-risk youth, Lois made her wishes to the board more explicit in a letter the following year:

"I prefer to work more directly. I can put books directly into the hands of children who have never had them, *now*—without hoping that it may be done some day in such a roundabout manner."[36]

Since 1975 the foundation's Library Grant Program has become its top priority, providing funds to libraries specifically "earmarked for purchasing books for young people." Through the foundation, Lois's passion for social justice translates into providing children with the stuff of dreams "that can open . . . a door / To another life / unknown before," as her poem "A Book Can Take Me," cited above, points out.[37]

Lois died on September 11, 1974, a month shy of her eighty-first birthday. Emma Celeste shared the sad news with Clyde:

> My mail was delayed, placed in the wrong box, so I just got a letter from Marie Ram saying Lois died Sept. 14. Stephen Covey phoned Marie Sept 14. She was in Mease Hospital in Florida four weeks with emphesema [*sic*] and one week at home in bed with Kathy Covey Stephen's new wife as cook nurse companion and comfort. Lois had a legal paper stating no injections or drugs were to be given her to prolong the end. Lois was buried Sept 14 at 2:30 beside her husband Arthur in a Florida cemetery. . . . I thought her husband was buried "up north" perhaps she had him re-intered [*sic*].[38]

Emma Celeste was as confused about the dates as she was about Arthur's burial. On September 13, 1974, Lois was interred next to her husband at Sylvan Abbey Memorial Park in Clearwater, Florida. Her headstone bears the simple inscription "Friend of Children," just as she would have wanted to be remembered.[39]

The first use of the phrase "Friend of Children" appeared as the title of a thirty-page booklet produced by Lippincott in 1958, most likely to promote the works of Lois to prospective bookstore, school, or library purchasers. The opening vignette contains a charming anecdote that captures the essence of Lois's strengths:

> A small boy came up to the librarian's desk. "Please," he said, "I want a book by my friend, Lois Lenski."
>
> The librarian smiled. "Your friend?" she said. "Do you *know* her?"

The little face fell.

"Well, er . . . no, I never saw her, but . . ." The boy looked up again. "I have one of her books at home. She signed her name in it and said she was my friend."

The next time the boy came, he proudly displayed his autographed copy: "With love, your friend, Lois Lenski."

All the letters that Lois Lenski writes to her "fans" are signed, "Your friend, Lois Lenski." And that is what she is, the friend of all children."[40]

This anecdote also brings to mind another young fan of Lois's, Mary Scott from Whittier, California, who first wrote on June 23, 1931, to tell the author, "I am an admirer of you'r [sic] book, Little Girl of Nineteen Hundred . . . I am a little girl 8 years old and want to write a story about a city girl's vacation. I started like this Jean Allen was sitting in a hammock. But I am at a great loss at what to say now. I wondered if you could tell me how you get your nice ideas." Five years later, Mary sent Lois a handmade card on folded rice-like paper to mark the author's forty-third birthday. The cover features a colored-pencil drawing of a girl and the words "A Girl to her Favorite Author," with the signature, Mary Scott, in the bottom right-hand corner. She has meticulously drawn light pencil lines so that all the words line up correctly between them. Once the card is open, the following poem appears:

> Oh you who wrote my dearest books,
> I wonder if you knew
> That I would steal away
> Alone to quiet secret nooks
> Where I could weigh
> Your every word and
> Dream about it too.
> I wonder if you thought of me
> O you who wrote my books
> I wonder if you struggled hard
> And if your hopes came true.
> I wonder all about your life,
> Your joys, your friends, your looks.

I wonder if you longed for fame,
As other people do.
I wonder if you thought of me
O you who wrote my books.

On the back page, Mary drew a candle and an open book beneath, and on the pages of the book she's written, "Happy Birthday Lois Lenski 1936." Lois undoubtedly answered Mary's letter as she did each child who wrote and was clearly moved by her poem. Lois placed it opposite a third half-title page in *Journey into Childhood* but dated it there "1950," very likely because she had kept only a typed (and undated?) copy of the poem and may have misremembered when it had been sent.[41] In 1968 Lois copyrighted "Dear Child," a probable answer to Mary's poem, and used it to introduce the last chapter in *Adventure in Understanding*—the only time it was ever published. Stephen Covey included "Dear Child" in two of his talks, one "on the occasion of the dedication of the Lois Lenski Elementary School in Littleton, Colorado on October 14, 1979," and the other delivered on April 10, 1999, when he accepted the Kerlan Award from the Kerlan Collection of Children's Literature at the University of Minnesota on behalf of his mother. It speaks eloquently to Mary Scott and to all of Lois's readers—from the very

Illustration from a Christmas card Lois Lenski designed. Courtesy of the Lois Lenski Papers, Special Collections, Butler Library, Buffalo State College.

youngest fans of Mr. Small to those who discovered her when they were in elementary or middle school.

> To you
> who read my books
> and write to me,
> This poem will
> my answer be.
>
> All my books are stories true,
> Of boys and girls and what they do.
> Their lives may be strange,
> Their customs new,
> Yet underneath
> They are much like you.
> Outside different, inside akin,
> Brothers and sisters under the skin.
>
> To you
> my love I send,
> I am your friend,
> A friend of children here and there,
> A friend of children
> everywhere.[42]

My Journey to Lois Lenski

My own journey to this biography began many years before I systematically started the research. Looking through my files when writing one of the final chapters, I came across a letter dated 1992 from the De Grummond Collection of Children's Literature at the University of Southern Mississippi. I must have inquired about their holdings on Lois Lenski, and library staff responded affirmatively. At the time I was writing my dissertation in American history at Tulane University that became the biography *Rabbi Max Heller: Reformer, Zionist, Southerner* (1997)—a far cry from children's literature—yet I must have been thinking about Lois while immersed in southern Jewish history. I am so glad that I waited to write about her until after I retired from my position at the Wisconsin Historical Society where I researched, wrote about, and edited materials produced for classrooms (mostly fourth-grade) on the history of the state. Engaging young students and their teachers in the many real stories of Wisconsin history and the cultures that contribute to it made me much more alert to the challenges and delights of reaching a young audience. I retired *in order to* write this biography. I finally fulfilled a lifetime dream: I got to know Lois.

I began by acquiring and reading or rereading her books. April

Hoffman, then librarian at Randall Elementary School in Madison, told me that many school librarians were discarding older books, and she offered to gather any Lenski books she could from her colleagues. Since the 1980s, I'd been scouring used bookstores and antique malls looking for Lenskis, and the box from April helped build my small collection. By then, the Internet booksellers arrived on the scene, and I was able to fill in the entire historical and regional series. I told the folks at the Cooperative Children's Book Center at the University of Wisconsin that I was on a mission, and the staff proved incredibly helpful: director emeritus Ginny Moore Kruse, director Kathleen T. Horning, and librarian Megan Schliesman, all of whom encouraged me and pointed me to resources to provision my research journey. After one of their annual book sales, someone on the staff sent me a small promotional record produced under the auspices of publisher Henry Z. Walck in 1963, *A Message from Lois Lenski*. When I played the "A" side, I heard Lois talking about "The Making of a Picture Book." The "B" side contained a sampling of Lenski-Bulla songs from the record *Frank Luther Sings Lois Lenski Songs*. Hearing Lois's warm voice reinforced my determination to begin in earnest.

Lois Lenski's family members, especially her late son, Stephen, have been very gracious. Stephen oriented me to the vast amount of materials she spread so liberally in archives and libraries around the country, telling me which were the most critical to visit. He also generously answered many questions about his childhood and his parents and put me in touch with George Nicholson, the longtime agent for the Lois Lenski Covey Foundation. George offered pertinent suggestions and tremendous support for the biography and was briefly my literary agent before his untimely death. Stephen's son, Michael, took over leadership of the Lois Lenski Covey Foundation after his father's death and continues to support her legacy as she so wisely intended. He put me in touch with other family members, helped me navigate the vagaries of research in various collections, read a draft of the manuscript when I completed it, and allowed me access to many family photographs and family letters. Step-daughter Margaret's son Alan and his wife, Linda, and daughter, Eleanor Landauer; David and Robert Chisholm; and nephew Gerhard E. Lenski and his daughter, Katherine Lenski Sherpa, shared photographs, analysis, insights, and delight in her memories and in my work. From Kathy Sherpa, I learned about a beautiful photograph of Lois as a child owned by another great-niece, Jan Ferne Haueisen, and she and her husband, Bill, made it available for this publication. She also reached out to other members of Lois's extended Lenski descendants who shared some of their memories.

Beyond the Lenski family, I found people who remembered Lois or had direct association with her. When I googled Lois's hometown of Anna, Ohio, I saw that the Shelby County Historical Society's front page and leading article featured "Return to Skipping Village" (www.shelby-countyhistory.org/schs/archives/women/llenskiwomena.htm), written by Ann Marguerite Ressler of Dayton, Ohio. R. C. H. Lenski had trained Marguerite's father, Rev. F. J. Mittermaier, at Capital University, and he served as pastor of St. Jacob Lutheran Church in Anna some years after R. C. H. had retired. Marguerite grew up in the same parsonage that had been Lois Lenski's home in Anna and shared her memories of Anna some decades later as well as her parents' perceptions of Lois, when she returned to Anna for a visit after Marguerite had left home. We spent delightful hours at the Resslers' home and still continue our warm correspondence. Before I visited Harwinton, the local librarian put me in touch with one of Lois's former neighbors, Joan Anderson Kirchner, who remembered Lois from the decades in which she and Arthur split their time between Harwinton and Tarpon Springs. Joan spent the day with my husband and me, regaling us with stories, introducing us to Arthur's extant murals in the Torrington area, gaining access to Greenacres, which was on the real estate market at the time, and introducing us to Jane Reynolds Pallokat. Jane, like Joan, lives on Harmony Hill Road and spent childhood summers with her grandparents, who lived directly across from the Coveys. She shared memories of accompanying her grandmother, who often drove Lois on her seemingly endless (to Jane, anyway) searches for exotic plants for her rock garden. Jane also shared her grandmother's collection of materials related to the Coveys. Joan continued to put me in touch with others who had some association with Lois and came to visit Wisconsin, where I introduced her to Arthur's Kohler murals. Joan also put me in touch with the Covey's across-the-road neighbor, Marjorie Smith Olson, who had modeled for Lois and graciously described how still she had to sit and how difficult it was to accomplish this task.

Just like Lois, I enjoy collaborating. I organized a group of women interested in children's literature and/or Lois Lenski and works of her contemporaries. We call ourselves Madison Friends of Lois Lenski and meet regularly, as we have done for the past four years. Anne Altshuler, Alice Appen, Susan Daugherty, April Hoffman, Madge Klais, and Peggy Marxen have been the stalwarts, reading and discussing the work of Lois and her contemporaries and critiquing my chapters as I drafted them. Susan also admirably proofread the final pages. The group continues to read historical Newbery Award winners and classical regional writers for children and adults. My two major manuscript editors, friends Ann Boyer and Christine Schelshorn, decided they were more interested in editing than in talking about children's literature. Ann splendidly edited the complete manuscript that went off to the University of Oklahoma Press, and many revisions later, Christine contributed her own accurate and well-considered edits of the ultimate revised version, just as she had done for many of my projects for the Wisconsin Historical Society.

Lois Lenski deposited her materials in many university and college libraries and archives, and in several museum and public library collections. Some institutions, particularly the University of Oklahoma, the University of North Carolina at Greensboro, Capital University, Buffalo State College, and Illinois State University have especially impressive collections, with many primary documents and illustrations in addition to her publications. Others like the University of Southern Mississippi, Arkansas State University, the University of Minnesota, Syracuse University, and Florida State University have medium-sized collections that include original manuscripts and illustrations, and even the smaller collections have original as well as published materials. Quite often, collections developed because of one librarian's respect for children's literature. At Florida State, for example, the Lenski collection "was started in the 1950s as a result of a request by Louise Richardson, who was head of FSU Special Collections at the time. She contacted Mrs. Lenski, asking for 'even just a page or drawing from Strawberry Girl.'" And the collection grew from the two illustrations Lois originally sent.[1] Originally Lenski sent only these drawings, but in 1958 Lenski presented Strozier Library with a substantially larger collection of her books, original drawings, articles, and other miscellaneous items. Since that time, the purchase of many additional Lenski books has added to the overall interest and value of the collection.

Lois, often with the help of Marie Ram, worked hard to compile duplicates of significant photographs for various collections and place them in albums. She also assembled a variety of sketches and illustrations-in-process in addition to the final renderings that she sent to her publishers so student librarians and elementary student teachers could get a real sense of the work that went into making books for young readers. I joke that she placed things all over the country, from the University of California and the University of Wyoming to Florida State and Syracuse with ample deposits in the Midwest and South, because she was trying to discourage any would-be biographer, preferring her own *Journey into Childhood* as the last word on her life. Actually, I believe she was reaching out to those undergraduates and graduate students in elementary education and library science who would guide the reading for coming generations of children. Librarians at some of these institutions recognized the value of collecting contemporary children's literature and sought materials from well-known authors. In other cases, Lois received several honorary doctorates or other honors (Capital University, University of North Carolina at Greensboro, the University of Southern Mississippi, and the University of Minnesota come to mind), and Lois returned the favor by presenting these institutions with collections. Whatever her original intent, tracking down and mining these collections became an immensely exciting, if challenging, aspect of the research.

As my husband and I drove down to visit our families in Texas in 2010, I happened to glance at our AAA guidebook for Missouri, which, quite surprisingly, mentioned that William Jewell College in Liberty had a Lois Lenski collection. We drove to the college on our way back to Madison and spent several hours photocopying articles written by Lois or biographical in nature, mostly from fairly obscure, religiously oriented publications not mentioned in any secondary materials. I also saw Lois's original lithographs there for the first time, the artwork that she'd stopped producing once she became a full-time author-illustrator. After I retired the following year, I began archival journeys in earnest, visiting the largest repositories, as Steven (Stephen) Covey had suggested. Carolyn Shankle and David Gwynn at the Martha Blakeney Hodges Special Collections and University Archives, University Libraries, at the University of North Carolina at Greensboro helped me secure illustrations from the marvelous Lois Lenski papers housed there. In addition to manuscripts, illustrations, and photographs principally related to *Bayou Suzette*, *Blue Ridge Billy*, and *Peanuts for Billy Ben*, this collection houses Lois's extensive library of early American children's literature and some of the toys she designed for manufacture.

The Milner Library Special Collections at Illinois State University has published online a complete list of all the books that Lois Lenski wrote and illustrated and her speeches and articles (http://library.illinoisstate. edu/unique-collections/lois-lenski/work.php). ILSU archivists Maureen Brunsdale and Mark Schmitt gave me complete access to the Lois Lenski materials there, which include the incomparable scrapbooks for *San Francisco Boy*, *Corn Farm Boy*, and *Houseboat Girl*. Through them, I was able to track down James Sue, the real "San Francisco Boy," who still lives in the city; Debbie Story Saylors and Irene Story Freeman, who shared memories of the summer when Lois Lenski was doing research on their family's houseboat for *Houseboat Girl*; and "Corn-Farm Boy" Noel Leinen, now living in Nebraska. These encounters reinforced my enthusiasm for her work and the impact it made on the children about whom she was writing. Closer to publication, Matthew Cook scanned all the illustrations from the collection that I needed.

Other archivists who were extremely welcoming included Dan DiLandro and Margaret Hatfield at the Edward H. Butler Library Special Collections at Buffalo State College, who made me very much at home among the manuscripts; Malissa Davis, Brady Banta, and David Doughan at the Archives and Special Collections, Dean B. Ellis Library, Arkansas State University–Jonesboro; and Ellen Ruffin at the de Grummond Collection, McCain Library and Archives, University of Southern Mississippi, Hattiesburg. Other collections with invaluable Lenski resources include the largest and most beautifully organized at the Western History Collections, University of Oklahoma Libraries, Norman; Blackmore Library, Capital University, Columbus, Ohio, where Steve Long was very helpful during my second visit and closer to publication; Kerlan Collection, Children's Literature Research Collection, Elmer L. Andersen Library, University of Minnesota; and Syracuse University Library. I obtained letters related to *San Francisco Boy* from the Lois Lenski Collection at Bancroft Library, University of California at Berkeley, and materials related to *Judy's Journey* from the Division of Home Mission Records, 1950–1964, National Council of Churches of Christ in the United States, Presbyterian Historical Society, Philadelphia, Pennsylvania. Archivist Linnea Anderson at the Social Welfare History Archives, Elmer L. Andersen Library, University of Minnesota, helped me navigate the Child Study Association of America Records and the Association of Junior Leagues of America Records there, while Naomi Williamson and Rusty Smith at the Clyde Robert Bulla Collection, Philip A. Sadler Collection, at the James C. Kirkpatrick Library, University of Central Missouri, Warrensburg, guided me to correspondence between Lois and her longtime collaborator and co-author. Although I did not visit Florida State University, Lisa Girard, Special Collections manager, facilitated my request for an illustration from the Lois Lenski Collection there. Katherine Kunau at the Cedar Rapids Art Museum showed me the Lois Lenski illustrations held by the Cedar Rapids Public Library, which once again reminded me of the many librarian allies Lois made across the country. Cedar Rapids Library director Dara Schmidt granted permission to use one of them. And Rich Messina at the *Hartford Courant* granted permission to reproduce a photograph from the newspaper archives.

Children's literature historian and critic Leonard S. Marcus offered advice to help me get started; Stephen Geiger, Wisconsin Lutheran Seminary, Mequon, Wisconsin, helped me understand more about R. C. H. Lenski's importance to the Lutheran Church; Julia Mickenberg advised me about secondary materials related to mid-twentieth-century cultural history; and an unnamed reader for the University of Oklahoma Press alerted me to Gary D. Schmidt's *Making Americans: Children's Literature from 1930 to 1960* (2013), which was immensely helpful. More friends than I can thank recalled their own Lois Lenski stories, many of which made it into the manuscript, and Elaine Maney, Kathy Gilbert, Nancy Smith, Lois Charles, Robin Halpren-Ruder, Marcie Ferris, Shirley Barnes, Linda Shriberg, Karen Goodin, and Sarah Brooks, among others, cheered from the sidelines. And it was *beshert* (Yiddish for "meant to be") that Kent Calder, our good friend and former editorial director at the Wisconsin Historical Society, should have accepted a position as acquisitions editor at the University of Oklahoma Press just as I had finished my manuscript. Since the Lois Lenski collection at OU is the most prominent of any institution, I am thrilled that the press decided to publish my biography. Along with Kent Calder, the OU Press production team for the project included assistant managing editor Stephanie Evans, who patiently walked me through the process; Daniel Simon, copyeditor, whose keen eye and sensitivity to continuity of style improved the flow of the text; Anna Maria Rodriguez, production coordinator; Tony Roberts, cover designer and production manager; Julie Rushing, book designer; Shannon Gering, production assistant; and Sarah Smith, editorial assistant, who prepared the manuscript files for copyediting. An especially heartfelt thanks goes out to Don Whisenhunt for preparing the index.

My adult children, Benjamin and Matthew Sontheimer, urged me to pursue my research and writing, but it never would have been accomplished without the encouragement of my exceptionally supportive husband, country music historian Bill C. Malone, who works on his manuscripts on his laptop in the armchair across from me working on mine. Would that Arthur had been there for Lois as Bill has been for me!

BOOKS WRITTEN AND ILLUSTRATED BY LOIS LENSKI

Categorized by the Special Collections department of Milner Library, Illinois State University

AUTOBIOGRAPHICAL NOVELS

Skipping Village. Stokes, 1927.

A Little Girl of Nineteen Hundred. Stokes, 1928.

EARLY PICTURE BOOKS

Jack Horner's Pie: A Book of Nursery Rhymes. Harper, 1927.

Alphabet People. Harper, 1928.

The Wonder City: A Picture Book of New York. Coward, 1929.

The Washington Picture Book. Coward, 1930.

Benny and His Penny. Knopf, 1931.

Johnny Goes to the Fair: A Picture Book. Minton Balch, 1932.

The Little Family. Doubleday Doran, 1932.

Gooseberry Garden. Harper, 1934.

Little Baby Ann. Oxford University Press, 1935.

Sugarplum House. Harper, 1935.

The Easter Rabbit's Parade. Oxford University Press, 1936.

Susie Mariar. Oxford University Press, 1939; Walck, 1968.

EARLY STORY BOOKS

Two Brothers and Their Animal Friends. Stokes, 1929.

Spinach Boy. Stokes, 1930.

Two Brothers and Their Baby Sister. Stokes, 1930.

Grandmother Tippytoe. Stokes, 1931.

Arabella and Her Aunts. Stokes, 1932.

Surprise for Mother. Stokes, 1934.

MR. SMALL SERIES

The Little Auto. Oxford University Press, 1934; Walck, 1959.

The Little Sail Boat. Oxford University Press, 1937; Walck, 1960.

The Little Airplane. Oxford University Press, 1938; Walck, 1959.

The Little Train. Oxford University Press, 1940.

The Little Farm. Oxford University Press, 1942.

The Little Fire Engine. Oxford University Press, 1946.

Cowboy Small. Oxford University Press, 1949.

Papa Small. Oxford University Press, 1951.

Songs of Mr. Small. Oxford University Press, 1954.

Policeman Small. Walck, 1962.

HISTORICAL NOVELS

Phebe Fairchild: Her Book. Stokes, 1936.

A-Going to the Westward. Stokes, 1937.

Bound Girl of Cobble Hill. Lippincott, 1938.

Ocean-Born Mary. Stokes, 1939.

Blueberry Corners. Stokes, 1940.

Indian Captive: The Story of Mary Jemison. Stokes, 1941.

Puritan Adventure. Lippincott, 1944.

DAVY BOOKS

Animals for Me. Oxford University Press, 1941.

Davy's Day. Oxford University Press, 1943; Walck, 1959.

A Surprise for Davy. Oxford University Press, 1947; Walck, 1959.

A Dog Came to School. Oxford University Press, 1955.

Big Little Davy. Oxford University Press, 1956.

Davy and His Dog. Oxford University Press, 1957.

Davy Goes Places. Walck, 1961.

AMERICAN REGIONAL SERIES

Bayou Suzette. Stokes, 1943.

Strawberry Girl. Lippincott, 1945.

Blue Ridge Billy. Lippincott, 1946.

Judy's Journey. Lippincott, 1947.

Boom Town Boy. Lippincott, 1948.

Cotton in My Sack. Lippincott, 1949.

Texas Tomboy. Lippincott, 1950.

Prairie School. Lippincott, 1951.

Mama Hattie's Girl. Lippincott, 1953.

Corn-Farm Boy. Lippincott, 1954.

San Francisco Boy. Lippincott, 1955.

Flood Friday. Lippincott, 1956.

Houseboat Girl. Lippincott, 1957.

Coal Camp Girl. Lippincott, 1959.

Shoo-Fly Girl. Lippincott, 1963.

To Be a Logger. Lippincott, 1967.

Deer Valley Girl. Lippincott, 1968.

OTHER PICTURE BOOKS

Forgetful Tommy. Greenacres Press, 1943.

Let's Play House. Oxford University Press, 1944.

My Friend the Cow. National Dairy Council, 1946.

Ice Cream Is Good. National Dairy Council, 1948.

Mr. and Mrs. Noah. Crowell, 1948.

SEASONS SERIES

Spring Is Here. Oxford University Press, 1945; Walck, 1960.

Now It's Fall. Oxford University Press, 1948.

I Like Winter. Oxford University Press, 1950; Walck, 1960.

On a Summer Day. Oxford University Press, 1953.

RELIGIOUS

Living with Others. Hartford (Conn.) Council of Churches, 1952.

ROUNDABOUT AMERICA SERIES

Peanuts for Billy Ben. Lippincott, 1952.

We Live in the South. Lippincott, 1952.

Project Boy. Lippincott, 1954.

We Live in the City. Lippincott, 1954.

Berries in the Scoop. Lippincott, 1956.

We Live by the River. Lippincott, 1956.

Little Sioux Girl. Lippincott, 1958.

We Live in the Country. Lippincott, 1960.

We Live in the Southwest. Lippincott, 1962.

We Live in the North. Lippincott, 1965.

High Rise Secret. Lippincott, 1966.

SONG BOOKS

We Are Thy Children. Music by Clyde Robert Bulla. Crowell, 1952.

Songs of the City. Music by Clyde Robert Bulla. E .B. Marks, 1956.

Up to Six, Book I. Music by Clyde Robert Bulla. Hansen Music, 1956.

READ-AND-SING SERIES

I Went for a Walk. Music by Clyde Robert Bulla. Walck, 1958.

At Our House. Music by Clyde Robert Bulla. Walck, 1959.

When I Grow Up. Music by Clyde Robert Bulla. Walck, 1960.

POETRY AND SHORT STORIES

The Life I Live: Collected Poems. Walck, 1965.

Lois Lenski's Christmas Stories. Lippincott, 1968.

City Poems. Walck, 1971.

Florida, My Florida: Poems. Florida State University Press, 1971.

Sing a Song of People. Little, Brown, 1987.

Sing for Peace. Herald Press, 1987.

DEBBIE BOOKS

Debbie and Her Grandma. Walck, 1967.

Debbie and Her Family. Walck, 1969.

Debbie Herself. Walck, 1969.

Debbie and Her Dolls. Walck, 1970.

Debbie Goes to Nursery School. Walck, 1970.

Debbie and Her Pets. Walck, 1971.

Source: http://library.illinoisstate.edu/unique-collections/
lois-lenski/work.php

NOTES

INTRODUCTION

1. Lois Lenski (LL), *Strawberry Girl* (Philadelphia: Lippincott, 1945); Bertha E. Mahony and Elinor Whitney included a biographical sketch of Lois and a list of the works she had illustrated at the point in which they compiled *Contemporary Illustrators of Children's Books* (Boston: The Bookshop for Boys and Girls and Women's Educational and Industrial Union, 1930), 46; Watty Piper, *The Little Engine That Could,* illustrated by LL (New York: Platt & Munk), 1930; LL, *The Little Family* (New York: Doubleday, Doran, 1932); LL, *The Little Auto* (New York: Oxford University Press, 1934); LL, *Phebe Fairchild: Her Book* (1937); LL, *Indian Captive: The Story of Mary Jemison* (1941), both published by Frederick A. Stokes.

2. LL, "Seeing Others as Ourselves," in *Newbery Medal Books: 1922–1955 with Their Authors' Acceptance Papers and Related Material Chiefly from the Horn Book Magazine,* Horn Book Papers, vol. 1, ed. Bertha Mahony Miller and Elinor Whitney Field (Boston: Horn Book, 1955), 286.

3. Gary D. Schmidt, *Making Americans: Children's Literature from 1930 to 1960* (Iowa City: University of Iowa Press, 2013), xix; Leonard S. Marcus, *Minders of Make-Believe: Idealists, Entrepreneurs, and the Shaping of American Children's Literature* (Boston: Houghton Mifflin, 2008).

4. Leonard Kniffel, "Reading for Life: Oprah Winfrey," *American Libraries Magazine,* May 25, 2011, www.americanlibrariesmagazine.org/article/reading-life-oprah-winfrey.

5. In the first revised edition of May Hill Arbuthnot's influential *Children and Books* (Chicago: Scott, Foresman, 1957), 422, she cites Doris Gates's *Blue Willow* (1940), a "runner-up" (later designated Honor Book) for the Newbery Award and the first book dealing with migrant workers.

6. LL, *Papa Small* (1951), *Cowboy Small* (1949), *The Little Auto* (1934), *The Little Train* (1940), *Let's Play House* (1944), all originally published by Oxford University Press.

7. Steven Covey was named Stephen Covey but later changed the spelling of his first name. I will use the original spelling throughout the biography.

8. Stephen Covey, unrecorded telephone conversation with the author, early 2009.

9. As the director of School Services at the Wisconsin Historical Society (1995–2011), I authored and co-authored many books for students and teachers in the state, among them, with Catherine M. Greene and Jefferson J. Gray, *Great Ships on the Great Lakes* (Spring 2013); with Terese Allen, *The Flavor of Wisconsin for Kids* (Spring 2012); with Kori Oberle: *Wisconsin: Our State, Our Story,* a textbook for fourth-grade classrooms and the accompanying teacher's edition (Malone, Oberle, and Susan O'Leary) and student activity guide (Malone, Oberle, O'Leary, and Mary McMullen) (2008); with Nikki Mandell, *Thinking Like a Historian: Rethinking History Instruction—A Framework to Enhance and Improve Teaching and Learning* (2008); with Jon Kasparek: *Voices and Votes in Wisconsin: How Democracy Works* and the accompanying teacher's guide co-authored with Jon Kasparek and Erica Schock, *Wisconsin History Highlights: Delving into the Past* (2004); with Amy Rosebrough: *Water Panthers, Bears, and Thunderbirds: Exploring Wisconsin's Effigy Mounds* (2003), all published by the Wisconsin Historical Society Press.

10. LL, *The Little Fire Engine* (1946), *Spring Is Here* (1943), *On a Summer Day* (1953), *Now It's Fall* (1948), *I Like Winter* (1950), all originally published by Oxford University Press.

11. Peggy Marxen, note to author, March 14, 2014; "Interview: Oprah Winfrey Entertainment Executive," February 21, 1991, Chicago, Illinois, www.achievement.org/autodoc/printmember/win0int-1; Leonard Kniffel, "What Is Your Favorite Book? Is It the Same as Oprah's?" American Library Association, May 25, 2011, http://atyourlibrary.org/culture/what's-your-favorite-book-it-same-oprah's.

12. LL, *Journey into Childhood: The Autobiography of Lois Lenski* (Philadelphia: J. B. Lippincott, 1972); Lee Bennett Hopkins, emails to author, June 10 and June 12, 2011.

13. LL, *Adventure in Understanding: Talks to Parents, Teachers and Librarians, 1944–1966* (Tallahassee: The Friends of the Florida State University Library, 1968).

14. Typically, a librarian interested in children's literature at one of the institutions wrote to Lois, as did Louise Richardson at Florida State University. Then head of Special Collections in 1958, Richardson wanted to know "if there were a possibility of our library's getting the manuscript of Strawberry Girl. . . . Even a drawing or a sheet would be a treasure." Perhaps she had not anticipated that Lois's reply included a query to ask if the library might want a Lois Lenski collection. A little over a year later, at a luncheon in Lois's honor, she presented the manuscript of *Strawberry Girl* to Florida State in addition to books, lithographs, and other materials (*Ad Lib*, Florida State University Library Staff Association newsletter, vol. 8, no. 1, "The Lois Lenski Collection at Florida State University Library," April 6, 1966, Box 6, Literary Scrapbook, LL Collection, Blackmore Library, Capital University).

CHAPTER 1

1. Lois Lenski (LL), "Autobiography (A Start)," to Stephen Covey, February 15, 1940, Box 22, Folder 28, Lois Lenski Collection, Western History Collections, University of Oklahoma Libraries, Norman (OU).

2. RCH Lenski to LL, postcard dated Aug. 30 (no year specified), Box 3, Lois Lenski Collection, Blackmore Library, Capital University, Columbus, Ohio (CU).

3. Both Marietta's family (the Youngs) and the Lenskis maintained a long association with Capital University, where many descendants have been ordained or have graduated in secular fields, and Jan Ferne Haueisen (Lois's great-niece) confirmed that Paul was indeed the father of the twins, and that his family remained in the Jackson, Michigan, area (interview with author, April 23, 2015).

4. "Autobiography (A Start)"; LL, *A Little Girl of Nineteen Hundred* (New York: Frederick A. Stokes, 1928), 73–87; LL, *Journey into Childhood: The Autobiography of Lois Lenski* (Philadelphia: J. B. Lippincott, 1972), 17, 46.

5. "Autobiography (A Start)"; LL, *Journey*, 13–14. "We children, even when very young, went to both Sunday morning and evening services, including those that were in German. My father preached in both languages and we listened, although we did not understand German. My father was a German scholar, his parents, although they were not German, spoke nothing else. No German was spoken in our home, at my mother's request" (LL, *Journey*, 73).

6. "Autobiography (A Start)."

7. LL, *Journey*, 14–15.

8. LL, *Journey*, 20; Marguerite Mittermaier Ressler, "Return to Skipping Village— Anna, Ohio," Shelby County Historical Society, April 2000, www.shelbycounty-history.org/schs/archives/women/llenskiwomena.htm.

9. LL, *Journey*, 60–61.

10. LL, *Journey*, 19, 71–72.

11. LL to Marie Ram (MR), February 5, 1954, Box 47, Folder 3, OU.

12. LL, *Journey*, 75–76; Marguerite Mittermaier Ressler, interview with author, Dayton Ohio, June 4, 2011.

13. "Autobiography (A Start)."

14. LL, *Journey*, 40–41, 75.

15. LL, *Journey*, 52–53.

16. LL, *Journey*, 20–23.

17. LL, *Journey*, 19–20; LL, *Skipping Village: A Town of Not So Very Long Ago* (New York: Frederick A. Stokes, 1927); LL, *Little Girl.*

18. LL, *Journey*, 23–36.

19. LL, *Journey*, 37.

20. Ibid.

21. LL, "Place and People," Eleanor Weir Welch Lecture, Milner Library, Illinois State University, Normal, Illinois, July 20, 1965, in LL, *Adventure in Understanding: Talks to Parents, Teachers, and Librarians* (Tallahassee: Friends of the Florida State University Library, 1968), 174–75.

22. LL, "Getting Books from Life (A Portion)," Reading Conference, Kent State University, Kent, Ohio, July 7, 1955, in *Adventure in Understanding,* 85–102; "Place and People," 196. Ann Boyer pointed out that Lois's rhyme fits exactly the Christian hymn "Come, Thou Long Expected Jesus," handwritten note on draft of author's manuscript.

23. Although R. C. H. was a regular pastor in Anna, he later earned his doctor of divinity and became the dean of the seminary at Capital University, where he had studied. He wrote many works, most distinctively, the twelve-volume *Lenski's Commentary on the New Testament,* written from a conservative theological perspective. According to the website Logos Bible Software, "Thorough as a student of Greek, R. C. H. Lenski interprets the books of the New Testament with meticulous exegetical research while providing an original, literal translation of the text" (www.logos.com/product/3911/lenskis-commentary-on-the-new-testament).

24. LL, *Journey,* 38–39.

25. LL, *Journey,* 39; 73–74; Ressler interview with author, Dayton, Ohio, June 4, 2011.

26. LL, *Journey,* 39; Maud Hart Lovelace, "Lois Lenski," *Horn Book* 22, no. 4 (July 1946): 276.

27. LL, *Journey,* 39–40, 44; LL to Mary Davis Coupe, December 12, 1948, Box 13, Folder 1, OU.

28. "Autobiography (A Start)"; LL, *Journey,* 42; Kathy Lenski Sherpa (LL's great-niece), in an email to the author, February 16, 2013, mentioned that Marietta may have died from pernicious anemia, which also affected Kathy's grandfather, Gerhard, and Lois throughout their adult lives.

29. "Autobiography (A Start)"; LL, *Journey,* 44–48.

30. LL, *Journey,* 48.

31. LL, *Journey,* 77.

32. LL, *Journey,* 64–69. Christmas remained precious to Lois throughout her life, and many of her books contain a variety of Christmas traditions. In 1968 Lippincott published *Lois Lenski's Christmas Stories,* most of which had previously appeared in other publications, cited in the opening pages (iv–v); Gary D. Schmidt cites David I. Macleod's observations in *Age of the Child* that in the late nineteenth century, no one considered a separate literature for children. Both adults and children enjoyed books like *Rebecca of Sunnybrook Farm* (1903), *Adventures of Huckleberry Finn* (1884), or *Little Lord Fauntleroy* (1886), all best-sellers (Schmidt, *Making Americans,* xi).

33. LL, *Journey,* 40–41.

34. LL, *Journey,* 54.

35. LL, *Journey,* 53–54.

36. LL, *Journey,* 55–56.

37. LL, *Journey,* 55–57.

38. LL, *Little Girl,* 135–44, quoted on 144.

39. Ibid, 147.

40. Ibid, 200–217, quoted on 216–17.

41. LL, *Journey*, 78.

42. R. C. H.'s congregants thought that their pastor believed his children were "too good" for the local school and resented that attitude, according to the daughter of one of the pastors who followed him in the Anna pulpit (Ressler telephone interview with author, November 18, 2013).

43. LL, *Journey*, 78–79.

44. LL, *Journey*, 79–80.

45. LL, "My Ohio Beginnings," *Ohioana Quarterly*, Spring 1970; Ressler, "Return to Skipping Village—Anna, Ohio"; Ressler interview with author, June 4, 2011.

CHAPTER 2

1. To reconstruct her life as autobiography, Lois asked Mabel Pugh to return all the letters that Lois had written to her over the years from the beginning of their friendship in 1916 when they were both art students in New York. Mabel wrote to Lois, October 23, 1969, "Here they are! I wanted to re-read all of them, and still think published just as they are they would be a success." Lois Lenski Collection, Box 46, Folder 15, Western History Collections, University of Oklahoma Libraries, Norman (ou).

2. Handwritten draft of chapter for *Journey into Childhood: The Autobiography of Lois Lenski* (Philadelphia: J. B. Lippincott, 1972), Box 23, Folder 4, OU.

3. LL, *Journey*, 83.

4. LL, *Journey*, 84; Thomas E. French, Carl L. Svensen, Jay D. Heisel, and Byron Urbanick, *Mechanical Drawing* (New York: McGraw-Hill, 1990); Thomas E. French and Jay D. Heisel, *Mechanical Drawing: Board and CAD Techniques* (New York: McGraw-Hill/Glencoe, 2002).

5. LL, *Journey*, 85.

6. LL, *Journey*, 85–86.

7. Mark K. Smith, "Johann Heinrich Pestalozzi: Pedagogy, Education and Social Justice," *Infed*, accessed July 17, 2015, http://infed.org/mobi/johann-heinrich-pestalozzi-pedagogy-education-and-social-justice, "Kindness ruled in Pestalozzi's schools: he abolished flogging, much to the amazement of outsiders," 3.

8. Mark K. Smith, "Friedrich Froebel (Fröbel)," *Infed*, 1997, www.infed.org/mobi/fredrich-froebel-frobel; and "Froebel Gifts," *Froebel USA*, accessed July 17, 2015, www.froebelgifts.com.

9. "Maria Montessori," *American Montessori Society*, accessed July 17, 2015, www.amshq.org/Montessori-Education/History-of-Montessori-Education/Biography-of-Maria-Montessori.aspx.

10. Lois was quoting herself from an unidentified letter in "Let Your Child Draw; Don't Teach Him," *Better Homes and Gardens*, May 1935, 26.

11. LL, "Say Yes to Life," in the pamphlet *The Lois Lenski Collection in the Florida State*

University Library, comp. Nancy Bird (Tallahassee: The Friends of the Florida State University Library, 1966), 13–14.

12. LL, *Journey,* 89.

13. Ibid, 89–90.

14. Ibid, 90.

15. Ibid; LL, "New York, 1915–1918," Box 22, Folder 20, OU.

16. Mabel Pugh (1891–1986) had a lengthy career as an artist, working in New York as an illustrator featured in various periodicals and also represented in exhibitions at the National Academy of Design, Brooklyn Museum, and in the 1939 World's Fair. She moved back to Raleigh, North Carolina, in 1936 to teach art and art history at her undergraduate alma mater, Peace College, retiring in 1960. See "Mabel Pugh," *The Johnson Collection,* accessed July 26, 2015, www.thejohnsoncollection.org/mabel-pugh. Thanks to Lois's correspondence that Mabel saved over the years, we know much about Lois's life that would have otherwise been lost. Two other correspondents and friends, Emma Celeste Thibodaux (1940s) and Marie Ram (1950s), also contributed their Lenski letters, and all three sets of materials are part of the Lenski Collection at OU.

17. "The Art Students League of New York," *The Art Students League of New York,* accessed July 27, 2015. www.theartstudentsleague.org/About/History.aspx; "Frank Vincent DuMond," *Florence Griswold Museum,* accessed July 27, 2015, http://florencegriswoldmuseum.org/collections/online/fox-chase/fox-chase-frank-vincent-dumond; "F. Luis Mora and the Expression of Beauty," *Mattatuck Museum,* accessed July 27, 2015, http://mattatuckmuseum.org/collections/mora/artist.html; "Kenneth Hayes Miller," *American Art at the Phillips Collection,* accessed July 27, 2015; www.phillipscollection.org/research/american_art/bios/miller-bio.htm. Realist painter Kenneth Hayes Miller was an important teacher at the Art Students League whose better-known contemporaries included Reginald Marsh, Edward Hopper, and George Bellows. Matthew Baigell, "Kenneth Hayes Miller," *Butler Institute of American Art,* accessed July 27, 2015; www.butlerartcollection.com/artist.php?artistId=2358.

18. Among many others, the Smithsonian holds the works of all three artists; DuMond and Mora are both in the collection of the National Academy of Design Museum; the Metropolitan Museum of Art has works of Mora and Miller; in addition, the Florence Griswold Museum and the Virginia Museum of Fine Arts contain works by Du Mond; Yale University Art Gallery holds works by Mora; and the Whitney Museum, the Los Angeles County Art Museum, and the Phillips Collection hold works by Miller, "Frank Vincent Dumond Papers," Archives of American Art, Smithsonian Institution, accessed August 29, 2015, www.aaa.si.edu/collections/frank-vincent-dumond-papers-7453; "The Kenneth Hayes Miller Papers," *Archives of American Art Journal* 13, no. 2 (1973), 19–24; "F. Luis Mora and the Expression of Beauty," Mattatuck Museum, accessed July 27, 2015, http://mattatuckmuseum.org/collections/mora/artist.html.

19. LL, *Journey,* 91; "Art Student in New York, Making Ends Meet, Flower Girl,

Back in N.Y., Mural Assistant, Dark Days Ahead," notes for autobiography, Box 23, Folder 5, OU.

20. LL, "New York, 1915–1918."

21. Ibid.

22. "Art Student in New York," 118; LL to Mabel Pugh (MP), November 18, 1917, Box 46, Folder 1, OU; "Guide to the Broadway Tabernacle Church and Society Papers, 1835–1980," *New York Historical Society*, accessed January 22, 2015, http://dlib.nyu.edu/findingaids/html/nyhs/broadwaytabernacle/bioghist.html.

23. Rebecca Zurier and Robert W. Snyder, "Introduction," in Zurier, Snyder, and Virginia M. Mecklenburg, *Metropolitan Lives: The Ashcan Artists and Their New York* (New York: National Museum of American Art, 1995), 13–27.

24. "Art Student in New York," 112; LL, *Journey*, 93.

25. "Art Student in New York," 112; LL, *Journey*, 93.

26. LL, *Journey*, 95–96; LL to MP, July 23, 1916, and August 18, 1916, Box 46, Folder 1, OU.

27. LL, *Journey*, 97.

28. While Molly's parents were British, she grew up in New Zealand, where her father and uncle were instrumental in founding the University of Otago in Dunedin. Molly and her older sister, Margaret, traveled to England to study art and music, respectively (telephone interview with Molly's grandson, Alan Chisholm, November 21, 2013).

29. Biographical information from Jean Fitzgerald, "A Finding Aid to the Arthur Sinclair Covey Papers, 1882–1960, in the Archives of American Art," *Archives of American Art*, Smithsonian Institution, accessed July 17, 2015, www.aaa.si.edu/collections/findingaids/covearth.htm.

30. LL to MP, October 29, 1916, Box 46, Folder 1, OU.

31. Ibid, March 12, 1917, Box 46, Folder 1, OU; LL, *Journey*, 98–99.

32. LL to MP, May 13, 1917, Box 46, Folder 1, OU; LL, *Journey*, 98–99.

33. LL to MP, May 13, 1917, Box 46, Folder 1, OU; LL, *Journey*, 98–99. Other paperback picture books that Lois produced for Platt and Munk before 1920 included *Dolls from Fairy Land, Dolls from the Land of Mother Goose*, and *Mother Goose Cut-Outs*. Lois "always considered these pot-boilers, not real books" ("Art Student in New York," 118–19).

34. LL to MP, November 18, 1917, Box 46, Folder 1, OU; LL, "New York, 1915–1918."

35. LL to MP, April 14, 1918, Box 46, Folder 2, OU.

36. LL, *Journey*, 101–103.

37. "Art Student in New York," 124.

38. LL, *Journey*, 103–104; "The Great Pandemic: The United States in 1818–1919," *United States Department of Health and Human Services*, accessed July 17, 2015, www.flu.gov/pandemic/history/1918/the_pandemic/influenza/index.html.

39. LL, *Journey*, 104.

40. LL to MP, March 31, 1919, and June 21, 1919, Box 46, Folder 2, OU.

41. LL to MP, July 27, 1919, and August 10, 1919, and December 3, 1919, Box 46,

Folder 2, OU; "Charles Livingston Bull, 1874–1932, Painter," *National Museum of Wildlife Art of the United States,* accessed July 17, 2015, www.wildlifeart.org/collection/artists/artist-charles-livingston-bull-307. Peter Newell illustrated an edition of *Alice in Wonderland* and later published his own humorous books, among them *The Hole Book, The Rocket Book,* and *Topsys and Turvys.* See "Peter Newell's eBooks," *nonsenselit.org,* accessed July 17, 2015, www.nonsenselit.org/newell.

42. Lois saved no personal correspondence with Arthur in any of the archival collections she established before her death.

43. In addition to his teaching at the Art Students League, Boardman Robinson painted murals, later moving to Colorado Springs where he founded the Fine Arts Center ("Boardman Robinson," *Labor Arts,* accessed July 28, 2015, www.laborarts.org/exhibits/themasses/bios.cfm?bio=boardman-robinson).

44. LL to MP, February 26, 1920, and August 14, 1920; Box 46, Folder 2, OU.

45. "Walter Bayes, 1869–1956," *Tate,* accessed July 28, 2015, www.tate.org.uk/art/artists/walter-bayes-713; LL to MP, November 26, 1920; Box 46, Folder 2, OU.

46. LL to MP, November 26, 1920, Box 46, Folder 2, OU.

47. Barbara Bader, *American Picturebooks from Noah's Ark to The Beast Within* (New York: Macmillan, 1976), 6–7.

48. Leonard Marcus, *Minders of Make Believe: Idealists, Entrepreneurs, and the Shaping of American Children's Literature* (Boston: Houghton Mifflin, 2008), 64–65, 73–76, quote from 76.

49. Ibid, 76; John Lane was one of the initial founders of the Bodley Head, which published a wide variety of books ("About the Bodley Head," *The Bodley Head,* accessed July 28, 2015, www.bodleyhead.co.uk/aboutus.asp).

50. LL, *Journey,* 108.

51. Bader includes a quote from Boutet de Monvel as discussed by Norman Hapgood in his description of the illustrator's style in an 1898 issue of *McClure's Magazine.* Explaining his method of dealing with the limitations of reproduction, Boutet de Monvel said, "Gradually, through the process of elimination and selection, I came to put in only what was necessary to give the character." Bader commented that Monvel "allowed little shadow, and the resulting combination of unaccented outline and flat tone was called Japanese," though lithographic reproduction actually produced "thin, soft colors," actually quite different in effect (Bader, *American Picturebooks,* 4).

52. Alice Robinson to LL, May 11, 1922, Box 3, Lois Lenski Collection, Blackmore Library, Capital University, Columbus, Ohio (CU).

53. LL to MP, December 26, 1920, Box 46, Folder 2, OU.

54. LL to MP, February 6, 1921, Box 46, Folder 2, OU; LL, *Journey,* 108–109.

55. LL to MP, March 1, 1921; Box 46, Folder 2, OU.

56. In a letter from Italy, Lois told Mabel that painters found Florence "the most important place of all." But Lois felt that "Perugia is the loveliest spot I've ever

seen in my life. I'm actually hypnotized with the beauty of it . . . a town out of a fairy tale—the kind I love to draw—so here for the first [time] I've started sketching (in pencil)" (April 25, 1921, Box 46, Folder 2, OU).

57. LL, *Journey*, 109–11; Kathy Lenski Sherpa, "Lois Lenore Lenski," *Lenski Family Tree*, accessed July 28, 2015, http://trees.ancestry.com/tree/2974738/person/-1759760637/fact/57601588215.

CHAPTER 3

1. Lois Lenski (LL) to Mabel Pugh (MP), June 21, 1921, Box 46, Folder 4, Lois Lenski Collection, Western History Collections, University of Oklahoma Libraries, Norman (OU).

2. LL to Esther Ferne, April 29, 1921, quoted in LL, *Journey into Childhood: The Autobiography of Lois Lenski* (Philadelphia: J. B. Lippincott, 1972), 111–12.

3. Ibid.

4. LL to MP, June 10 and June 26, 1921, Box 46, Folder 4, OU.

5. LL, *Journey*, 114.

6. LL to MP, August 28, 1921, Box 46, Folder 4, OU; LL, *Journey*, 115–17.

7. LL, *Journey*, 117.

8. Jacalyn Eddy, *Bookwomen: Creating an Empire in Children's Books* (Madison: University of Wisconsin Press, 2006), 3–4.

9. LL, *Journey*, 85.

10. Anita Clair Fellman, *Little House, Long Shadow: Laura Ingalls Wilder's Impact on American Culture* (Columbia: University of Missouri Press, 2008), 122–23; Leonard S. Marcus, *Minders of Make-Believe: Idealists, Entrepreneurs, and the Shaping of American Children's Literature* (Boston: Houghton Mifflin, 2008), 101.

11. Marcus, *Minders*, 101–102; Lindsey Wyckoff, "About Lucy Sprague Mitchell," *Bankstreet Library Research Guides*, July 11, 2015, http://libguides.bankstreet. edu/content.php?pid=315616&sid=2585717; "The Principles of Progressive Education," *The Park School*, 2015, www.parkschool.net/about/philosophy/principles-of-progressive-education.

12. Marcus, *Minders*, 72, 76–78.

13. Alan Chisholm, telephone interview with author, November 21, 2013.

14. LL, *Journey into Childhood*, first draft, "Personal Life, 1921–1929," Box 23, Folder 6, OU; LL, *Journey*, 120.

15. LL, *Journey*, 115.

16. LL, *Journey*, 114–15.

17. Lois quoted from the letter to Esther she had written from Rome, LL, *Journey*, 112.

18. LL, *Journey*, 117.

19. Anne Scott MacLeod, *American Childhood: Essays on Children's Literature of the Nineteenth and Twentieth Centuries* (Athens: University of Georgia Press, 1994), 158; LL, *Journey*, 127. Like Louise Seaman at Macmillan, May Massee was another early

giant in American children's book publishing as the founding children's book editor at Doubleday, Page, and Company (1923) and Viking (1932) ("The May Massee Collection," William Allen White Library, Emporia State University, 2015, www.emporia.edu/libsv/archives/collections/may-massee-collection.html).

20. MacLeod, *American Childhood*, 158.

21. LL, *Journey*, 117–18, 127–28.

22. Review of *Jack Horner's Pie: A Book of Nursery Rhymes*, *New York Times Book Review*, December 4, 1927, 36; Review of *Jack Horner's Pie: A Book of Nursery Rhymes*, *Booklist* 24, no. 7 (April 1928): 286–87; Josiah Titzell, "Lois Lenski: A Serious Artist with a Sense of Humor," *The Publishers' Weekly* (October 25, 1930), 1969. This article also contained a photograph of Lois and examples of her illustrations.

23. J. J. Sedelmaier, "Watty Piper's 1930 'The Little Engine That Could,'" *Print*, September 10, 2012, www.printmag.com/obsessions/watty-pipers-1930-the-little-engine-that-could; Lawrence Levine, "American Culture and the Great Depression," *Yale Review* 74, no. 2 (1985): 197–226, cited by Fellman, *Little House*, 57.

24. LL to MP, December 31, 1922, Box 46, Folder 4, OU. *Nativity*, one of the paintings in the New York Water Color Club, sold for sixty dollars, and Lois showed other works in 1924 at the Detroit Institute of Art, the Independent Exhibition, the Newark Museum, and in New York, at the New Gallery and the Whitney Studio Club, the Art Institute of Chicago (scrapbook, Box 3, Lois Lenski Collection, Blackmore Library, Capital University [CU]).

25. LL, *Journey*, 123.

26. Ibid; Bobbie Malone, "Arthur Covey's Kohler Murals: Honoring the 'Dignity and Nobility' of Men Who Work," *Wisconsin Magazine of History* 93, no. 2 (Winter 2009–2010): 28–37. Arthur later created industrial-themed murals for the Norton Company of Worcester, Massachusetts (1925–27), and "Bridgeport Manufacturing" for the post office in Bridgeport, Connecticut (1935). "Arthur Covey Achievements: Highlights in the Life of the Artist," in booklet "Southwestern College Collection of Art by Arthur Covey," undated, Southwestern College, Winfield, Kan.; Arthur Sinclair Covey Papers, 1882–1960, Archives of American Art, Smithsonian Institution; "Post Office Murals—Bridgeport, CT," *The Living New Deal*, accessed July 17, 2015, http://livingnewdeal.berkeley.edu/projects/post-office-mural-bridgeport-ct.

27. LL to MP, May 12, 1924, Box 46, Folder 4, and October 21, 1925, Box 46, Folder 5, OU.

28. LL to MP, undated (Lois later wrote "1925 or '26" in the upper right-hand corner), Box 46, Folder 4, OU; LL, *Journey*, 123, 148; LL, "Private life, 1921–1924," 146, Box 23, Folder 6, OU.

29. LL, *Journey*, 132–33.

30. LL to MP, February 28, 1926, Box 46, Folder 5, OU.

31. LL to MP, October 21, 1925, Box 46, Folder 5, OU.

32. LL, *Journey*, 125–26; LL to MP, March 21, 1926–April 28, 1926, Box 46, Folder 5, OU.

33. LL, *Journey*, 133; RCH Lenski to LL, October, 1927, Box 50, Folder 4, OU.

34. LL, *Journey*, 133–34; LL, "Professional Work, 1920–1930," Resource Materials for *Journey into Childhood*, 173; Box 23, Folder 7, OU.

35. Frances Sharp to LL, Box 10, Ohio file, Lois Lenski Collection, Syracuse University Library; LL, *Journey*, 79.

36. From 1926 to 1929, Arthur served as president of the National Society of Mural Painters (Arthur Sinclair Covey Papers, Archives of American Art, 1882–1960, Smithsonian Institution, 2015, www.aaa.si.edu/collections/arthur-sinclair-covey-papers-7531/more).

37. LL, *A Little Girl of Nineteen Hundred* (New York: Frederick A. Stokes, 1928).

38. Marian C. Dodd, "An Unusual Book," *Saturday Review of Literature* 4, no. 20 (December 10, 1927): 438.

39. LL, *Skipping Village: A Town of Not So Very Long Ago* (New York: Frederick A. Stokes, 1927), 15; two examples of anthologies containing "People": Nancy Larrick, ed., *On City Streets: An Anthology of Poetry* (New York: M. Evans, 1968), 43; Elizabeth A. Thorn et al., *Out and Away Language Experience Reading Program* (Toronto: W. J. Gage, 1965), 212. Lois received many requests for reprinting "People" in all kinds of anthologies (for which LL, and not Stokes, retained complete rights and received compensation), including *Very Young Verses* for Houghton Mifflin, 1944–45 ($25); Westminster Press, 1946 ($15); Oxford University Press, 1947 ($25); Ginn and Company, 1948 ($25); American Printing House for the Blind, 1953 (no charge); D. C. Heath, 1948 ($25); *Our English Language* (grade 2) for American Book Company, 1956 ($15); Grosset & Dunlap, 1956 ($25); Doubleday, 1957 ($25); *Beginning Language Arts Instruction with Children*, Charles E. Merrill Books, 1961 ($25); *The Sound of Poetry*, Allyn and Bacon, 1961 ($25); Encyclopaedia Britannica Press, 1966 ($25); Harcourt Brace, 1968 ($25); *The World of Language*, Follett, 1969 ($30), Box 1, Folders 6–9, OU; LL, *The Life I Live: Collected Poems* (New York: Henry Z. Walck, 1965), 15. School districts such as Los Angeles, Duluth, and New York City requested permission to reprint the poem, as did the Unitarian Church and the Episcopal Church for use in their own publications (Box 1, Folders 6–9, OU).

40. A review of "A Little Girl of Nineteen Hundred," *Saturday Review of Literature* 5, no. 16 (November 10, 1928): 357; Mark Graham Bonner, review of *A Little Girl of Nineteen Hundred*, *New York Times Book Review*, December 16, 1928, 28.

41. LL to Marie Ram (MR), January 30, 1954, Box 47, Folder 3, OU.

42. LL to MR, April 30, 1928, Box 46, Folder 6, OU; LL, *Journey*, 202; Stephen Covey, telephone conversations with author, 2008–2010.

43. LL to MP, December 29, 1928, Box 46, Folder 6, OU.

44. Ibid.

CHAPTER 4

1. Lois Lenski (LL) to Mabel Pugh (MP), January 30, February 12, and February 28, 1929, Box 46, Folder 6, Western History Collections, University of Oklahoma Libraries, Norman (OU); *Journey into Childhood: The Autobiography of Lois Lenski* (Philadelphia: J. B. Lippincott, 1972), 137.

2. LL to MP, June 23, 1929, Box 46, Folder 6, OU. Pediatric nurse Anne Altshuler reminded me that the primary concern for all newborns today is "the need for skin-to-skin holding . . . that is important in keeping the baby's temperature, heart beat and respirations stable, reducing cortisol levels (stress hormones) that rise with separation, facilitating breastfeeding, preventing infection by colonizing the new baby with the mother's protective microbiome, and enhancing bonding. This is a vast change from birth practices that occurred in hospital settings in 1929" (email to author, March 27, 2015).

3. LL to MP, June 23, 1929, OU; LL, *Journey*, 138, 144; Greenacres is now part of the Burlington–Harmony Hill Roads Historic District, and the Jonathan Balch house dates from about 1770 ("Burlington–Harmony Hill Roads Historic District," *Living Places*, 1997–2015, www.livingplaces.com/CT/Litchfield_County/Harwinton_Town/Burlington-Harmony_Hill_Roads_Historic_District.html; LL, "The Story of *Phebe Fairchild Her Book*," *Horn Book* 13, no. 6 (November–December 1937): 394.

4. "Personal 1930's," first draft of LL, *Journey into Childhood*, 175–76, Box 23, Folder 8, OU; LL, "The Legend of Mrs. Sprightly," *Parents' Magazine* (September 1933): 20–21, 58. A typescript of the essay is the most successful of several similar satiric pieces, undated, although probably written in the 1930s in a three-ring binder, "Anecdotes Based on the Personal Experiences of Lois Lenski," which Stephen Covey sent to his niece, Katherine Lenski Sherpa, who shared the notebook with the author.

5. Box 24, correspondence with *Better Homes and Gardens* regarding "Let Your Child Draw" (1934) for the article published in May 1935, 26–27; and with *Parents' Magazine* regarding "Christmas Is What You Make It" (1935), Folders 5 and 6, OU.

6. Ibid, 176.

7. LL to MP, August 15, 1932, Box 46, Folder 8, OU.

8. Ibid, 178; LL, *Journey*, 139.

9. Marjorie Smith Olson, interview with author, March 24, 2014. Marjorie was eighty-seven years old at the time of the interview, which would make her three years older than Stephen—and just about the right age for *The Little Family*.

10. LL, *The Little Family* (New York: Random House, 1932), unnumbered.

11. Dorothy Bryan to LL, December 6, 1932, Box 1, Folder 33, OU.

12. MacLeod, *American Childhood*, 166. In *American Children's Literature and the Construction of Childhood* (New York: Twayne, 1998), Gail Schmunk Murray notes that authors of the 1930s "strove for exacting physical detail and attempted to realistically portray children's abilities and emotions. Yet the family setting

into which this more realistic child was placed remained highly idealized" (147).

13. Miriam Sieber Lind, "Friend of the Family," *Christian Living*, November 1956, 3.

14. Barbara Bader, *American Picturebooks: From Noah's Ark to the Beast Within* (New York: Macmillan, 1976), 73–77.

15. Bader, "A Second Look: The Little Family," *Horn Book* 61 (March–April 1985): 169.

16. Joel E. Brown, Portland, Maine, review of "The Little Family (Lois Lenski Books)," *Amazon.com*, February 15, 2008, accessed July 28, 2015, www.amazon. com/Little-Family-Lois-Lenski-Books/product-reviews/0375810773/ref=dp_ top_cm_cr_acr_txt?showViewpoints=1. All posted reviews on the site gave *The Little Family* five stars (top rating); the book was most recently reprinted in 2002.

17. Dorothy Bryan to LL, December 6, 1932, Box 1, Folder 33, OU.

18. LL, "Picture Books," *Journey into Childhood*, first draft, 240, Box 23, Folder 10, OU; LL, *Journey*, 140; LL, *The Little Auto* (New York: Henry Z. Walck), 1934.

19. Lois's 1930s picture book titles include *Johnny Goes to the Fair* (New York: Minton Balch, 1932); *Gooseberry Garden* (New York: Harper & Brothers, 1934); *Sugarplum House* (New York: Harper & Brothers, 1935); *Little Baby Ann* (New York: Oxford University Press, 1935).

20. May Hill Arbuthnot, *Children and Books*, rev. ed. (Chicago: Scott, Foresman, 1957), 398.

21. When I arranged an initial telephone interview with Steven Covey (he changed the spelling of his first name later in life to distinguish himself from Stephen Covey, co-founder of the Franklin-Covey Company), December 27, 2008, he introduced himself by asking me, "Did you know that Mr. Small is now nearly eighty?"

22. LL, "Picture Books," *Journey into Childhood*, First draft, 241, Box 23, Folder 10, OU.

23. Grace Hogarth, "'Our Noisy Years Seem Moments,'" *Horn Book* 50, no. 5 (October 1974): 67.

24. LL, *Journey*, 162–63.

25. LL, "Picture Books," OU; "Henry Z. Walck," *New York Times*, December 26, 1984, www.nytimes.com/1984/12/26/obituaries/henry-z-walck.html.

26. Bader, "A Second Look," 171.

27. Bader, *American Picturebooks*, 77.

28. Charlotte Huck and Doris A. Young, *Children's Literature in the Elementary School* (New York: Holt, Rinehart, 1961), 101; Steven Covey, "My Artistic and Literary Heritage," unpublished and undated typescript that he sent to the author.

29. LL, *Journey*, 139; Marjorie Smith Olson interview with author, March 24, 2014.

30. Arbuthnot, *Children and Books*, 399; LL, "Picture Books," OU.

31. Unidentified writer, undated, but with note penciled in another's handwriting, "1st Grade: Notes written by practice student in group at teacher's request," Box 5, Folder 15, OU.

32. Gretchen Murray to LL, April 3, 1940, Box 5, Folder 15, OU; LL, *The Little Train* (New York: Oxford University Press, 1940), unnumbered. Later in the year, Horace Mann students had lots of suggestions for Lois: "Let Mr. Small be a fireman sometime. Make him be a life-saver, a farmer, a policeman, a milkman, a street car man, a bus driver, a subway engineer, a butcher, a mailman, a doorman, a tailor, or a elevator man in some of your books" (Edith Baker's First Grade to LL, December 9, 1940, Box 8, Lois Lenski Collection, Blackmore Library, Capital University, Columbus, Ohio).

33. LL to Emma Celeste Thibodaux (ECT), June 10, 1945, Box, 48, Folder 5, OU.

34. Cited by Leonard Marcus, *Why Picture Books Matter: The Sixteenth Annual Charlotte Zolotow Lecture* (Madison: UW-Madison Friends of the CCBC, 2014), 14.

35. Josiah Titzell, "Lois Lenski: A Serious Artist with a Sense of Humor," *Publishers' Weekly* (October 25, 1930), 1969; Eunice Blake (EB) to LL, April 8, 1946; LL to EB, April 12, 1946; EB to LL, May 7, 1946, Box 8, Folder 15, OU.

36. According to the press release, "Mrs. Trieschman, a former nursery-school teacher who has read many stories to three- and four-year-olds, said, 'The figure 2,000,000, impressive as it is, represents only a small part of the children who have known and enjoyed Davy and Mr. Small'" ("Literary Scrapbook, 1950–1968," Box 6, CU).

37. Bill C. Malone, *Singing Cowboys and Musical Mountaineers* (Athens: University of Georgia Press, 1993), 73–74. Children's author and illustrator Holling C. Holling's *The Book of Cowboys* was published by Platt and Munk in 1936.

38. *Texas Tomboy* was published by Lippincott and is fully discussed in chapter 8.

39. LL to Mary Davis Coupe, August 6, 1948, Box 13, Folder 1, OU.

40. Mary Davis Coupe to LL, August 17, 1948, and September 15, 1948, Box 13, Folder 1; LL, *Cowboy Small* (New York: Oxford University Press, 1949), unnumbered. For the "two-color scheme," Lois chose a warm cinnamon as the accent color.

41. LL to Mary Davis Coupe, September 5, 1948, Box 13, Folder 1, OU.

42. Victoria S. Johnson, "Books for Children," *World Topics Year Book 1961* (Lake Bluff, Ill.: Tangley Oaks Educational Center), unnumbered; Marie L. Ram (MR), "Mr. Small—Ambassador: Second-Graders in Buffalo and Mexico City Have Successful Cultural Exchange," *New York State Education*, October, 1962, 28–29.

43. Bader, "A Second Look," 170.

44. LL, *Papa Small* (New York: Oxford University Press, 1951), unnumbered.

45. May Hill Arbuthnot, *Children and Books* (Chicago: Scott, Foresman, 1957), 398.

46. LL, "Picture Books," *Journey into Childhood*, first draft, 246, Box 23, Folder 10, OU.

47. LL, *Journey*, 170–72; LL, *Davy's Day* (New York: Oxford University Press, 1943); *A Surprise for Davy* (New York: Oxford University Press, 1947); *A Dog Came to School* (New York: Oxford University Press, 1955); *Big Little Davy* (New York: Oxford University Press, 1956); *Davy and His Dog* (New York: Oxford University Press, 1957); *Davy Goes Places* (New York: Henry Z. Walck, 1961); telephone interview with Alan Chisholm, November 21, 2013.

48. LL to MR, February 5, 1954, Box 47, Folder 3, OU; LL, *Debbie and Her Grandma* (New York: Walck, 1967); *Debbie Herself* (New York: Walck, 1969); *Debbie and Her Family* (New York: Walck, 1969); *Debbie and Her Dolls* (New York: Walck, 1970); *Debbie Goes to Nursery School* (New York: Walck, 1970); *Debbie and Her Pets* (New York: Walck, 1971).

49. "General Comments by LL on MR's dissertation: An Analysis of the Lois Lenski Literature from a Sociological Point of View" (typed, with Ram's thesis), University of Buffalo School of Education, February 1958, Lois Lenski Collection, Edward H. Butler Library Special Collections at Buffalo State College, Buffalo, New York (BSC).

50. LL to MP, March 5, 1933, and July 20, 1933, Box 46, Folder 8, OU.

51. The Lois Lenski Collection at Syracuse University Library contains the very handsome *Story Parade* covers and interior illustrations for many issues (Box 17, Folder 8, Syracuse University, Syracuse, N.Y.); *Child Life* correspondence related to a double-page spread illustrated cartoon series, which Lois entitled "Tickletown," resides in Box 2, Folder 14, OU; the collection also holds other correspondence relating to articles and illustrations from that period in Box 27, Folders 1–53.

52. "Arthur Covey Achievements: Highlights in the Life of the Artist," in booklet "Southwestern College Collection of Art by Arthur Covey," undated, Southwestern College, Winfield, Kan.; "Murals Depicting Washington's Life," *New York Herald Tribune*, February 14, 1932, 5; Karen Berman, "A man who made walls come to life," *Bridgeport (Conn.) Telegram*, April 20, 1983, p. 4. Arthur taught pictorial composition, probably very much on an ad hoc basis, at the National Academy Schools in New York between 1929 and 1942; "Arthur C. Covey Papers, 1882–1960, Biographical Information," *Archives of American Art*, Smithsonian Institution, accessed July 28, 2015, www.aaa.si.edu/collections/arthur-sinclair-covey-papers-7531/more; "Arthur Covey," *The Living New Deal*, 2012, http://livingnewdeal.berkeley.edu/projects/post-office-mural-bridgeport-ct; "Arthur C. Covey," *National Academy Museum*, accessed July 28, 2015, www.nationalacademy.org/collections/artists/detail/381; "Torrington Remembers John Brown," *New York Times*, January 15, 1978, p. 17.

CHAPTER 5

1. LL, *Journey into Childhood: The Autobiography of Lois Lenski* (Philadelphia: J. B. Lippincott, 1972), 144; "Personal 1930's," first draft of *Journey*, 191, Box 23, Folder 8, Lois Lenski Collection, Western History Collections, University of Oklahoma Libraries, Norman (OU); Alan Chisholm, telephone conversation with author, November 21, 2013.

2. Lois Lenski (LL) to Marie Ram (MR), February 5, 1954, Box 47, Folder 3, OU. Joan Kirchner, who grew up in the 1950s on the neighboring farm to the north and remembers the Coveys, is a Drake family descendant, the family that had

once owned Greenacres. Her grandfather, who lived next door, was the farmer ("with one hand") who provided the milk to the Covey family. Joan still lives on part of his property, and she told me that "for at least six generations, three families have lived on Harmony Hill Road in a one-mile stretch" (email from Joan Kirchner, November 6, 2013). Greenacres was for sale during the summer of 2012, and Joan graciously made arrangements with a realtor who allowed the author to visit the property.

3. Michael Kammen, *Mystic Chords of Memory: The Transformation of Tradition in American Culture* (New York: Alfred A. Knopf, 1991), 305, 338–39, 347, 352–70.

4. Ibid, 307–308, 321–25, 387.

5. Richard Gary Wilson, *The Colonial Revival House* (New York: Harry N. Abrams, 2004), 6, 9.

6. LL, *Journey*, 150–51. "First settled in 1731 and 'incorporated' in 1737, Harwinton has had a proud and very interesting history. From its beginning as a 'Western Land' to serving as today's 'Eastern Gateway' to Litchfield County, Harwinton is a town that has strived to maintain its history and rural environment" (Roger Plaskett, "Welcome to Harwinton's History," *Harwinton Historical Society*, accessed July 29, 2015, www.harwintonhistory.com).

7. LL, "The Story of *Phebe Fairchild Her Book*," *Horn Book* 13, no. 6, (November-December 1937), 395–96; first draft of *Journey*, 219, Box 23, Folder 9, OU.

8. LL, "Story," 397; Gary D. Schmidt, *Making Americans: Children's Literature from 1930 to 1960* (Iowa City: University of Iowa Press, 2013), xxi.

9. LL, *Journey*, 397.

10. Ibid, 152–53.

11. First draft of *Journey*, 218–19; LL, *Journey*, 154–55.

12. May Lamberton Becker, ed. "With decorations by Lois Lenski," *Golden Stories of New England* (New York: Dodd, Mead, 1931), v.

13. Ibid, 4.

14. According to the Newbery Award website, "The Newbery Medal is awarded annually by the American Library Association for the most distinguished American children's book published the previous year." Newbery Medal winners carry a gold seal on their book jackets. Since 1971, the runners-up for the award have been known as Newbery Honor Books (a designation applied retroactively as well), and they bear a silver medal on their jackets ("How the Newbery Came to Be," *Association for Library Services to Children*, accessed July 29, 2015, www.ala.org/alsc/awardsgrants/bookmedia/newberymedal/aboutnewbery/aboutnewbery).

15. Rachel Field, *Hitty: Her First Hundred Years* (New York: Mcmillan, 1929).

16. LL, *Journey*, 155; LL, *Phebe Fairchild Her Book* (New York: Frederick A. Stokes, 1936), vii, 225.

17. William P. Alexander to LL, October 27, 1941; Helen Dean Fish (HDF) to LL, October 23, 1935, Box 2, Folder 32, OU; Field, *Hitty*, 3–4.

18. HDF to LL, April 18, 1936, Box 2, Folder 32, OU.

19. Ibid; LL to HDF, April 30, 1936; HDF to LL, May 1, 1936; John A. Lowe to LL, December 2, 1941, Box 2, Folder 32, OU.

20. HDF to LL, May 25, 1936; LL to HDF, May 27, 1936, Box 2, Folder 32, OU.

21. HDF to LL, May 25, 1936; LL to HDF, May 27, 1936, Box 2, Folder 32, OU.

22. Lois's collection of early-nineteenth-century children's books is in the Lois Lenski Collection in the Martha Blakeney Hodges Special Collections and University Archives, University Libraries, University of North Carolina at Greensboro (UNCG).

23. LL, *Phebe Fairchild*, 52–53.

24. Ibid, 312.

25. May Lamberton Becker, review of *Phebe Fairchild: Her Book*, *New York Herald Tribune Books*, November 8, 1936, 10.

26. Anne T. Eaton, review of *Phebe Fairchild: Her Book*, *New York Times Book Review*, December 27, 1936, 10.

27. Marilyn Leathers Solt, "The Newbery Medal and Honor Books, 1922–1981: 'Phebe Fairchild: Her Book,'" in *Newbery and Caldecott Medal and Honor Books: An Annotated Bibliography* (New York: G. K. Hall, 1982), 61–62.

28. LL to Mabel Pugh (MP), August 30, 1936, Box 46, Folder 9, OU. Lois censored all letters that she deposited in various collections, very likely deleting anything she deemed too revealing about her personal life.

29. LL, *Journey*, 146–47; LL, "Professional and Domestic Life," Box 51, File 3, Lois Lenski Collection, Kerlan Children's Literature Research Collection, Elmer L. Andersen Library, University of Minnesota, Minneapolis; Stephen Covey, "My Literary and Artistic Heritage," unpublished and undated manuscript sent by Stephen Covey to author, January 2009.

30. LL, "Professional and Domestic Life."

31. LL to MP, December 2, 1936, Box 46, Folder 9, OU.

32. LL, *Journey*, 134–35; Stephen Covey mentioned that Lois suffered from pernicious anemia and tried one remedy after another for many years (telephone interview with author, December 2008).

33. First draft of *Journey*, 175; LL, *Journey*, 135–36; Stephen Covey commented that Lois was always a devout Lutheran, although she attended the Episcopal Church in Connecticut, since there was no local Lutheran congregation, and in his words, "She lived her faith" (telephone interview with author, December 2008).

34. LL to MP, December 2, 1936, Box 46, Folder 9, OU.

35. All the historical books were published by J. B. Lippincott, Philadelphia.

36. Megan E. VanderHart, "In Pursuit of Womanhood: How Lois Lenski's Little Girls Learn to Change Their World," 2, M.A. thesis, Hollins University, Roanoke, Virginia, 2003.

37. LL, *A-Going to the Westward* (Philadelphia: J. B. Lippincott, 1937), x.

38. HDF to LL, April 6, 1937, Box 3, Folder 1, OU; Gerhard Lenski to LL, July 27, 1937, Lois Lenski Collection, Syracuse University Library, Syracuse, New York.

39. Helen Fuller Orton, *The Treasure in the Little Trunk* (New York: Doubleday, 1932), 53; LL to HDF, April 27, 1937, Box 3, Folder 1, OU.

40. Sara E. MacPherson, review of *A-Going to the Westward*, *Library Journal* 62, no. 15 (November 15, 1937): 882.

41. Anne T. Eaton, "Early New England," *New York Times Book Review*, December 4, 1938, 11.

42. LL, *Ocean-Born Mary* (Philadelphia: J. B. Lippincott, 1939), 381.

43. LL, *Blueberry Corners* (Philadelphia: J. B. Lippincott, 1940), xiii–xiv

44. Ibid; LL, *Journey*, 161. According to Joan Kirchner, the large blueberry patch at Greenacres undoubtedly inspired the author, and Joan enjoyed picking berries there when she was growing up in the 1950s (Joan Kirchner interview with author, August 27, 2012); LL, "Getting Books from Life," *Adventures in Understanding* (Tallahassee: Friends of the Florida State University Library, 1968), 87–102.

45. "Personal 1930's," first draft of *Journey*, 195.

46. Maud Hart Lovelace, *Betsy-Tacy* (1940); *Betsy-Tacy and Tib* (1941); *Betsy and Tacy Go Over the Big Hill* (originally published as *Over the Big Hill*, 1942); *Betsy and Tacy Go Downtown* (1943), all published originally by Thomas Y. Crowell, New York. The books are all included with original LL illustrations in *The Betsy-Tacy Treasury* (New York: First Harper Perennial Modern Classics Edition, 2011), with an essay, "Maud Hart Lovelace and Her World," at the end, which includes a short biography of LL, mentioning her work on the illustrations for the series (45). Thanks to Anne Altshuler for calling attention to this important commission for Lois's illustrations and its possible implications for bringing increased recognition to her own books for this age group.

47. LL, "Research for INDIAN CAPTIVE," undated typescript, 1, 2, 4, Lois Lenski Collection, UNCG.

48. Ibid, 6, 10–11; LL, *Indian Captive: The Story of Mary Jemison* (Philadelphia: J. B. Lippincott, 1941), ix–x.

49. *Letchworth State Park Information*, 2012, www.Letchworthpark.com; LL, "Research for INDIAN CAPTIVE," 7–9; *Indian Captive*, endpapers.

50. First draft of *Journey*, 230, Box 23, Folder 9, OU.

51. Anne Altshuler's questions helped clarify the analysis of this paragraph (Anne Althshuler to author, January 8, 2014); Madge Klais to author, email, December 24, 2013.

52. LL, *Indian Captive*, x.

53. LL, "Research for INDIAN CAPTIVE," 11–12.

54. Alice M. Wetherell, review of *Indian Captive: The Story of Mary Jemison*, *Library Journal* 66, no. 19 (November 1, 1941): 952; May Lamberton Becker, review of *Indian Captive: The Story of Mary Jemison*, *New York Herald Tribune Books*, November 2, 1941, 10; K. S. W., review of *Indian Captive*, *New Yorker* 107, no. 43 (December 6, 1941): 115–16; Anne T. Eaton, "Mary Jemison," *New York Times Book Review*, December 28, 1941, 9.

55. William P. Alexander to LL, October 27, 1941; Clark Wissler to HDF, April 12, 1941; John A. Lowe to LL, December 2, 1941; HDF to LL, January 22, 1942; HDF to LL, May 18, 1942; Natalie Mayo to HDF, June 25, 1942; Box 6, Folder 9, OU.

56. Walter Edmonds, *The Matchlock Gun* (New York: Dodd, Mead, 1941); thanks to April Hoffman for this insight.

57. LL to MP, December 4, 1943, Box 46, Folder 10, OU.

58. Lillian N. Riess to LL, December 6, 1960, Box 6, Folder 9, OU. The Coach House Press, Chicago, published a catalog of plays for children's theater, which is undated. On page 9, there's an advertisement for *Indian Captive*, "*adapted by Gertrude Breen, with a foreword on Chamber Theatre by Dr. Robert Breen: Casts: 3 to 5 men, 6 or 7 women, 5 girls, 2 boys, extras as desired; Doubling possible. Excellent for all-women casts; Sets: Played in drapes, bare stage, or with simple set pieces; Playing time: 1:15; Scripts, $1.00; Royalty, $15.00.* A very moving story—easily staged—of a white girl captured by the Indians, her struggle to keep her identity as a white girl, and the dramatic events that finally lead her to remain with the Indian tribe. Based on an authentic character of early American history." (Lois Lenski Collection, E. H. Butler Library at Buffalo State College, Buffalo, New York [BSU]); Lois also wrote *White Girl Captive: A Play in Three Acts for Boys and Girls*, "Based on the book *Indian Captive:* The Story of Mary Jemison by the same author," undated typescript, UNCG.

59. Email from Kathy Lenski Sherpa to author, February 9, 2014. Kathy continued, "That first, lonely summer, we wrote weekly. (Can you imagine how dear that was, for her to answer each and every one of my letters?) Over time, our letters became monthly." The two did not meet until the following summer, when her grandfather celebrated the fiftieth anniversary of his ordination.

60. Author visit to Mary Ann Sander's classroom, Lakeview School, Wind Lake, Wisconsin, May 20, 2011; Sander to author, email, January 10, 2014; Louise Erdrich, *The Birchbark House* (New York: Hyperion, 1999).

61. LL to MR, July 27, 1952, Box 47, Folder 1, OU.

CHAPTER 6

1. Gary D. Schmidt, *Making Americans: Children's Literature from 1930 to 1960* (Iowa City: University of Iowa Press, 2013), xxiv.

2. William Stott, *Documentary Expression and Thirties America* (New York: Oxford University Press, 1973), 3.

3. Stott, *Documentary Expression*, 51; Schmidt, *Making Americans*, xxvii.

4. Lois Lenski (LL), *Journey into Childhood*, New York: J. B. Lippincott, 1972, 48.

5. Ibid, 180.

6. LL, quoting Marjorie Kinnan Rawlings's passage: "There are worlds within worlds. It seemed to him a shocking thing that no man could see beyond the rim of his own. Perhaps there lay the ultimate wisdom, to see all life, all

living, with the acute awareness one brought to one's own," in "Seeing Others as Ourselves," Newbery Award Acceptance Paper, read June 18, 1946, at the Sixty-Fifth Annual Conference, American Library Association, Buffalo, New York, and published in *The Horn Book* 22, no. 4 (July 1946): 285.

7. LL, "Regional Children's Literature," in *Adventure in Understanding* (Tallahassee: Friends of the Florida State University Library, 1968), 52–53.

8. Ibid, 54.

9. LL, "Stories Behind My Regionals," 2, photocopied typescript provided courtesy of the Lois Lenski Covey Foundation.

10. Stott, *Documentary Expression*, 105.

11. Ibid, 49.

12. Ibid, 21.

13. LL, "Stories Behind My Regionals," 4; Schmidt, *Making Americans*, 85–86. Where Schmidt viewed Lenski's strengths, Gail Schmunk Murray, *American Children's Literature and the Construction of Childhood* (New York: Twayne Publishers, 1998), found didacticism: "Lenski chose from available facts to make the plots work didactically. Most of her characters are poor, white, and not well-educated, but Lenski does not turn them into victims. Children almost always reside in an intact, nuclear family and, even if working in the cotton field or harvesting vegetables, enjoy outdoor games and family-centered activities" (157). Murray does not seem to consider that children find ways to amuse themselves regardless of circumstances.

14. LL, "Stories Behind My Regionals," 6.

15. Anne Altshuler, member of the Madison Friends of Lois Lenski, emphasized the importance of these incidents in an email (February 16, 2013).

16. LL, "Are Your Books True?" in *Adventure in Understanding*, 83.

17. Schmidt, *Making Americans*, 88–89.

18. LL, *Journey*, 187.

19. Ibid, 187–88.

20. Impressive albums of *Bayou Suzette* photographs are housed in the Lois Lenski collections at both the de Grummond Collection, McCain Library and Archives, University of Southern Mississippi, Hattiesburg, and the Lois Lenski Papers, 1800–1974, Mss 015, Martha Blakeney Hodges Special Collections and University Archives, University Libraries, University of North Carolina at Greensboro (UNCG).

21. LL to Mabel Pugh (MP), Christmas 1942, Box 46, Folder 10, Lois Lenski Collection, Western History Collections, University of Oklahoma Libraries, Norman (OU).

22. Helen Dean Fish (HDF) to LL, October 30, November 5, and December 8, 1942, Box 6, Folder 22, OU.

23. LL, "Stories Behind My Regionals," 1, 11. In an undated letter from Stephen Covey to the author, circa 2009, he wrote, "I do not believe there was a conscious decision on her [Lois's] part to write 'Regional' stories. They came

about naturally, as a result of her involvement with families in a variety of regions throughout the United States. As time went on, her 'fans' (children) who read her regional stories would write to her asking her to write a story about them. Thus the 'Regional' stories evolved."

24. LL, "Stories Behind My Regionals," 1.

25. LL, "My Purpose," in *Lois Lenski: An Appreciation,* ed. Charles M. Adams, Friends of the Library of the Women's College, University of North Carolina at Greensboro, April 1963, Lois Lenski Papers, 1800–1974, Mss 015, Martha Blakeney Hodges Special Collections and University Archives, University Libraries, University of North Carolina at Greensboro (UNCG) and cited by LL in the introduction to "Stories Behind My Regionals," 6.

26. LL, "Seeing Others as Ourselves," *Horn Book* 22, no. 4 (July 1946): 295.

27. George P. Wilson, "Lois Lenski: Her Regional Dialect," in *Lois Lenski: An Appreciation,* 26–27.

28. Charlotte Huck and Doris A. Young, *Children's Literature in the Elementary School* (New York: Holt, Rinehart, 1961), 170.

29. Sandra Dutton, "The Poetry of Talk: Musings on Dialect," *Horn Book Magazine* 87, no. 6 (November/December 2011): 52.

30. LL, "Stories Behind My Regionals," 18.

31. LL to HDF, December 29, 1942, Box 6, Folder 22, OU.

32. Arthur Sinclair Covey Papers, Series 6, Project Files, Box 1, folders 76–93, Smithsonian Archives of American Art; Bobbie Malone, "Arthur Covey's Murals: Honoring the 'Dignity and Nobility' of Men Who Work," *Wisconsin Magazine of History* 93, no. 2 (Winter 2009–2010): 28–36.

33. "Artist: Arthur Covey," *The Living New Deal,* accessed July 29, 2015, www.livingnewdeal.org/artists/arthur-covey; "Torrington Remembers John Brown," *New York Times,* January 15, 1978, 17; "Arthur Covey Achievements: Highlights in the Life of the Artist," in booklet "Southwestern College Collection of Art by Arthur Covey," undated, Southwestern College, Winfield, Kan.

34. LL, "Regional Children's Literature," 53.

35. LL, *Journey into Childhood,* 182.

36. LL to Emma Celeste Thibodaux (ECT), October 3, 1955, Box 48, Folder 12, OU.

37. Another insightful link suggested by Anne Altshuler.

38. Jeanne B. Peyregne to LL, October 17, 1943; Evelyn Peters to LL, November 24, 1943; unidentified newspaper clipping, Box 6, Folder 25, OU.

39. LL, "Emma Celeste Thibodaux," undated, handwritten note, Lois Lenski Collection, Edward H. Butler Library Special Collections, Buffalo State College (BSC).

40. HDF to LL, December 8, 1942, Box 6, Folder 22, OU.

41. LL, "Stories Behind My Regionals," 18.

42. "It's not terribly surprising that Lois Lenski, who was known for writing children's books with a regional flavor, would have a copy of Marjorie Kinnan Rawlings'

When the Whippoorwill in her collection. A first edition with Lenski's signature on the front flyleaf is in the Lighthouse Books, ABAA collection of interesting and unusual books" (Michael Slicker, "Lois Lenski and the Marjorie Rawlings Book," *Lighthouse Books, ABAA*, February 1, 2011, www.oldfloridabookstore.blogspot. com/2011/02/lois-lenski-and-marjorie-rawlings-book.html).

43. Charles Reagan Wilson, "Crackers," in *Encyclopedia of Southern Culture*, ed. Charles Reagan Wilson and William Ferris (Chapel Hill: University of North Carolina Press, 1989), 1132.

44. LL, "Stories Behind My Regionals," 20–21.

45. Ibid, 18.

46. Ibid, 22–23A.

47. HDF to LL, July 6, 1945, Box 6, Folder 27, OU.

48. HDF to LL, October 2 and November 5, 1942, Box 6, Folder 27, OU.

49. LL, "Seeing Others as Ourselves," 283, 292.

50. LL, "The Inside Story of Getting a Medal," typescript, BSC; LL to MP, August 6, 1946, Box 6, Folder 11, OU.

51. Harold Rugg, *An Introduction to American Civilization: A Study of Economic Life in the United States* (New York: Ginn, 1929), iii–vi.

52. Rugg and Louise Krueger, *The Building of America*, vol. 5 of the Elementary School Course in the Rugg Social Science Series (Boston: Ginn, 1936), v-vi.

53. LL, "Seeing Ourselves as Others," 289.

54. Leland B. Jacobs, "Lois Lenski's Regional Literature," *Elementary English* 30, no. 5 (May 1953): 263.

55. Prudence Cutright, gen. ed., Macmillan Social-Studies Series (1958). *Living Together in the United States* was the volume aimed at the fifth grade, for example.

56. Margaret Owensby, "A Guidance Unit based on *Boom-Town Boy*," and Virginia Umstead, "This Land of Ours," undated typescripts, Box 22, Folder 2, OU.

57. Paul R. Hanna, Clyde F. Kohn, Helen F. Wise, and Robert E. Lively, *Living and Learning Together and Guidebook to Accompany In All Our States.* (Chicago: Scott, Foresman, 1965), 13, 161.

58. LL, *Boom Town Boy* (New York: J. B. Lippincott, 1948), 169.

59. Wendell Willkie, *One World* (New York: Simon & Schuster Pocket Books, 1943), 2, 164–66; Schmidt, *Making Americans*, 85.

60. LL, "Regional Children's Literature," in *Adventure in Understanding*, 51–52, 63–64.

61. Flora Straus, "Let Them Face It: Today's World in Books for Boys and Girls," *Horn Book* 21 (January–February 1945): 63–64.

62. Lois illustrated Cornelia Meigs's *Mother Makes Christmas* (New York: Grosset & Dunlap, 1940).

63. Cornelia Meigs, ed., *A Critical History of Children's Literature*, rev. ed. (New York: Macmillan, 1969), 407. Other contemporaries mentioned as writing in this vein were Florence Crannell Means and Eleanor Estes, both of whom were outstanding children's authors themselves. In 1946, when *Strawberry Girl*

was awarded the Newbery Medal, Means received a Newbery Honor for *The Moved-Outers*, a book on Japanese internment. She situated most of her other books in the West and focused on children of other minorities, especially American Indians. Eleanor Estes received the Newbery Medal in 1951 for *Ginger Pye*, while three of her 1940s publications—*The Hundred Dresses, The Middle Moffat*, and *Rufus M.*—were selected as Newbery Honor books. Estes located her stories in fictional Cranbury, Connecticut, the small town based on her home in West Hartford.

64. Email to author, September 22, 2010. The writer prefers to remain anonymous.

65. On March 18, 2014, country music historian Bill C. Malone, pointed out to the author that Ashe County was also an important center of old-time music, documented in the CD *Music from the Lost Provinces: Old Time String Bands from Ashe County, North Carolina and Vicinity, 1927–1931*, Old Hat CD 1001, Old Hat Records, 1997.

66. LL to MP, August 3, 1946, Box 46, Folder 11, OU.

67. In an undated, handwritten note, Lois wrote that "Miss Thibodaux was a great help with *Judy's Journey*, the migrant children being very similar to the Louisiana backwoods children she knew so well" (BSC).

68. LL, *Judy's Journey* (Philadelphia: J. B. Lippincott, 1947), x–xi.

69. Hugh Johnson to LL, November 17, 1946, Box 8, Folder 16, OU.

70. LL, *Judy's Journey*, 101–106.

71. Anne Altshuler, email to author, January 28, 2013.

72. Dorothy Aucott to LL, July 21, 1947, Box 8, Folder 17, OU.

73. Mrs. Hugh Grant Straus, chairman, Children's Book Committee to Lois Lenski, January 15, 1948 (carbon), Box 11, Folder 105, Child Study Association of America Records, Social Welfare History Archives, University of Minnesota, Minneapolis.

74. Alice Ring to LL, Mildred Powell to LL, folder entitled "Fan Letters Written to Lois Lenski, 1946–1953," Box 9, Lois Lenski Collection, Blackmore Library, Capital University, Columbus, Ohio.

75. "Letter from Lois Lenski" [dated November 15, 1965] in mimeographed "Juvenile Book Fare," February 1966, "presenting Juvenile Books, Their Authors and Illustrators with Other Notes of Interest to Bookshops, Libraries, and Schools," 1–2, Box 1, folder 2, Lois Lenski papers, de Grummond Children's Literature Collection, Special Collections, McCain Library, University of Southern Mississippi, Hattiesburg.

CHAPTER 7

1. William Stott, *Documentary Expression in Thirties America* (New York: Oxford University Press, 1973), 164, on Robert Park and quote from Ernest Burgess commenting on Paul Cressey's *Taxi-Dance Hall*.

2. Lois Lenski (LL), "Foreword," *Bayou Suzette* (Philadelphia: J. B. Lippincott,

1943), n.p.; "Foreword," *Strawberry Girl* (Philadelphia: J. B. Lippincott, 1945), xiii, for example.

3. LL, "Are Your Books True?" in *Adventure in Understanding* (Tallahassee: Friends of the Florida State University Library, 1968), 75.

4. Anita Clair Fellman, *Little House, Long Shadow: Laura Ingalls Wilder's Impact on American Culture* (Columbia: University of Missouri Press, 2008), 170.

5. LL to Emma Celeste Thibodaux (ECT), December 8, 1948, Lois Box 48, Folder 5, Lois Lenski Collection, Western History Collections, University of Oklahoma Libraries, Norman (OU).

6. LL to ECT, June 8, 1951, Box 48, Folder 6, OU.

7. LL, "Out of a Paper Sack," *Horn Book Magazine* 25, no. 6 (July 1949): 299–309.

8. LL to ECT, June 10, 1945, Box 48, Folder 5, OU.

9. LL, "Emma Celeste Thibodaux," undated, handwritten note, Lois Lenski Collection, Edward H. Butler Library Special Collections, Buffalo State College (BSC).

10. The Association of Junior Leagues of America promoted educational radio programs throughout the United States during the late 1940s and contracted with Gloria Chandler Recordings to produce the "Books . . . Bring Adventure" series. *Bayou Suzette* and *Strawberry Girl* were among those books in the series at the time the Yarbro School children were listening in the fall of 1946 (Box 9, Folder 87 and Box 30, Folder 293, Association of Junior Leagues of America Records, Social Welfare History Collection, Elmer L. Andersen Library, University of Minnesota).

11. LL, "Stories Behind My Regionals," 54, photocopied typescript provided courtesy of the Lois Lenski Covey Foundation.

12. LL to "Dear Boys and Girls of Blytheville," October 19, 1946, Box 10, Folder 1, OU.

13. "I, Bridgeton, N.J., Aug. 12, 1946, Negro Migrants," Notebooks, Box 5, Lois Lenski Collection, Blackmore Library, Capital University, Columbus, OH (CU).

14. LL, "Stories Behind My Regionals," 54–55.

15. Ibid, 55–58.

16. Ibid, 58–60.

17. Ibid, 60–61.

18. "Arkansas—1947—Cotton," Notebooks, Box 2, CU.

19. LL to Minnie Foster, July 3, 1948, OU.

20. LL to Alice Marie Ross, November 17, 1947; January 10, 1948; July 20, 1948; LL to Minnie Foster, summer 1948, six pages from letter to Minnie Foster [cover page inscribed by LL]; LL to Minnie Foster, August 2, 1948; "Lois Lenski—Real Live Author," speech given by Alice Marie Ross, April 17, 1970, at meeting of Library Association of Northeast Arkansas, Jonesboro, typescript photocopy, Lois Lenski Collection, Lois Lenski Collection, Archives and Special Collections, Dean B. Ellis Library, Arkansas State University–Jonesboro (ASU).

21. Alice Marie Ross; Gail Schmunk Murray, *American Children's Literature and the Construction of Childhood* (New York: Twayne Publishers, 1998), 158; Gary D.

Schmidt, *Making Americans: Children's Literature from 1930 to 1960* (Iowa City: University of Iowa Press, 2013), 88–89.

22. LL, "Stories Behind My Regionals," 65–66.

23. LL, "A Story from Strangers," originally an address to the Friends of the Library, Strozier Library, Florida State University, Tallahassee, 1966, collected in LL, *Adventure in Understanding* (Tallahassee: Friends of the Florida State University Library, 1968), 160–61.

24. HDF to LL, September 17, 1948, Box 11, Folder 6, OU.

25. LL, *Cotton in My Sack* (Philadelphia: J. B. Lippincott, 1949), 121–22.

26. LL to HDF, September 18, 1948, Box 11, Folder 6, OU.

27. LL to Clyde Robert Bulla (CRB), carbon copy, March 12, 1949, Box 11, Folder 7, OU.

28. LL, *Cotton in My Sack* (Philadelphia: J. B. Lippincott, 1949), xiii. Five of the other regionals (*Prairie School, Mama Hattie's Girl, Corn-Farm Boy, Flood Friday,* and *Coal Camp Girl*) also contain songs with Lois's lyrics and Clyde's music.

29. "THE COTTON PLAY as acted at a rural school in Arkansas," typescript carbon copy, Box 11, Folder 11, OU; photographs from ASU.

30. Hubert A. Johnson to LL, March 8, 1949, Box 11, Folder 7, OU.

31. Hubert A. Johnson to LL, December 15, 1949, Box 13, Folder 4, OU.

32. Lois Lenski, undated handwritten note, BSC.

33. Lois Lenski, "TEXAS TOMBOY: Getting the Material for the Book; My Trip to Texas, April, 1948," Box 13, Folder 7, OU.

34. LL to HDF, carbon copy, August 18, 1949, Box 13, Folder 4, OU.

35. Hugh Johnson to LL, December 15, 1949, Box 13, Folder 4, OU.

36. Daniel T. Walden to LL, November 17, 1949, Box 13, Folder 4, OU.

37. LL, *Texas Tomboy* (Philadelphia: J. B. Lippincott, 1950), 93–93; LL, "A Biography: Arthur Covey's Boyhood and Youth," in the catalog [undated] of the Southwestern College Collection of Art by Arthur Covey, Southwestern College, Winfield, Kan.; Arthur Covey, "Opening of the Cherokee Strip to Settlement," September 16, 1898, lithograph, Arthur S. Covey Collection, Photo #28, Western History Collections, University of Oklahoma Libraries, Norman.

38. Lelah Belle Davis Bird to LL, October 15, 1950, Box 13, Folder 10, OU.

39. Mrs. J. N. Davis to LL, September 6, 1950, Box 13, Folder 10, OU.

40. Lynda Johnson Robb to LL, July 10, 1968, Box 51, File 13, Lois Lenski Collection, Kerlan Collection, Children's Literature Research Collection, Elmer L. Andersen Library, University of Minnesota, Minneapolis.

41. LL, "Stories Behind My Regionals," 77–78.

42. Ibid, 78–83.

43. LL to HDF, September 8, 1950, Box 13, Folder 12, OU.

44. "I'm enclosing the *Atlantic Monthly* review. . . . She gave it top place on her list of Christmas 1951 books. *Child Life* makes it one of their '10 best books of 1951.' I'm getting fine letters about the book from South Dakota people who

know this life & how true the book is. I was so mad—one Texas paper scoffed at the book 'as a thriller,' & said 'we are asked to believe that all this is true!' I wrote the book editor a scathing reply, & they printed it too, testifying to the utter truth of this book, the truest I've written!" (LL to ECT, February 10, 1952, Box 48, Folder 7, OU); Edrie Van Dore, "'Prairie School' Tells True Tale for Child; Courage of Children in Great 1949 Blizzard Inspires Well-Illustrated Lois Lenski Book," *The Hartford (Conn.) Times*, September 17, 1951; "Miss Lenski's real understanding of her prairie children makes this another distinguished contemporary regional story," Jennie D. Lindquist and Siri M. Andrews, "Early Fall Booklist," *Horn Book* 27, no. 5 (September–October 1951): 329.

45. LL to ECT, February 10, 1952, Box 48, Folder 7, OU.

46. Ibid.

47. In Arbuthnot's revised edition of *Children and Books* (1957), she annotates (under the topic "Negroes") several titles by both African American and white authors and lists more in the bibliography, among them: Arna Bontemps, *Sad-Faced Boy* (Houghton, 1937); Marguerite De Angeli, *Bright April* (Doubleday, 1946); George Faulkner and John Becker, *Melindy's Medal* (Messner, 1945); and Mabel Leigh Hunt, *Ladycake Farm* (Lippincott, 1952), all for elementary readers. She cites Florence Crannell Means's *Great Day in the Morning* (Houghton, 1946) and *Shuttered Windows* (Houghton, 1938) for older students (413–16, 442).

48. LL, "Stories Behind My Regionals," 87.

49. LL, "Stories Behind My Regionals," 87–89.

50. LL, "Stories Behind My Regionals," 90–92. A notebook labeled "Miscellaneous Material, 1949," CU, contains notes, observations, oral interviews, descriptions, such as the following from pages 85–92: 7 P.M. Feb 12, 1950 stone church on Rte 19—1/2 block from Hattie's. Choir singing as we went in," with notes on the sermon, the singing, and that the song the choir was singing was "He's All I Need," from a record by Rosetta Tharp; LL to Marie Ram (MR), October 4, 1953, Box 47, Folder 2, OU.

51. LL to MR, October 4, 1953, Box 47, Folder 2, OU; "Material for expressions in the North came from children in 2 schools in the North, where Negroes predominated: Potter School, Saginaw, Michigan Elem. School, East Chicago, Ill where my niece was teaching & where I visited & interviewed a number of children" ("For experiences in the South, from Negro children in Union Academy School, Tarpon Springs, Fla.," undated handwritten notes by Lois Lenski, BSC).

52. LL, *Mama Hattie's Girl* (Philadelphia: J. B. Lippincott, 1953), n.p.

53. Ibid.

54. Ibid, iv.

55. CRB to LL, September 3, 1953, Box 45, Folder 8, OU.

56. LL, *Mama Hattie's Girl*, 44–45, 100–101, 156–57.

57. *Virginia Kirkus' Bookshop Service* 21, no. 17 (September 1, 1953): 580; Augusta Baker, *Library Journal* 78, no. 18 (October 15, 1953): 1858. The books mentioned in footnote 47 would be among those Baker would want in a library's collection; the review in the *Bulletin of the Children's Book Center* at the University of Chicago (vol. 7, no. 4, December 1953) argued that the problems presented in *Mama Hattie's Girl* were too complex for upper elementary students to understand (31). They lacked "a background for interpreting books of this kind and in their hands the book becomes a serious misrepresentation of the way of life among Negroes in both the North and South." Thanks to Kathleen T. Horning of the Cooperative Children's Book Center at the University of Wisconsin–Madison for pointing out these reviews.

58. LL to MR, October 4, 1953 and November 22, 1953, Box 47, Folder 2, OU.

59. "Separate Is Not Equal: *Brown v. Board of Education*," National Museum of American History, Behring Center, accessed August 31, 2001, http://americanhistory.si.edu/brown/history/index.html; LL to MR, August 6, 1954, Box 47, Folder 3, OU; Walter Dean Myers, "Where Are the People of Color in Children's Books?" *New York Times*, March 16, 2014, Sunday Review, 1, 6; Lois's niece was her sister Esther's daughter, Jean Ferne, who taught physical education at Riley School in East Chicago (author interview with Jan Ferne Haueisen, April 23, 2015).

60. LL to MR, April 11, 1954, Box 47, Folder 3, OU.

61. LL, "Otherness," in *Adventure in Understanding*, 109–11.

62. LL to ECT, July 25, 1952, Box 48, Folder 7, OU.

63. LL, "Stories Behind My Regionals," 93–94; Ruth H. Wagner, "Corn-Farm Boy: Here Is the Story behind the Story" (*Midland Schools*, Iowa State Education Association, October 1954): 10–11.

64. LL, *Corn-Farm Boy* (Philadelphia: Lippincott, 1954), viii.

65. LL to ECT, November 18, 1952, Box 48, Folder 8, OU.

66. Wagner, "Corn-Farm Boy," 11.

67. LL, "Stories Behind My Regionals," 95–96.

68. LL, *Corn-Farm Boy*, ix. Madge Klais, a member of the Madison Friends of Lois Lenski group, responded to this statement. Lois "clearly rejects the idea of creating a story arc. The whole paragraph is very insightful, I think, because it illuminates Lenski's notion of fiction, which seems to me to be a fore-runner of the 'fictional non-fiction.' . . . It also seems to me that she has a real disdain for the concept of 'literature' and how it is taught and critiqued" (email to the author, July 3, 2012).

69. LL, "Stories Behind My Regionals," 99.

70. LL to MR, November 22, 1953, Box 47, Folder 2, OU.

71. Celeste Frank to LL, August 14, 1954, Lois Lenski Collection, Milner Library, Illinois State University, Normal (ILSU).

72. "'Arkansas Cotton Children' to Mrs. Celeste Frank and Women's Club, Remsen, Iowa," September 24, 1954, ILSU.

73. LL to MR, Sept 24, 1954, Box 47, Folder 3, OU.

74. Wagner, "Corn-Farm Boy," 12.

75. Ibid.

76. Ibid, 180.

77. *Corn-Farm Boy* scrapbook, ILSU.

78. Phone interview with Noel Leinen, March 20, 2013.

CHAPTER 8

1. Hubert Johnson to Lois Lenski (LL), November 21, 1950, Box 13, Folder 4, and November 23, 1951, Box 13, Folder 26, Lois Lenski Collection, Western History Collections, University of Oklahoma Libraries, Norman (OU).

2. The Roundabouts consisted both of short-story collections by region with similar titles—*We Live by the River* (1956), *We Live in the City* (1956), *We Live in the Country* (1960), *We Live in the Southwest* (1962), and *We Live in the North* (1965)—and chapter books about a protagonist, more like simplified Regionals—*Project Boy* (1954), *Berries in the Scoop* (1956), *Little Sioux Girl* (1958), and *High Rise Secret* (1966). When Lois was doing research for *We Live in the South*, she wrote Emma Celeste that she had recently bought "Faulkner's 'Collected Works' & Carson McCullers' 'Ballad of the Sad Café'—really her complete works—so will be steeping myself in their interpretations of the Deep South. . . . I read Faulkner's 'Barn Burning' last night—Oh, his long-winded sentences are powerful—they keep me panting & out of breath, but how they do build up to a climax!" (LL to ECT, July 6, 1951 Box 48, Folder 6, OU).

> I've just bought Faulkner's "Collected Works" & Carson McCullers' "Ballad of the Sad Café"—really her complete works—so will be steeping myself in their interpretations of the Deep South. Haven't read much of either—only short stories. What vivid emotion they pile up—when I read him, I feel that I don't know or understand these people at all—He knows their very hearts & souls. His little boy in "Barn Burning" makes my "Timmy" seem a paper-doll in comparison. Of course we can't write like Faulkner for children & I don't intend to try—but I do want to write as truthfully & honest as I can.

3. Marie Ram (MR), "The Story Behind the Lois Lenski Collection," in *The Lois Lenski Collection in the Edward H. Butler Library* (Buffalo, N.Y.: State University College at Buffalo, 1972), foreword, n.p., Edward H. Butler Library Special Collections, Buffalo State College, Buffalo (BSC).

4. Marie Ram (MR) to LL, August 20, 1950, Box 47, Folder 1, OU.

5. The project was built "on a dump on a filled-in stone quarry at Kensington and Fillmore Avenues in Buffalo" (MR, "The Story Behind the Lois Lenski Collection"); taped interview with MR after her retirement, conducted by Bruce Andrew, Edward H. Butler Library, Buffalo State College, 1975, BSC; MR to LL, August 20, 1950, Box 47, Folder 1, OU.

6. LL to MR, October 10, 1950, Box 47, Folder 1, OU.

7. MR, "The Story Behind the Lois Lenski Collection"; taped interview with Marie Ram (MR) after her retirement, conducted by Bruce Andrew, Edward H. Butler Library, Buffalo State College, 1975 (BSC).

8. Marie Ram cites Leland Jacobs's unpublished dissertation, "Democratic Acculturation in American Children's Historical Fiction" (Ohio State University, 1945) and the work of Hilda Taba et al., *Literature for Human Understanding* (Washington, D.C.: American Council on Education, 1948), for establishing the methodology that she adapted for her unpublished master's thesis, "The Regional Stories of Lois Lenski," Buffalo State College, 1952, 19 (BSC).

9. LL to MR, July 14, 1952, Box 47, Folder 1, OU.

10. LL to MR, August 30, 1952 Box 47, Folder 1, OU.

11. LL to MR, January 8, 1953, Marie Ram materials, BSC.

12. Taped interview with MR, after her retirement, conducted by Bruce Andrew, Edward H. Butler Library, Buffalo State College, 1975, BSC.

13. LL to MR, October 4, 1953, Box 47, Folder 2, OU.

14. The relationship of the Roundabouts was even closer to the Lippincott market for textbooks than the Regionals had been. Hugh Johnson reported to Lois, "All the educational salesmen were very enthusiastic about the Roundabout America books at the sales conference last week. . . . The Educational Department . . . will be entirely responsible for the promotion and sale of the textbook edition of these two books" (Hugh Johnson to LL. November 23, 1951, Box 13, Folder 26, OU).

15. "Review of *Project Boy* written by a Project Mother," signed "Mrs. Allen H. Larson" (all copied in LL's handwriting), Marie Ram scrapbooks, BSC.

16. MR, "The Story Behind the Lois Lenski Collection"; taped interview with MR, BSC.

17. LL, foreword to *High-Rise Secret* (Philadelphia: J. P. Lippincott, 1966). In the Lois Lenski Collection at the de Grummond Collection, McCain Library and Archives, University of Southern Mississippi, Hattiesburg, boxes 3–5 contain materials pertinent to the research and the publication of the book. Folder 2 has a notebook put together by LL, entitled "Background Material / Letter / High-Rise Secret / Lois Lenski," which contains notes from Lou Larson all about moving into the high-rise. These form the most complete manuscript materials and working drawings for this, Lois's last Roundabout.

18. LL to MR, August 23, 1953, Box 47, Folder 2, OU.

19. LL to Emma Celeste Thibodaux (ECT), August 23, 1954, Box 48, Folder 10, OU.

20. "Provides fine social studies background," *Scholastic Teacher,* March 31, 1967, 20.

21. LL, *San Francisco Boy* (Philadelphia: J. B. Lippincott, 1955), x.

22. LL, "Stories Behind My Regionals," 103–104, photocopied typescript provided courtesy of the Lois Lenski Covey Foundation.

23. Clara Ingram Judson's *The Green Ginger Jar (They Came from China): A Chinatown Mystery* (Boston: Houghton, 1949) and Joseph Krumgold's . . . *and now Miguel*

(New York: Crowell, 1953) are among the authors and titles to which Lois may have been referring (cited in Arbuthnot, *Children and Books*, 643).

24. LL to Helen Dean Fish (HDF), January 20, 1953, Box 15, Folder 25, OU.

25. Christine A. Behrmann, "Fish, Helen Dean, 1889–1953," in *Pioneers and Leaders in Library Services to Youth: A Biographical Dictionary*, ed. Marilyn Lea Miller (Westport, Conn.: Libraries Unlimited, 2003), 70–71.

26. LL to ECT, February 17, 1953, Box 48, Folder 9, OU.

27. LL, "Stories Behind My Regionals," 105–106.

28. Dina Gianni to LL, April 21, 1953, Carton 1, Folder 19, Lois Lenski Collection, Bancroft Library, University of California at Berkeley (UC-B).

29. James Sue to LL, undated, *San Francisco Boy* scrapbook, Lois Lenski Collection, Milner Library, Illinois State University, Normal, IL (ILSU).

30. LL, "Stories Behind My Regionals," 105–106.

31. LL, *San Francisco Boy*, 39.

32. Ibid, 38.

33. Dina Gianni to LL, September 28, 1955, Carton 1, Folder 19, Lois Lenski Collection, Bancroft Library, University of California at Berkeley.

34. LL to MR, May 29, 1954, Box 47, Folder 3, OU.

35. Leliah B. Cain to LL, April 28, 1953, Carton 1, Folder 19, UC-B.

36. LL to ECT, September 25, 1955, Box 48, Folder 12, OU.

37. "San Francisco Boy," typescript translation, *San Francisco Boy* scrapbook, ILSU.

38. Author's telephone interview with James Sue, December 4, 2011.

39. LL, "Stories Behind My Regionals," 111; "Foreword," *Houseboat Girl* (Philadelphia: J. B. Lippincott, 1957).

40. LL, "Stories Behind My Regionals," 111; "Foreword," *Houseboat Girl*. The Lois Lenski Collection at Illinois State University's Milner Library has a superb collection of background materials for *Houseboat Girl*.

41. Harlan Hubbard, *Shantyboat: A River Way of Life* (Lexington: University of Kentucky Press, 1977), 259–60.

42. *Memphis (Tenn.) Commercial Appeal*, front page, October 3, 1954; small notice (very likely from Blytheville, Ark., undated, unattributed), both in complete notebook, "Background Material / Houseboat Girl / Lois Lenski 1957 / Notes and Outline, Letter, Questions, and Answers," ILSU.

43. LL, "Stories Behind My Regionals," 112.

44. LL, *Houseboat Girl*, 7.

45. Ibid, 59.

46. Eunice Blake to LL, February 7, 1957; LL to Eunice Blake, February 22, 1957, Box 17, Folder 16, OU.

47. LL, "Picture Map of Houseboat Voyage," *Houseboat Girl*.

48. LL, "Stories Behind My Regionals," 116.

49. Irene Story to LL, undated but with typed introductory note signed L. L., ILSU; LL, *Houseboat Girl*, 42–44.

50. Irene Story to LL, February 8, 1957, ILSU.

51. Lou Story to LL, October 9, 1957; Harlan Hubbard to Lois Lenski, October 10, 1957, in "HOUSEBOAT GIRL, Post Publication Letters," ILSU.

52. Lou Story to LL, January 3, 1958, ILSU.

53. Irene Story to LL, May 5, 1958, ILSU. Lois continued to stay in touch with the Story family. Two years later, she wrote her daughter-in-law, Yolanthe, that the family were nearly "penniless" over the previous winter, with no fishing available for the father, "no money for children's school lunches & they are too proud to accept the 'free' lunches which are provided for the poor children. So I have been helping them—the mother (a fine woman) insists she will pay it back, when they get 'on their feet again'" (LL to Yolanthe Covey, April 4, 1960, letters to Stephen and Yolanthe Covey, courtesy of their children).

54. Author's telephone conversation with Irene ("Dago") Story Freeman, October 10, 2012.

55. Author's telephone conversation with Debbie Story Saylors, October 8, 2012.

56. Author's telephone conversations with Irene Story Freeman and Debbie Story Saylors, cited above; Michele Longworth, "Houseboat Girl Returns to Ohio River," *Metropolis Planet*, September 5, 2012, 1 and 8A.

57. An unsigned review of *We Live in the Country* in *The Junior Bookshelf* 25, no. 5 (November 1961): 271.

58. May Hill Arbuthnot, *Children and Books* (Chicago: Scott, Foresman, 1957), 423.

59. Bradford Koplowitz, "Lois Lenski and the Battle between Fact and Fiction," *Journal of Youth Services in Libraries* 5, no. 1 (Fall 1991): 97, 101; Gary D. Schmidt, *Making Americans: Children's Literature from 1930 to 1960* (Iowa City: University of Iowa Press, 2013), 88–89; In Paul Theroux's article "The Story Behind Thomas Hart Benton's Incredible Masterwork," he discusses the *America Today* mural sequence that Benton originally painted for the New School for Social Research in 1929, which has recently been installed permanently in the Metropolitan Museum of Art. Theroux quotes what Benton said about the "veracity" of his composition. Paul Theroux, "The Story Behind Thomas Hart Benton's Incredible Masterwork," *Smithsonian Magazine*, December 2014, www.smithsonianmag.com/arts-culture/story-behind-thomas-hart-bentons-incredible-masterwork-1-180953405/?no-ist. Theroux's quote from Benton—"Every detail of every picture is a thing I myself have seen and known. Every head is a real person drawn from life"—could have been spoken by Lois with the same sort of self-assurance.

60. Ralph Jennings interview with LL at her studio in Harwinton, 1957, Tape 1 of 3, Box 13, Lois Lenski Collection, Special Collections at the Jackson Library, UNC–Greensboro.

61. Ibid.

62. Email from Amy McFarland to author, December 10, 2012.

63. LL, "Place and People," in *Adventure in Understanding* (Tallahassee: Friends of the Florida State University Library, 1968), 194–95.

CHAPTER 9

1. Mrs. Hugh Grant Straus, chairman, Children's Book Committee to Lois Lenski, January 15, 1948 (carbon), Box 11, Folder 105, Child Study Association of America Records, Social Welfare History Archives, University of Minnesota, Minneapolis.

2. Edith E. Lowry (EL) to Lois Lenski (LL), February 25 and May 4, 1948, LL to Lowry, May 10, 1948, Lois Lenski Migrant plays, Box 12, Folder 20, Division of Home Mission Records, 1950–1964, National Council of Churches of Christ in the United States, Presbyterian Historical Society, Philadelphia, Pennsylvania (Home Mission).

3. LL, *Judy's Journey*, xi; LL to Lowry, May 20, 1948, Home Mission.

4. LL to EL, June 18, 1949; EL to LL, June 20, 1949; LL to EL, December 7, 1949, Home Mission.

5. LL to Emma Celeste Thibodaux (ECT), January 24, 1949, Box 48, Folder 5, Lois Lenski Collection, Western History Collections, University of Oklahoma Libraries, Norman (OU).

6. LL to EL, December 7, 1949, Home Mission.

7. Ibid.

8. LL, "Play-Acting Real," Box 9, Folder 17, Lois Lenski Collection, Special Collections, Jackson Library, UNC-Greensboro.

9. LL and Clyde Robert Bulla (CRB), "Strangers in a Strange Land," song for the play *Strangers in a Strange Land*, by Lois Lenski (New York: Department of Publication and Distribution, National Council of Churches, 1952).

10. LL to ECT, May 6, 1952, Box 48, Folder 7, OU; LL to CRB, January 29, 1952, Box 37, Clyde Robert Bulla Papers, Sadler Research Collection of Literature for Children and Young Adults, James C. Kirkpatrick Library, University of Central Missouri, Warrensburg (UCM–W).

11. LL to CRB, Oct 5, 1953, UCM-W.

12. LL to CRB, January 29, 1952, Box 37, UCM-W; Lois Lenski, *A Change of Heart* (New York: Department of Publication and Distribution, National Council of Churches, 1952), 7.

13. Ibid, 22.

14. LL, *The Bean Pickers* (New York: Department of Publication and Distribution, National Council of Churches, 1952), 20.

15. Ibid, 7; "History of *Brown v. Board of Education*," United States Courts, www.uscourts.gov/educational-resources/get-involved/federal-court-activities/brown-board-education-re-enactment/history.aspx.

16. LL to Marie Ram (MR), August 30, 1952, Box 47, Folder 1, OU.

17. "Migrant Plays by Lois Lenski," 1, Migrant plays, Home Mission.

18. Ibid, 2; LL to ECT, July 19 and July 25, 1952, Box 48, Folder 7, OU.

19. M. R. Cooke, Torrington National Bank and Trust Company, to National Council Churches of Christ in America, Home Missions Division, June 13, 1958; EL to LL, June 29, 1959, Home Mission.

20. LL, "A Story from Strangers," in *Adventure in Understanding* (Tallahassee: Friends of the Florida State University Library, 1968), 169–70.

21. LL, "Living with Others," *Thoughts of God for Boys and Girls* 17, no. 2, (Hartford: The Connecticut Council of Churches, 1952), 9, 3.

22. Ibid, 4.

23. LL to ECT, July 31, 1952, Box 48, Folder 7, OU.

24. Ibid.

25. LL to ECT, June 8, 1951, Box 48, Folder 6, OU.

26. LL to Emma ECT, July 31, 1952, Box 48, Folder 6, OU.

27. LL and CRB, *We Are Thy Children: Hymns for Boys and Girls* (New York: Thomas Y. Crowell, 1952), 1, 10.

28. Elizabeth Riley (ER) to LL, January 22, 1952, Box 14, Folder 2, OU.

29. LL to ER, January 26, 1952, Box 14, Folder 2, OU; LL to CRB, Jan. 29, 1952, Box 37, UCM–W.

30. ER to LL, January 22, 1952 and LL to Riley, January 26, 1952, OU.

31. LL and CRB, *We Are Thy Children: Hymns for Boys and Girls*, unnumbered.

32. Ibid, 27.

33. Ibid, n.p.

34. On February 2, 1952, Lois had written to Emma Celeste: "I've just found out that the intense pain I've been having in my hip joints for the past 6 months is 'osteo-arthritis'—the crippling kind that ties you all up in knots! It seems it is apt to follow pernicious anemia & the alkaline stomach condition which I will always have" (Box 48, Folder 7, and September 6 and 18, 1952, Box 48, Folder 8, OU).

35. LL to ECT, September 6, 1952, Box 48, Folder 8, OU.

36. Louise S. Bechtel, untitled review of *We Are Thy Children* in "Books for Boys and Girls," *New York Herald Tribune*, Nov. 30, 1952, 8. Years before, Louise Seaman had been the first children's book editor, hired by Macmillan, as noted in chapter 3 (Marcus, *Why Picture Books Matter*, 76); "Guide to Louise Seaman Bechtel Papers, 1877–1980," *Vassar College Libraries*, accessed July 29, 2015, http://specialcollections.vassar.edu/findingaids/bechtel_louise_seaman.html#d0e53.

37. Searching the Internet for Frank Luther, one finds many of his singles and albums for children from the 1930s through the 1950s available on eBay, with listings such as the following Decca recordings: *Fairy Tales*, 1946; *Babar Stories*, 1947; *Winnie the Pooh and Christopher Robin*, 1948; *The Birthday Party Record*, 1950.

38. LL, *Journey into Childhood: The Autobiography of Lois Lenski* (Philadelphia: J. B. Lippincott, 1972), 165.

39. LL and CRB, *Songs of Mr. Small* (New York: Oxford University Press, 1954), unnumbered, 8–9.

40. LL with music by CRB, *I Went for a Walk* (New York: Oxford University Press, 1958); *At Our House* (New York: Henry Z. Walck, 1959); *When I Grow Up*

(Henry Z. Walck, 1960); Patricia Cummings to LL, December 4, 1956, and November 26, 1958, Box 17, Folder 22, OU.

41. LL to Henry Z. Walck, April 4, 1960, and Walck to LL, May 13, 1960, Box 15, Folder 15, OU.

42. The Lois Lenski Collection in the Edward H. Butler Library Special Collections at Buffalo State College has a copy of *Frank Luther Sings Lois Lenski Songs* and the accompanying promotional material.

43. LL to ECT, April 19–June 15, 1953, "Stories in Sound / Sound Stories," undated typescript with handwritten notes (LL handwriting), unidentified typescript (recognized by the author as from ECT), and titled "Picture Music" in pencil by LL as June, '53; quote, LL to ECT, June 8, 1953, Box 48, Folder 9, OU.

44. LL to ECT, June 8 and June 15, 1953, Box 48, Folder 9, OU.

45. LL and CRB, *Up to Six, Book I: Picture Music for the Pre-School Child* (New York: Chas. H. Hansen Music Corp., 1956), copy, UCM-W.

46. Lois Lenski, "Let Your Child Draw; Don't Teach Him," *Better Homes and Gardens*, May 1935, 26; LL and CRB, *Up to Six.*

CHAPTER 10

1. Lois Lenski, *Journey into Childhood: The Autobiography of Lois Lenski* (Philadelphia: J. B. Lippincott, 1972), 197.

2. LL, *The Life I Live: Collected Poems* (New York: Henry Z. Walck, 1965), n.p.

3. The diet included lamb, chicken, rice, or potatoes. She could eat no wheat. LL to Yolanthe Covey, October 7, 1968, letters from Yolanthe and Stephen Covey, courtesy of their children. Email from Nolan Doesken to Jan Ferne Haueisen, May 4, 2015, shared with the author in an email, May 13, 2015.

4. Michael Covey to author, telephone conversation, April 13, 2009, and email, March 10, 2014.

5. LL, "Let Them Create," *Horn Book* 28, no. 1 (February 1952): 9–10; "Say Yes to Life," in *The Lois Lenski Collection in the Florida State University Library* (Tallahassee: Friends of the Florida State University Library, 1966), 13–14.

6. Telephone conversation with Marilyn Reynolds Coronado, February 18, 2014; LL, "Kathy's Chickens," *We Live in the Country* (Philadelphia: Lippincott, 1960), 13–47.

7. LL to Emma Celeste Thibodaux (ECT), November 2, 1951, Box 48, 6, Lois Lenski Collection, Western History Collection, University of Oklahoma Libraries, Norman (OU); email from Robert Reynolds to Jane Pallokat, February 13, 2014, forwarded with message from Jane Pallokat to author.

8. Author interview with Joan Anderson Kirchner, Torrington, Connecticut, August 12, 2012; "Let Them Create," 19; LL, *Journey*, unnumbered photographic insert between 112–13.

9. Stephen Covey, "My Literary and Artistic Heritage," unpublished and undated manuscript sent to author by Stephen Covey; "The Works of Lois Lenski,"

Ohioana Authors, www.ohioana-authors.org/lenski/works.php; LL, *The Life I Live,* 76.

10. Author's telephone interview with Michael Covey, April 13, 2009, and with Alan Chisholm, November 21, 2013.

11. LL, "Stories Behind My Regionals," 87, photocopied typescript provided courtesy of the Lois Lenski Covey Foundation.

12. LL to ECT, December 8, 1948, Box 48, Folder 5, OU; LL, *Journey,* 198.

13. LL, *Journey,* 199.

14. LL to ECT, November 20, 1951, Box 48, Folder 6, OU; Kathy Sherpa, email to author, February 9, 2014.

15. LL sent identical notes to Mabel Pugh and to Clyde Robert Bulla (CRB), February 6, 1960, Box 46, Folder 14, OU; Clyde Robert Bulla Papers, Box 37, Sadler Research Collection of Literature for Children and Young Adults, James C. Kirkpatrick Library, University of Central Missouri, Warrensburg; LL, *Journey,* 201.

16. *Southwestern College Collection of Art by Arthur Covey,* printed, undated, unnumbered, Southwestern College, Winfield, Kan.

17. LL to CRB, August 26, 1960, Clyde Robert Bulla Papers, Box 37.

18. Arthur Sinclair Covey Papers, Archives of American Art, Smithsonian Institution, www.aaa.si.edu/collections/arthur-sinclair-covey-papers-7531.

19. LL, *Journey,* 201–203.

20. LL to CRB, June 11, 1962, Clyde Robert Bulla Papers, Box 37.

21. Ibid; LL, *Journey,* 202.

22. Mimeographed letter from LL to "My dear Library friends," September 1956, Lois Lenski Collection, Milner Library, Illinois State University, Normal.

23. Marilyn Doesken Perry, "Marilyn Doesken Perry's report of summer 1960 visit with Lois Lenski at her home, Greenacres, near Harwinton, Conn, plus information from 1966 and 1968," email attachment from Jan Ferne Haueisen, forwarded to the author, June 28, 2015.

24. The certificate and hood from Wartburg College, the hood and program from Capital University, the Regina Medal, the Newbery, and the medallion from the University of Southern Mississippi can all be found in the Lois Lenski Collection, Blackmore Library, Capital University, Columbus, Ohio; Sister M. Julianne, O.P., "Regina Medal Award 1969 Presentation," *Catholic Library World* 41 (September 1969): 15.

25. "Miss Lenski Accepts," *Catholic Library World* 41 (September 1969): 19.

26. LL, *The Life I Live: Collected Poems* (New York: Henry Z. Walck, 1965), n.p.

27. Ibid, 225–33.

28. Ibid, 26.

29. Ibid, 145, 159.

30. Ibid, 111.

31. LL, *Journey,* 64–67; *Lois Lenski's Christmas Stories* (Philadelphia: Lippincott, 1968), viii; LL to Stephen and Yolanthe Covey, December 20, 1960, letters to Stephen and Yolanthe Covey, courtesy of their children.

32. LL, "The Pink China Bonbon Dish" (Minneapolis: Augsburg Publishing House, 1939), 49–54, *Lois Lenski's Christmas Stories*, 35–52; *A Little Girl of Nineteen Hundred*, 55–64; LL, *Journey*, 50–51; "Beyond the Rim of Our Own World," *Child Guidance in Christian Living* (November 1950): 6–7.

33. Michael Covey email to author, March 14, 2014.

34. LL to Kathy Lenski Sherpa, March 12, 1972, Kathy Sherpa private collection.

35. Ibid.

36. Quote from Lois Lenski letter, August 12, 1968, in "Informational Paper for the Directors of the Lois Lenski Covey Foundation, Inc.," February 26, 2010, in the possession of Michael Covey and used with permission.

37. Lois Lenski Covey Foundation, www.loislenskicovey.org; LL, "The Life I Live," 159.

38. ECT to CRB, October 10, 1974, Clyde Robert Bulla Papers, Box 37.

39. "Lois Lenski," *Find a Grave*, last updated July 8, 2002, www.findagrave.com.

40. "Lois Lenski, Friend of Children" (Philadelphia: J. B. Lippincott, 1958), 3.

41. Mary Scott to LL, June 23, 1931, and 1936, "California," Folder 2, Boxes 9–10, Children's letters, 1927–1950, Lois Lenski Collection, Syracuse University; LL, *Journey*, 10.

42. LL, "Dear Child," in *Adventure in Understanding: Talks to Parents, Teachers and Librarians, 1944–1966* (Tallahassee: Friends of the Florida State University Library, 1968), 226; Stephen Covey sent the author copies of his speeches.

AFTERWORD

1. "The Lois Lenski Collection at FSU," *Florida State University Libraries*, accessed July 17, 2015, https://loislenski.omeka.net/collections/show/5.

INDEX

Page numbers in italics indicate illustrations.